SECOND BUMPER BOOK
—OF—
WEYMOUTH

SECOND BUMPER BOOK
OF
WEYMOUTH

MAUREEN ATTWOOLL

DORSET BOOKS

First published in Great Britain in 2009

British Library Cataloguing-in-Publication Data
A CIP record for this title is available from the British Library

ISBN 978 1 87116 461 9

DORSET BOOKS
Dorset Books is a Partnership Between
Dorset County Council & Halsgrove

Halsgrove House,
Ryelands Industrial Estate,
Bagley Road, Wellington, Somerset TA21 9PZ
Tel: 01823 653777   Fax: 01823 216796
email: sales@halsgrove.com

Part of the Halsgrove group of companies
Information on all Halsgrove titles is available at: www.halsgrove.com

Printed and bound in Great Britain by CPI Antony Rowe Ltd., Wiltshire

INTRODUCTION

The Second Bumper Book of Weymouth follows the same format as the original *Bumper Book of Weymouth* – an alphabetical listing of all kinds of information about the town and the villages which surround it. History is usually presented chronologically or by subject, but the A–Z encyclopaedia-style arrangement provides the Weymouth story in a different way. There is a guide to using the book overleaf.

This is a personal choice of entries, based on many local history enquiries received during my years at Weymouth Library, discussions with other local historians and a fascination with the history of the town I have enjoyed living in for most of my life. The entries are, as far as possible, different from those in *Bumper Book I* and I hope that this book stands alone, as well as being a companion to the first volume. To avoid space-consuming repetition, some entries do inevitably refer the reader to the first *Bumper Book*, and some of the information in that volume has been updated to keep up with events which have occurred since it was published in 2006. History does not stand still when the compiler stops compiling and even as this book was being typeset, some of the entries it contains needed to be amended to bring them up to date. Several errors in the first *Bumper Book* have also been corrected in this volume. As in the first *Bumper Book*, 'Further reading' suggestions follow individual entries rather than being included in a separate bibliography.

The entries are necessarily brief in a work of this kind and there is still much, much more to learn about the town and the events and personalities which have shaped its history.

ACKNOWLEDGEMENTS

Weymouth has two excellent and accessible sources of information on the town's history - Weymouth Library and Weymouth Museum - and my thanks are due to the staff of both these establishments for their help and patience in my research. At the Library the whole team has helped in various ways and I'm grateful to the Managers there, Chris McManus and Marie Trevett, for their co-operation. At Weymouth Museum archivist Richard Samways and fellow volunteer Margaret Morris are ever-helpful and assiduously track down obscure local facts - my thanks to them and also to David Carter and David Stonier (who copied, at short notice, a large and unwieldy photograph of William Gladstone's visit to Weymouth for the book). Old place names have been traced in early deeds at the Dorset History Centre, Dorchester, where I also made extensive use of microfilmed pre-Victorian local newspapers.

Special thanks are due to Brian Jackson who shares his encyclopaedic knowledge of the town so willingly and he, Andy and Jenny Miller, Joe Ward and Bill Macey have provided illustrations for the book. Thanks too, to those who supplied individual illustrations:- Gerry and Graham Coleman (for the photo of their father John Coleman), Mr and Mrs Graham Davies (for the photo of Mrs Davies' great-grandfather, Charles Clay, at the Springhead Hotel), Ronald Erridge (the HMS Mars memorial at Cobh), Mrs Elizabeth Garrett (Tumbledown Farm) and Ted Legg (the 1911 Esplanade Arch). The family of the late Eric Ricketts gave permission for his drawings of the first Town Bridge and Fleet Church to be included. 'Roller Revellers' Pat Russell (nee Trevett) and Nina Fitzgerald (nee Wells) lent me the pictures of their youthful roller-skating days at the Pier Bandstand. Hazel Thorby supplied the photograph of Abbot's Court. World War II photographs of American forces are reproduced courtesy of the US Army. Other pictures are from my own collection and that of Weymouth Library. I apologise if any illustrations have not been properly acknowledged, but the copyright of old photographs is often difficult to trace.

Others who have contributed are Wendy Brown, Nigel Cooper, John Cranny, John Dancy, Lindsay Fry, Pauline Jessett, Peter Love, John Mann, Peter Metcalfe, Stuart Morris, John and Chris Munroe, Colin Parr, Colin Pomeroy, Geoff Pritchard, Ted Tranter and the secretaries of various schools and institutions who supplied opening dates. My thanks to all and to anyone whose name I may have inadvertently omitted. Any mistakes in the book are, of course, my own.

Last, but by no means least, thanks to my husband David, whose patience and forbearance were tested to the limit as, yet again, his home was taken over by 'local history'.

THE SECOND BUMPER BOOK OF WEYMOUTH
HOW TO USE THIS BOOK

The Bumper Book is arranged in A – Z format. If you are looking for a specific subject – a person, a building etc. look under the surname or building name. For example Eli Bridle will be listed under **BRIDLE, Eli** and Brentry Villa will be under **BRENTRY VILLA**. If another entry relevant to the subject is mentioned in the entry you have looked up, it will be highlighted in **Bold Type**. If you are searching for village information, try the village name e.g. **SUTTON POYNTZ** in the alphabetical sequence. There are also 'See' and 'See also' references to other entries which may provide more information. Rather than adding a bibliography at the end of the book, I have followed an entry with a 'Further reading' suggestion if a book has been published on that particular topic.

NOTE: Old street and terrace names have been identified, I hope accurately, from local maps, rate books, census returns and directories, but this is not an exact science and is complicated by factors such as proposed names which are not actually used, the duplication of names, the demolition of buildings and the occasional complete renumbering of streets. Any corrections or additions would be most welcome.

Abbot's Court

ABBOT'S COURT was a mansion in extensive grounds at the top of Radipole Lake. It was built and owned by John Bagg, three-times mayor of Weymouth who had to sell the property when his extravagant lifestyle led to bankruptcy in 1910. Next owner was Thomas Burberry of the famous clothing firm and later the house was divided into flats. It was demolished in 1987 and new flats built on the site kept the original house name.

Abbots Court, the mansion built by John Bagg.

ABBOTSBURY. ABBEY The abbey at Abbotsbury was founded in the 11th century, a wealthy and extensive establishment of which very little now remains, apart from the Tithe Barn, St Catherine's Chapel and the gable end of one

St Catherine's Chapel, Abbotsbury.

of the abbey buildings. The Abbey closed during the Dissolution of the Monasteries by King Henry VIII in the mid-16th century and its buildings were taken down, some of the stone being re-used – a gateway fashioned from abbey stone once led to the house of Sir Giles Strangways, but the house itself no longer exists having been destroyed during Civil War fighting. Other fragments of abbey stone can be found in houses and walls around the village. Still dominating the scene today is the hilltop chapel dedicated to St Catherine, a landmark and a seamark for those out in the treacherous waters of Lyme Bay. She is traditionally the patron saint of spinsters and those visiting the chapel can offer a prayer… *'A husband St Catherine, a handsome one St Catherine, a rich one St Catherine, a nice one St Catherine… and soon, St Catherine'.*

Abbotsbury Abbey's Tithe Barn.

ABBOTSBURY. CASTLE The original Castle, an 18th century mansion, was one of the homes of the Strangways family, Earls of Ilchester and was totally destroyed by fire on 7th February 1913. The owner, Mary, Countess of Ilchester, was not in residence at the time. The fire broke out in the late evening and spread rapidly, strong winds that night fanning the flames. There was no available water supply and the nearest fire engine, twelve miles away at Weymouth, would have taken some hours to reach Abbotsbury, too late to save the building. The Castle was rebuilt two years later but their new residence was never popular with the family,

The first Abbotsbury Castle.

After the fire of 1913 the Castle was demolished.

Its successor (below) was built in 1915 on the same site.

The Ilchester family disliked their Abbotsbury residence and pulled it down in 1934.

being damp and draughty, and it was demolished in 1934. There is still an 'Abbotsbury Castle' – an Iron Age hill fort to the northwest of the village.

ABBOTSBURY GARDENS The sub-tropical gardens were first laid out in the 1760s by the 1st Countess of Ilchester in a sheltered hollow close to the sea and to the first Abbotsbury Castle nearby. Later members of the family continued their development and the gardens now contain an array of rare and beautiful plants which are grown in a succession of individual gardens at different levels linked by winding paths.

ABBOTSBURY HILL. LAY-BY *see* REES JEFFERYS ROAD FUND

ABBOTSBURY. RAILWAY Direct travel by rail from Weymouth to Abbotsbury was possible from 9th November 1885 when the Abbotsbury Branch Line opened branching off the main line at Upwey Junction. After Upwey, the stops were Coryates Halt, Portesham and Abbotsbury. The development of the line stemmed from iron ore and stone quarrying industries in the latter two villages, although the goods traffic never lived up to expectations. The line closed on 1st December 1952. The buildings of Upwey, the first station on the line after Upwey Junction, now form part of a builder's yard at Broadwey, Coryates Halt is no more, Portesham Station has been converted to a residence and Abbotsbury Station was pulled down in 1963 to provide a bungalow's site.

Edwardian travellers at Abbotsbury station.

ABBOTSBURY. SWANNERY The Swannery dates back at least to mediaeval times and may pre-date the Abbey itself. The Mute Swans feed on the plentiful eel grass which grows in the brackish waters of The Fleet. This is supplemented at twice daily feeding time when hundreds of swans, together many other species of waterfowl, congregate to enjoy extra rations. Visitor numbers to the Swannery increase in early summer when baby swans are hatching.

ABBOTSBURY ROAD. HALL *see* WESTHAM CINEMA

A'COURT, Percy *see* A'COURT, William Charles

A'COURT, William Charles A livery stable proprietor of No.3 Gloucester Row who died 13th February 1900. He

Two modes of transport for the A'Courts – the Royal Hotel coach which picked up hotel guests and their luggage from the railway station in the early 1900s...

drove the new and splendid *Royal* four-horse coach to Moreton on its first outing in June 1886. Father of Percy A'Court who carried the business into the motor age and drove visiting royalty in the early years of the 20th century. Percy A'Court was Mayor of Weymouth and Melcombe Regis in 1925-26 and 1926-27.

...and a special passenger for Percy A'Court in 1912 when King George V visited Weymouth.

ACT OF PARLIAMENT CLOCK In 1797 William Pitt levied a tax on all clocks and watches with the inevitable result that few people carried watches. To overcome this lack of personal timekeeping many innkeepers installed clocks in their public rooms and these became known as 'Act of Parliament' clocks, the name continuing in use even though the Act was repealed the following year. One such clock, said to have originally hung in Gloucester Lodge, King George III's Weymouth residence, was lent to the borough council and displayed in the Guildhall for some years and later in the Timewalk, Brewer's Quay but it has now been returned to its owner, Salisbury Museum.

ACUTT, Arthur George Frederick Peaty
Established a naval and military outfitter's shop at No.3 Upper Bond Street in 1910. His son Arthur Bertie 'Roy' Acutt took over the business in 1934 and ran it almost until his death in 1982. Today (2009) the shop continues at the same address as a men's outfitters and is still run by the Acutt family.

ADDISON, Rev. Joseph and ADDISON, Rev. John Dupre
Joseph Addison (1786-1832) was curate of All Saints Church, Wyke Regis and also headmaster of the boys' school at Rodwell House, a post later held by his son, the Rev. John Dupre Addison, who was Vicar of Holy Trinity Church from 1863 -1884.

On the right, Rodwell House, now the Rodwell House Hotel.

ADELER, Edwin *see* PIERROTS

ADMIRAL'S BARGE 18th century deeds refer to a building of this name on the west side of St Thomas Street.

AERIAL VIEWS

From around 1960.

AEROPLANES It is difficult to imagine now that Weymouth was once a town with two airfields nearby – the first was at Lodmoor, a ground with rather primitive facilities in the very early days of flying and a little later Chickerell Airfield opened, dating from World War I (on land now the site of the Granby Industrial Estate). When aviation was in its infancy and the opportunity to see an aeroplane at close quarters was a rare occurrence, visits by early pilots caused quite a stir. Some were famous names – Claude Grahame-White and Benny Hucks among them. Weymouth's place in aviation history was assured on one

An aerial view of 1939, shortly before the start of WW2. The pier had been extended in 1933.

Samson's seaplane at Weymouth.

memorable day in 1912 when on 9th May Lieutenant Charles Samson made the first flight from the deck of a moving vessel, the battleship *HMS Hibernia,* during a week of great celebration when King George V reviewed and sailed with the Home Fleet. The fragile seaplanes of these pioneering flyers were prone to accidents and Samson's aircraft had already had a ducking before his historic flight, but it left him uninjured and soon in the air again. Later, his plane was caught by a gust of wind at Lodmoor and toppled over, Samson fortunately jumping out before it fell. His luck held again when the review ended. He was on board *HMS Hibernia* when he decided to continue the journey by plane. He took off from the deck but encountered heavy fog and once more came down on the water. The destroyer *Recruit* went to his assistance and the aircraft, with Samson still in his seat, was towed into Sheerness.

A big attraction the same year in July was the *Daily Mail* seaplane when it arrived here from Bournemouth on a tour of coastal resorts. After landing in the Bay, the plane was pulled onto the sands where it proved to be a crowd puller. The pilot gave exhibition flights for a week before leaving for Exmouth, his next venue. A rather unfortunate sight in the Bay was an Avro seaplane which put into Weymouth to pick up a passenger for a flight to Bournemouth on 9th

August 1919. As the plane rose from the water it crashed rather spectacularly, but fortunately all three on board were rescued.

The RAF Airfield at Chickerell was established in 1918 and on 23rd June 1924 a plane which had taken off from there made a forced landing opposite Greenhill with a damaged undercarriage. When all on board had been rescued, the plane was hauled up on the beach and dismantled before being taken back to Chickerell. Although Lodmoor's role as an airfield was short-lived, Chickerell continued to be used by civilian and military aircraft until October 1959. Portland naval base was also involved in flying activities and late in 1924 a seaplane intending to fly from Portland to Portsmouth struck the mast of a coal hulk and crashed in the harbour shortly after take-off, the four airmen on board being lucky to escape drowning when the plane turned over.

The Twenties also brought an aerial tragedy which was witnessed by thousands. It was a by-product of the 'Tidal Wave Hoax' of 29th May 1928 when a prophesy that Weymouth would be destroyed by a great tidal wave on that date made front page news in the national newspapers and brought visitors flocking to the town – quite the opposite effect to that feared by the publicity chiefs who fully expected them to stay away! The crowds were being entertained by an airman performing stunts over the bay, when the plane crashed into the sea, killing the pilot, although his companion was saved.

In the 1930s another RAF airfield opened a few miles from Weymouth. This was RAF Woodsford, renamed RAF Warmwell a year before World War II broke out. From here courageous young pilots took to the skies to engage in the dogfights witnessed by many locals during the 1940 Battle of Britain months. The 1940s saw both RAF and Luftwaffe aircraft downed around Weymouth. One Australian pilot shot down off Chesil Beach returned in 1983 to see the wreckage of his Hawker Hurricane plane recovered from the

Flights from HMS Hibernia.

A downed Second World War Junkers 88.

sea bed near Langton Herring. Far sadder was the fate of 21 year old Sergeant-Observer Tom Chambers, the navigator on board a De Havilland Mosquito which crashed on Portland in July 1944. An orphan, he grew up at Stormount, a Children's Home (since demolished) on Buxton Road, to which he always returned to spend his leave. He now lies in an RAF grave at Wyke Regis Cemetery, close to the site of his childhood home.

Further reading: *Wings over Weymouth* by Colin Pomeroy (Dovecote Press, 2005).

AIR CADETS HQ A new hut for Weymouth air cadets opened at Bincleaves on 9th July 1961. They had previously met in a hut at Radipole Lane.

AIR RAIDS 1940 and 1941 saw the area's most intensive WW2 bombing raids as Luftwaffe aircraft targeted Weymouth and Portland. Attacks continued into 1942 but from this year enemy bombers appear to have been mainly overflying the local area en route to attack inland towns and cities. A lull in the bombing raids during 1943 was followed by the last raid of the war – a particularly serious one on 28th May 1944, shortly before D-Day. Enemy bombs fell close to Dorchester Road at Lodmoor Hill, a cause of great concern as this was the main route American troops would use as they moved down to Weymouth Harbour for embarkation. Property close to the road was destroyed and it was several days before a buried unexploded bomb in Cranford Avenue was lifted and safely defused. The

raiders also laid mines in Portland Harbour, damaging a number of the landing craft assembled for the invasion.

The following list of air raid dates and areas on which bombs fell shows how widely the Weymouth and Portland area suffered (unless they were close to land, I have excluded the many enemy bombs which fell in the sea and also bombing raids on allied shipping in the Channel). The list has been compiled from published sources and from two unpublished diaries. In Weymouth, Peter Love was a schoolboy at the start of World War II and he meticulously recorded air raid alerts and bombing raids until March 1943 when he joined the RAF. On Portland, retired magistrate

A successful end to many hours work as the Cranford Avenue UXB is safely defused.

Not an air raid, but a pre-war Civil Defence exercise in a derelict Chickerell Road property.

Weymouth stayed put in the *Dorset Daily Echo* issue dated 28th November 1944 and *Portland was the first town to be bombed* in the *Dorset Daily Echo* issue dated 28th December 1944.

Brigade in Action: the history of the origin and development of the St John Ambulance Brigade in Weymouth, and its co-operation with the Civil Defence Services during the War 1939-1945 by D. G. F. Acutt (published in Weymouth, 1946).

Weymouth and Portland at War: Countdown to D-Day by Maureen Attwooll and Denise Harrison (Dovecote Press, 1993).

St Leonard's Road Methodist Church was damaged in Chapelhay air raids but remained in use. It has since been replaced with housing.

Jonathan Greenwood Comben kept a similar diary of wartime activity on the Island from 1940 until 1944. At a time when very little information appeared in local newspapers due to wartime press censorship, their invaluable records show clearly how life in the area was constantly disrupted by the frequency of air raid sirens, enemy planes overhead, anti-aircraft fire and bombing. The list which follows does not record the loss of life and destruction of property which occurred as a result of many of the raids. More details of where the bombs fell and the resulting casualties and damage can be found in: *Bombed 51 times,*

No. 12 Russell Avenue, the first Weymouth house to be destroyed by bombs, 27th July 1940.

Air Raids

Date	Location
1940	
30 June	Portland
4 July	Portland
7-12 July	Portland
17 July	Portland
27 July	Weymouth (Wyke Road area), Upwey
11 August	Chapelhay, Rodwell, Westham and Portland
14 August	Portland
15 August	Portland
17 August	Lodmoor Hill
18 August	Lodmoor Hill and Westham
19 August	Portland
25 August	Portland
27 August	Portland (off Chesil Beach)
28 August	Westham, Lanehouse and Portland
4-13 September	several 'tip and run' raids (no damage)
15 September	Portland
17 September	Portland
19 September	Portland
24 September	Portland Harbour
25 September	Portland
30 September	Rodwell
2 October	Portland
3 October	Weymouth (town, seafront)
5 October	Lodmoor and Portland
7 October	Chesil Beach (towards Fleet)
13 October	Portland (Chesil Beach)
19 October	Portland
20 October	Portland Harbour
21 October	Weymouth (Edward Street Bus Garage), Portland, Portland Harbour
5 November	Portland Harbour
14-17 November	Lodmoor Hill, Redlands, Radipole
17 November	Chapelhay
19 November	Rodwell, Wyke Regis, Portland (in sea)
24 November	Portland
30 November	Radipole
1 December	Portland (in sea near Breakwater)
1941	
2 January	Portland Harbour, Wyke Regis, Westham, Radipole
3 January	Lanehouse, Westham, Radipole, Preston, Chickerell
16-17 January	Pye Hill, Rodwell, Radipole, Preston, Wyke Regis, Portland
17-18 January	Weymouth (railway sidings), Radipole, Upwey, Preston, Osmington Hill
19 February	Portland (off Chesil Beach)
12 March	Portland
14 March	Portland
16 March	Portland (in sea)
20 March	Portland, Chickerell and Abbotsbury (all in sea)
4 April	Preston
7 April	Weymouth (in sea)
8 April	Osmington
11 April	Portland
14-15 April	Portland
15-16 April	Rodwell, Lanehouse, Westham, Lodmoor Hill, Southill, Portland
29-30 April	Portland (in sea)
1 May	Wyke Regis, Portland.
3-4 May	Weymouth (town centre) Pye Hill, Westham, Wyke Regis, Portland
4-5 May	Weymouth (railway station goods yard), Westham, Portland
6-7 May	Hope Square, Rodwell, Wyke Regis
8 May	Chapelhay
9-12 May	Chapelhay, Rodwell, Wyke, Portland
14-15 May	Weymouth (Sidney Hall car park)
28-29 May	Wyke Regis
30 May	Rodwell, Portland
4 June	Portland (off Chesil Beach)
5 June	Portland Harbour
9-10 June	Westham, Chickerell
8 July	Portland
13 July	Chapelhay
6 September	Ringstead
11-12-13 October	Rodwell, Wyke Regis, Portland Harbour
26 October	Portland
1 November	Westham
22 November	Portland, Portland Harbour
12 December	Portland
1942	
23 March	Rodwell (Castle Cove, bombs fell in sea), Portland
24 March	Nottington, Radipole, Chickerell, Preston, Portland.
2 April	Weymouth (town centre), Rodwell, Westham, Greenhill, Wyke Regis
8 April	Portland (apparently a British shell and something of a mystery)
9 April	Weymouth and Wyke Regis
13 April	Weymouth (Commercial Road), Granville Road, Portland
21 April	Portland Harbour
17 June	Portland
28 June	Pye Hill, Rodwell, Lanehouse, Upwey, Wyke Regis
29 June	Westham
2 July	Rodwell, Fleet, Portland
11 July	Wyke Regis
1943	
2 February	Portland
9-10 March	Preston, Portland
1944	
24 April	Overcombe
15 May	Portland
28 May	Lodmoor Hill and Portland Harbour

Clearing up in Ilchester Road after the raid of 11th August 1940.

Weymouth's worst raid on 2nd April 1942. The remains of the Fox Inn, St Nicholas Street.

There was still occasional activity at Chickerell Airfield in the late 1950s – this was TA training.

AIRPORT Plans to turn the former RAF Airfield at Chickerell into a civil airport for Weymouth were afoot in the early 1930s but nothing came of them, and the onset of WW2 brought the RAF back until the airfield closed in 1959. *See also* CHICKERELL AIRFIELD in *Bumper Book I*

ALBERT HOTEL This pub no longer exists. Standing on the corner of Park Street and King Street it is sometimes listed as being in Park Street but it was at No. 1 Richmond Terrace, part of King Street. It was later renamed the **Queen's Hotel**, but was pulled down in the 1930s to make way for the present hotel of the same name.

ALBERT HOUSE was in Derby Street.

ALBERT INN, The Square, Wyke Regis, dates from the mid-19th century.

ALDERNEY. WW2 EVACUEES *see* EVACUEES

ALEX VAN OPSTAL The Belgian passenger liner on voyage New York-Antwerp was the first WW2 casualty in the waters around Weymouth when she struck a mine on 15th September 1939 and sank off the Shambles lightship. Her crew and passengers, more than 60 people in all, were picked up by a Greek vessel and brought into Weymouth.

ALEXANDER TECHNIQUE A method of mind and body re-education designed to reduce stress and muscle tension. An early pioneer of Frederick Matthias Alexander's Principle in the 1930s in England was Gurney MacInnes who worked with the boys of the junior school at Weymouth College, the boys' public school, during the headmastership of A. G. Pite.
Further reading: *Teaching F. M. Alexander's technique in a boys' preparatory boarding school 1936-1939*, by Gurney MacInnes in *Conscious Control: a Journal of the F. M. Alexander Technique, Vol. 1, No. 2, Autumn 2007.*

ALEXANDRA GARDENS *Addition to the main entry in Bumper Book I:*
    The classical statues which once stood all around the Alexandra Gardens were installed during the mayoralty of Charles Jesty, Mayor of Weymouth and Melcombe Regis 1896-1898. They were purchased from Holnest Park, one of the Dorset seats of the Drax family.

ALEXANDRA HOUSE is now Nos. 33-34 The Esplanade. Currently (2009) The Cactus Tea Rooms and Bistro, which relocated here from the Pier in 2008.

ALEXANDRA INN, Charlestown is now known as 'The Alex'.

ALEXANDRA MAISONETTES, No. 5 Clarence Buildings are now No. 23 The Esplanade.

ALL SAINTS TERRACE is now part of All Saints Road, Wyke Regis.

ALLEN, Rear-Admiral William (1793-1864) Born in Weymouth, his active naval service finished in 1842, when he was placed on half-pay having returned from a expedition to the River Niger which, although he was not in command, proved to be a disaster. He was the author of a number of works including an account of the Niger expedition and a plan for the abolition of the slave trade in the West Indies. Also an accomplished artist he published volumes of his pictures made whilst travelling abroad and exhibited landscapes at the Royal Academy. He died in Weymouth in 1864.

ALLEN'S ROW was in East Street in the 19th century.

ALLIGATOR CLUB A jazz club set up for teenagers in 1958 in a room above a garage at No. 31 Hope Street. Following protests about noise and the suitability of the club for young people it closed later the same year.

ALMA PLACE Cottages on the east side of Radipole Lane.

Alma Place cottages, seen here after floods in July 1955.

ALMA TERRACE is now part of Dorchester Road at Broadwey. Also Nos.1-29 Alma Road, Westham.

ALPHA PLACE, Nos. 85-86, St Mary Street *see* BENSON & BARLING

ALUM WORKS In the 18th century Sir Richard Clavell of Smedmore tried to establish an alum works at Kimmeridge. He built a massive stone pier 100 feet long but the venture failed and the pier was destroyed in a gale in 1744.

AMERICAN INDIANS On 28th July 1766 a party of four Indian chiefs and three women arrived in Weymouth. They were eventually intending to journey to London to complain about encroachments on their lands. Whilst here they met William Pitt the Elder, who was staying in the town.

AMERICAN RED CROSS CLUB This was a WW2 club staffed by locals which provided social facilities – dances, meals, accommodation, a library, etc. – for the American troops stationed here prior to and following the D-Day landings. It opened in January 1944 above the Hawkes, Freeman store at Nos. 39 and 40 St Thomas Street and closed in August 1945.

AMERICAN WARSHIPS Occasional visits by vessels of the U.S. Navy were a feature of the first half of the 20th century. In November 1910 the arrival of the United States Atlantic Fleet coincided with Weymouth's **Grand Nautical Bazaar and Nelson 'Victory' Exhibition**. The US ships included the *Connecticut, Delaware, Michigan and North Dakota*, which, together with the Royal Navy's Home Fleet, must have provided a striking sight in Portland Roads. There was a 10-day visit by American warships *Arkansas, Florida* and *Utah* in July 1929 and in July 1952 the world's two largest battleships *USS Missouri* and *HMS Vanguard* (45,000 and 42,000 tons respectively) exchanged 17-gun salutes during an American fleet visit which included the heavy cruisers *Macon* and *Des Moines*, destroyers *Meredith* and *Sperry* and frigates *Burdo* and *Cobb*. Eighteen visiting ships of the US Atlantic Fleet battleship cruiser force in 1955 included the battleship *New Jersey*, destroyers *R L Wilson* and *Basilone* and supply ship *Salamone*. A nuclear submarine, *USS Nautilus*, was in the fleet of the United States Naval Squadron which arrived in October 1957 – Portland would also be the submarine's first port of call following an epic sea passage under the North Pole ice cap the following year. Other vessels in the US Naval Squadron on this occasion included *Grand Canyon, Shasta* and another submarine, *Ray*. Nuclear submarine visits in the Fifties and Sixties included *USS Triton* and *Skate*. A reminder of war but not a display of naval force came in 1964 when the Swedish American Line's passenger liner *Kungsholm* stopped off at Weymouth on 30th April. The American passengers, homeward bound from a European cruise, were presented with framed World War II mementoes of the US troops who embarked at Weymouth for the D-Day landings.

AMPTHILL, Lord and Lady The couple led the fight to prevent the erection of USAF wireless aerials at Ringstead on land held in trust for their son. There was a Public Inquiry into the Air Ministry's compulsory purchase order on 30th November 1959, which the Ampthills lost. The Air Ministry announced that 2 x 150 feet high dish type radio aerials would be built on the site. At the same time it was announced that 67 acres of land in the area would be derequisitioned – it had been used for a wartime radar station. *See also* RINGSTEAD

ANCHOR, displayed at Weymouth Ferry Terminal
The anchor was purchased from the Receiver of Wreck, HM Customs, Folkestone in May 1979. It had been dredged up off the Kentish coast by fishermen earlier in 1979. Restored at Weymouth, it was presented by Sealink UK Limited to Weymouth and Portland Borough Council on the opening of the Car Ferry Terminal Extension, 7th May 1980.

ANCHOR CLUB The Royal Naval Association's Anchor Club HQ was in the former Military Arms public house in Barrack Road from 1970 until 1987.

ANCHOR INN A pub of this name existed on the Weymouth side of the harbour in the 17th century. Another Anchor Inn/Beerhouse, possibly of 18th century date, stood opposite the Guildhall in Melcombe Regis.

ANDREWS, R. C. A butcher whose shop was originally at No. 6 St Mary Street (now part of the site of Marks and Spencer's store). In 1935 he moved across the street to No. 100 which had been totally demolished and rebuilt, previously the offices of the *Southern Times* newspaper. The architect of the new shop was **C. Lionel Stewart-Smith**, of No. 9, Royal Terrace, best known for his design of the Riviera Hotel at Bowleaze.

ANGERSTEIN, Reinhold Rucker (1718-1760)
Swedish industrial spy who travelled around Europe in the 1750s collecting information on developments in trade and technology for the Swedish government. He was in England and Wales from 1753-1755 and his diary, meticulously illustrated with views of places he visited and industrial processes he observed, includes his visit to Dorset in May 1754. His main interest locally was in the Portland stone quarries but he includes an interesting early description of sea bathing at Weymouth and of the dozen drawings of Dorset scenes, more than half are of the Weymouth and Portland area.

Further reading: *R. R. Angerstein's Illustrated Travel Diary 1753-1755: Industry in England and Wales from a Swedish perspective.* Translated by Torsten and Peter Berg with an introduction by Professor Marilyn Palmer. (Science Museum, London, 2001.)

ANTWERP TERRACE On the north side of Dorchester Road this terrace was nearing completion early in 1833. Known as the 'Antwerp Estate', houses in this area have had a variety of names – Antwerp Villas, Antwerp Lodge, Antwerp Bungalow. The terrace is now Nos. 203-209 Dorchester Road.

ANZACS *see* AUSTRALIAN GRAVES; WESTHAM CAMP; WESTHAM CINEMA

AQUARIUMS The 'sundeck' on the beach opposite York Buildings once had an aquarium below it. The structure was built around 1949-50 as a shelter and the aquarium seems to have existed in the 1960s. Other aquariums were at No. 50 The Esplanade in the early 1970s and the structure on Radipole Lake known as Noah's Ark, which is now a restaurant, originally opened in May 1966 as an aquarium.

ARCH on the Esplanade In 1911 a large temporary arch spanned the Esplanade roadway. It was constructed to celebrate two events in June that year – the Royal Counties Agricultural Show, held on Lodmoor from June 13th – 16th and the Coronation of King George V and Queen Mary on the 22nd. Decked out with greenery, flowers and flags it was topped with a model ship copied from one on the borough's

Celebrations in 1911.

coat of arms. The motto 'Weymouth Welcomes You' for the Show's visitors was supplemented by 'Long Live Our King and Queen' for Coronation week.

ARCH LIBERAL CLUB This Working Men's Club was founded in 1900. In November 1903 its premises in Chickerell Road were closed by the courts for six months due to drunken and rowdy behaviour. A new club, **Westham Working Men's Club**, opened at No. 1, Cromwell Road on 1st October 1904.

ARCH TERRACE is now Nos. 17-29 Chickerell Road. In 1901 the Census enumerator's sequence was Prince of Wales Road, Ilton Terrace, Selway Terrace, North View, Melrose Terrace, Chickerell Road, Lilac Cottage on the Marsh, Coburg Terrace, Fermain Terrace, Lulworth Terrace, Springfield Terrace and 16 houses at the back of Lulworth Terrace, Arch Terrace and cottages, south side of Town Lane [Town Lane is an alternative name for Chickerell Road].

ARCH VILLAS are now Nos. 31-53 Chickerell Road.

ARCOT VILLA, Lennox Street Was for sale in August 1878 and described as *'All that newly erected freehold villa residence called Arcot Villa with a carriage entrance, capital walled-in garden and front ditto enclosed by iron palisades, situate in Lennox Street, near Victoria Terrace' The premises front the south west and at the back are protected by a thick shrubbery from the north winds'.* Now No. 27 Lennox Street.

ARONIA This 200-ton, 145 feet long luxury yacht belonged to millionaire Jack Billmeir and was frequently berthed in Weymouth Harbour in the 1950s. Following a fight on board in October 1959, one of her crew was found dead with head injuries. The yacht's steward was found not guilty of murder but jailed for manslaughter. The two men were friends, had been drinking heavily and started fighting. Jack Billmeir was founder of the Stanhope Steamship Company.

ARTS CENTRE *see* WEYMOUTH AND SOUTH DORSET ARTS CENTRE

ASCOT GOLD CUP There is a tradition that the Ascot Gold Cup was one used by King George III when he stayed at Weymouth and he later presented it as a horseracing trophy, but no documentary evidence has yet been found regarding the Cup's history. It is presented on Ladies Day at Royal Ascot.

ASH, Bryer Born in a Somerset mining village, Bryer Ash came to Weymouth around 1900 to manage a small coal business for his uncle and built up an extensive chain of depots extending over several counties. He bought S. C. Collins coal company in 1943. In the latter part of his life he lived at Cleaves Cliff, Overcombe.

ASHE, Philip *see* CADE, John

ATTACK, HMS In January 1941, due to the intensity of bombing raids on Weymouth and Portland, it was decided to relocate the Portland shore base *HMS Osprey,* headquarters of anti-submarine warfare research, to Scotland. The vacated buildings were then occupied by *HMS Attack,* the operational base for Coastal Forces. Its MGBs (Motor Gun Boats) were kept busy intercepting German E-boats in the Channel and were supplemented by launches and anti-submarine and minesweeping trawlers. On 31st December 1945, *HMS Attack* at Portland ceased to exist and *HMS Osprey* was able to return.

AUGUST BANK HOLIDAY Bank Holidays were originally days in the year when banks were legally closed. After the passing of the Bank Holiday Act in 1871 these days were fixed in the calendar and soon became public holidays. The August Bank Holiday weekend combined with cheap rail travel brought visitors flocking to Weymouth and was one of the factors which changed the character of the resort. Genteel long holidays for the wealthy gave way to the 'trippers' who wanted short breaks and inexpensive accommodation for their families. Originally August Bank Holiday was the first Monday in August but in 1965 it was changed to the last Monday in August.

AUSTRALIAN AND NEW ZEALAND TROOPS *see* WESTHAM CAMP

AUSTRALIAN GRAVES Close to Newstead Road in Melcombe Regis Cemetery are the graves of a number of World War I Anzac soldiers who died in Weymouth. Some had been severely wounded in the unsuccessful Gallipoli campaign in 1915.

AVIATION *see* AEROPLANES

Anzac graves, Melcombe Regis Cemetery, Newstead Road.

BW Club for HM Forces

B

BW CLUB for HM Forces was run during WW2 by Mrs Dorothy King of the British Women's League of Abstinence at St John's Mission Hall in Chelmsford Street. Further reading: *Happy Recollections* by Dorothy B. King (1946).

BAGG, James W. Died at his residence in Hartford Terrace on 16th April 1904. Partner in the firm of builders and contractors J. and H. Bagg. Originally traded from Avenue Road but moved to larger premises in Commercial Road near Westham Bridge in 1902. The firm built the Electricity Generating Station on Westwey Road, completed in August 1904. He was brother of John Bagg, also a builder and three-times Mayor of Weymouth, whose lavish lifestyle led to bankruptcy in 1910. (More about John Bagg in *Bumper Book I.*)

BALLAST QUAY In the 19th century the Ballast Quay on the Weymouth side of the harbour was between the end of Hope Quay (now Nothe Parade) and the start of the Stone Pier. On Melcombe side the Ballast Quay was in the vicinity of today's Ferry Steps, near Devonshire Buildings. Terms such as 'Ballast Quay' and 'New Quay' and 'New Wharf' are used rather loosely in earlier documents making identification of locations difficult.

A long way to fall if the circus balloonists had not managed to disentangle their craft.

BALLOONISTS Sometime in the 1890s a trio of balloonists, publicising Sanger's Circus then being held on the Barrack Field at Lodmoor Hill, flew not very far at all before the ropes of their balloon became entangled with the weathervane on the spire of St John's Church. They fortunately managed to disentangle themselves and landed safely on the beach at Greenhill. The weathervane was less fortunate and was severely bent out of shape.

BALSTON, Edward (1778-1850) *see* CORFE HILL HOUSE

BANK COTTAGES are now in Dorchester Road at Broadwey.

BANK HOUSE, Bank Buildings, The Esplanade John Puckett, a corn merchant built what became known later as Bank House on land leased from the Corporation. It appears, if the date of a painting by Thomas Girtin is correct, that it was completed in 1798 although this date is rather at odds with Corporation records which suggest that it was still being built in 1801. By this time Puckett was heavily in debt and his bankers, William and John Bower and Charles Bowles acquired the lease. They in turn passed it on to Anna Buxton who married Edmund Henning in 1804. Edmund Henning was a banker (his bank later failed) and presumably it was his business which gave the building its name. In later years it was Voss's Boarding House, the Cherbourg Hotel, the Marine Hotel, the Edward Hotel and the Hotel Dumonts before being converted to apartments and renamed Edward Court. *See also* PUCKETT'S STORES

BANKS, Gladys Mrs G. I. Banks died in the Salisbury area in the 1950s and left money to build almshouses in Swanage or Weymouth. Houses off Wyke Road were built under the auspices of this charity in the 1980s.

BARGE which went aground in Weymouth Bay October 2007. *See LONG SAND*

BARNES, Frederick George Portland quarry owner of the largest Portland stone concern on the island. Member of Weymouth Town Council 1895-1898. Died 14th July 1913 at his residence, Glenthorne, Bincleaves, Weymouth.

BARRACK FIELD was the barrack square of the Georgian Radipole Barracks, off Dorchester Road at Lodmoor Hill – an area now enclosed by Westbourne and Alexandra Roads. Little remains of the Cavalry Barracks, apart from Radipole Terrace and York Villa. Originally built in 1798 and later enlarged, they were redundant by the 1820s and sold off. *See also* RADIPOLE BARRACKS in *Bumper Book I*

BARROW RISE at Wyke Regis takes its name from two Bronze Age barrows which were believed to have existed in the Camp Road vicinity, long since lost under housing and never excavated.

BARROWS The area all around Weymouth and its villages abounds in Long Barrows and Round Barrows, too many to list in this work, which describes just a few of particular interest. *See* BARROW RISE; BINCOMBE;

The General Gordon Hotel, seen here, was pulled down in the post-war Chapelhay clearance.

MUSIC BARROWS; REDLANDS.

Further reading: *Dorset barrows*, by Leslie Grinsell (Dorset Natural History and Archaeological Society, 1959) and *An inventory of the historical monuments of the county of Dorset. Volume 2, South East, in three parts,* (The Royal Commission on Historical Monuments, 1970).

BARTLETT, butcher As demolition of war damaged buildings at Chapelhay went on all around his shop in 1952, Bartlett the butcher carried on trading – an isolated shop in the midst of the demolitions. Much of the rubble from Chapelhay was transported to Radipole Lake to provide foundation for the new pathways planned to criss-cross the lake.

BATCHFOOT HOUSE Dating from the first half of the 19th century Batchfoot House is the former Rectory on the west side of Church Street, Upwey. It is now a residential home.

BATHING, MIXED *see* MIXED BATHING

BATTLE OF PORTLAND 1653 During the first Anglo-Dutch War of 1652-4, the Dutch Admiral Marten Van Tromp's warships were escorting a fleet of some 200 merchantmen back to Holland when they were intercepted in the Channel off Portland by the English fleet under Admiral Robert Blake on 18th February 1653. Battle

Butcher Bartlett's isolated Chapelhay shop. Chapelhay was particularly badly hit in WW2 air raids and its ruined streets were used for street fighting training during the war.

commenced and continued without any decisive result until early in the morning of the 20th when firing began again and continued all day. The English claimed a victory and the defeated Van Tromp and his battered ships anchored off Calais. The Dutch lost about six fighting ships and a number of vessels in the convoy were captured. Although some of the English ships were damaged, only one, the 32-gun *Sampson* was sunk. Admiral Blake was wounded in the action.

BATTLE OF THE NILE 1798 At Weymouth in October 1798 King George III received the news of Admiral Horatio Nelson's victory (on August 1) over the French fleet in Aboukir Bay. Wild celebrations followed and the King himself stopped passers-by on the Esplanade to acquaint them with Nelson's triumph. Salutes were fired by ships in the Bay and repeated by hundreds of troops lined up on the sands, a band played 'Rule Britannia' and 200 people dined at Stacie's Hotel. At Mr Wood's Library a subscription was opened for *'the wives and orphans of those brave men who so gloriously fell in the ever-memorable action at the mouth of the Nile'* to which the proceeds of theatre performances and a ball were donated.

BAYARD'S FARM at Upwey belonged in the mid-19th century to John Hardy Thresher. The Thresher family owned **Corfe Hill House**.

BAYHAM Prolific novelist Mary Elizabeth Braddon (1837-1915), writing as 'Miss Braddon' used the name Bayham for Weymouth in her novel *Dead Sea Fruit*. She is best known for her novel *Lady Audley's Secret*.

BAYLY, Edward A local solicitor who had a house and offices in High Street, Weymouth. He was one of the executors of the will of Governor Arbuthnot, which he was later accused of altering or forging. He apparently subsequently fled the town and escaped to America in 1811.

BAYLY, Edward, JP, (1810-1905) Built Claylands (later renamed Blackdown) on Buxton Road where he died in October 1905. For many years he was manager of Williams, Thornton and Sykes's Bank, Weymouth. The house still stands, on the corner of Cross Road, currently (2009) in use as a day nursery.

BAYTREE COTTAGES, Wyke Regis are now part of Shrubbery Lane.

BEACH COURT, Overcombe was built in 1981-2.

BEACH VOLLEYBALL The National Beach Volleyball Championships were first held at Weymouth in August 1983.

BEACH'S CHARITY Martha Beach's will of 1823 left a sum of money, the interest on which was to be divided between six poor women over the age of sixty in the parish of Wyke Regis. The funds were usually distributed at Christmas.

BEALE, John Elmes (1849-1929) Born in Weymouth, the son of a ship's captain. Following his apprenticeship to a draper, he moved to Bournemouth and in 1881 opened his first shop there – Fancy Fair, which later became Beales department store. He was Mayor of Bournemouth from 1902-1905. He had a property in Weymouth overlooking Portland Harbour – Clovelly in Belle Vue Road, which lost a large portion of its grounds in February 1904 due to cliff slippage, a problem which has recurred regularly along this stretch of the coast.

The first big landslip along Underbarn as Clovelly's garden slides down to the sea in 1904.

BEECHCROFT INFANT SCHOOL took its first pupils in April 1991 and was officially opened by Jessie Fry on 17th July 1992. The school is a Voluntary Aided Church of England Primary School and is built on the former annexe of Westham Secondary Modern School.

BEECHEY, Sir William He painted *George III at a Review* in which the King, seated on his horse Adonis, is viewing a mock battle between two companies of dragoons, together with other officers and members of the royal family. Copies of the picture are not uncommon and Weymouth Museum has a fine picture of the King on horseback copied from part of the original painting. When it was presented to the town in the will of Sir Richard Nicholas Howard (died 1905) it was thought to be by Sir William Beechey but modern thought tends towards a copy. It is a fine painting, nevertheless, and can be seen in Weymouth Museum.

BELGRAVE TERRACE (No. 1) was being advertised as No. 79 Dorchester Road in 1905.

BELLE VIEW COTTAGES are now in Dorchester Road, Upwey.

BENNETT, Vilat Hackfath (1864-1948) *Amendment and correction to the main entry in Bumper Book I:*

V. H. Bennett opened shops at Nos. 16 and 17 Park Street in about 1885. He later bought a small former toy shop in St Thomas Street and began acquiring adjoining property. He then purchased sites in St Mary Street and in July 1908 realised his ambition to have a walk-through store from St Mary Street to St Thomas Street, the new St Mary Street premises being designed by Crickmay and Sons. The next property he acquired here was the jeweller's shop on the corner of St Mary Street and Bond Street formerly owned by J. B. Cole. Big showroom extensions were the result. Other developments followed. In September 1924 the electrical firm of Brooking and Co., at Nos. 8-9 Bond Street was incorporated with V. H. Bennett & Co., under the management of Mr T. H. Escott (later becoming Bennett and Escott).

When V. H. Bennett was Mayor in 1918-1919 he prepared his own plans for a Weymouth War Memorial. These were rejected, so he instead presented the Armistice Shelter to the town which still stands in Greenhill Gardens. His last here home was 'Whitecross' on Buxton Road, now demolished, but apartments built on the site have retained the name of the old house. His brother Robert Bennett worked with him in the business.

BENNETTS WATER GARDENS In 1959 Norman Bennett started growing water lilies in the disused clay pits of Chickerell Brickworks and was soon exporting them worldwide. Since then the 8-acre site has been landscaped with tranquil walks around the lakes and outstanding displays of water lilies in flower throughout the summer and pond and moisture loving plants, a far cry from the area's former industrial use. The gardens include a small museum displaying the history of the Putton Lane Brickworks which were formerly on the site.

BENSLEY, Harry 'the man in the iron mask' The story goes that in a London club two men, both rich, were debating whether it would be possible for a man to walk round the world without being identified. Harry Bensley heard of the conversation between the 5th Earl of Lonsdale and American John Pierpont Morgan – who bet $100,000 dollars that it could not be done. Bensley took on the wager and set off on 1st January 1908, pushing a baby's pram and with a steel helmet covering his face. It was an extraordinary challenge – he was supposed to visit (and prove) that he'd travelled through 17 counties in England and 17 towns in foreign countries – and find a wife en route. He was certainly photographed in Weymouth complete with the disguise, but the end of the story is as odd as the beginning and no-one seems to know if he ever left England. Harry Bensley 'the man in the iron mask' died penniless in Brighton in 1956.

BENSON, Sir Frank The famous Shakespearian actor, appeared with his Company at the Pavilion Theatre from February 18th 1924 for one week.

BENSON AND BARLING were printers with a circulating library at No. 86 St Mary Street (in 2009 occupied by the Next clothing shop). The address was also known, with No. 85, as Alpha Place. When the printers sold up in 1853, Septimus Mace, a draper, took over, followed by jeweller John Vincent in 1867, who had relocated from No. 74. Vincents remained at the address for just over 100 years, closing in 1968.

BERE REGIS & DISTRICT MOTOR SERVICES took over Ellis and Betts garage at No. 148 Dorchester Road in 1953. The large coach firm had previously operated in Weymouth, but on a fairly small scale. The garage, its fascia bearing a model coach in the company's two-tone brown livery, closed in 1967. It is now (2009) the site of Lidl supermarket.

BETJEMAN, John His *'First and last loves'* published in 1952 contains an essay on Weymouth.

Betts' wood pond, long filled in, is now Park Street Car Park.

BETTS, George William Betts' Timber and Deal Yards and Steam Saw Mills, Weymouth had previously belonged to P. Dodson & Co. Philip Dodson was a well-known Weymouth builder and Mayor of Weymouth in 1855, 1857 and 1858 who committed suicide in 1860. Betts appears to have taken over the yard and timber pond in Commercial Road the following year. This later became Webb, Major & Co's yard, and is now Park Street Car Park. Betts' sawmills site is now occupied by the Bridges Medical Centre on the corner of Gloucester Street and Commercial Road, having

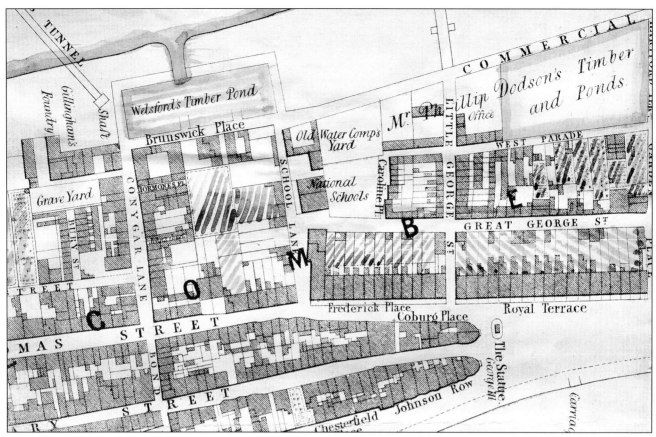

Dodson's Yard and Pond, Commercial Road on Pierse Arthur's Weymouth map of 1857. Later Betts Yard.

been the site of UBM Dibben's builders merchants' store in the 1980s. *See also* WEBB, MAJOR & COMPANY.

BEULAH HOUSE, Abbotsbury Road, Westham was occupied by Froom Bros., coal merchants in the early 1900s.

BEVAN, William Latham (1861-1934) First Bishop of Swansea and Brecon, was born in Weymouth and retired here, where he died in February 1934.

BIG RED ONE Many of the Americans who embarked at Weymouth and Portland for the D-Day landings on 6th June 1944 were part of the US 1st Division known as the 'Big Red One' after their distinctive shoulder patch, a red Arabic numeral 1 on an olive background. They landed in Normandy on a beach code-named 'Omaha' which became known as 'Bloody Omaha' after the US troops suffered 3,500 casualties there.

Initially, there were huge problems. Some landing craft sank before hitting the shore, drowning those on board. Men seasick from the crossing and weighed down with equipment and arms encountered mines and heavy firing from German guns in sheltered bunkers above the beach, out of reach of the fire from Allied warships offshore. With the dead and dying all around them, gradually small parties of men made their way across the beach and by evening, against all odds, the enemy guns were silenced and the Big Red One was established in France. *See also* POINTE DU HOC

BINCOMBE After the Norman Conquest, Bincombe was granted to the monastery of St Stephen at Caen and it eventually passed to St Stephen, Westminster. Following the Dissolution of the Monasteries in Henry VIII's reign it was granted to King's men Sir Richard Sackville and Richard Baker, being sold in 1570 to Caius College, Cambridge, the college to this day having an interest in the village. The barrows on Bincombe Hill, known as 'Bincombe Bumps' are the subject of an intriguing reference in Weymouth's earliest town guide published in 1785 by Peter Delamotte, in which he refers to two excavations in that decade. One was by the Duke of Gloucester and Mr Drax in the winter of 1781, during which an urn and warlike instruments were found, the second in 1784 carried out by the Duke of Northumberland, but nothing more is known about these 'digs'. More than one hundred and fifty years earlier **William Whiteway** described an unsuccessful excavation in the area in 1621.

BINCOMBE CHURCH From the 1720s the Rectors of Broadwey were also rectors of Bincombe and the parish of Bincombe-cum-Broadwey was consolidated in 1738. Bincombe Church tower has been extended, the new height being clearly shown in the stonework. The parish registers name the two young Hussars who were shot for desertion and buried in the churchyard on 30th June 1801 as Matthaus Tina and Christopher Bless. On duty guarding the royal family of King George III during his summer visit to Weymouth they had stolen a boat and unsuccessfully attempted to sail away from the town.

BINCOMBE SCHOOL The village school is thought to have opened in about 1876. It closed early in 1922.

BINCOMBE TUNNEL is the longest railway tunnel in Dorset, although its exact length seems to vary slightly depending on the measurer. A Dorset County Council survey probably provides the most accurate figure – that the tunnel is 751.940 metres or 822.322 yards long. The shorter adjacent tunnel is 38.21 metres or 41.79 yards long. The *Dorset County Chronicle* of 13th December 1849 announced *'The tunnel of the Railroad through Ridgeway Hill is at length completed'*.

BINCOMBE VALLEY PRIMARY SCHOOL, Culliford Way, Littlemoor The school, renamed in January 1999, was formerly known as Littlemoor Primary School.

BINDON COTTAGES are in Bryants Lane, Wyke Regis.

BINNIE, Alfred Maurice, F. Eng. (1901-1986) The distinguished engineer was not Weymouth-born, but he attended Weymouth College, the boys' public school, from 1910-1919.

BIRD FLU Strain H5N1 Bird Flu was confirmed at Abbotsbury Swannery in February 2008, its first appearance in Dorset. The outbreak was soon over.

BLACK ROD This name occurs in 17th and 18th century deeds as being a building on the south side of St Edmund Street but it is not clear if this was a house or perhaps at some time an inn. It also gave its name to a lane. In 1714 there was *'a house known by the name of the Black Rod in St Edmund Street...'* and a 1732 survey names *'a house formerly two tenements called the Black Rodd bounded on the west by an alehouse called the New Inn'* [the inn was in St Edmund Street]. Deeds of 1746 quote a building as being in *'a street commonly called the Corn Market in Melcombe Regis, on the east side and between a lane commonly called the Black Rod, on the north side of that lane with the Crown Inn on the north and west sides thereof...'*. The name Black Rod seems to have gone out of use by the mid-18th century.

BLACKSHIRTS *see* FASCISTS, BRITISH UNION OF

BLONDIN The famous tightrope walker performed his high wire act at Belfield Park on 14th October 1861 witnessed by a crowd estimated at some ten thousand, many having arrived on special excursion trains laid on for the occasion. A rope about 300 feet long was suspended between trees and said to be 60 feet above the ground, although some present felt it was not quite that high. Whatever the height, Blondin performed some spectacular feats – *'He walked along the rope, lay on his back and did somersaults. He walked backwards, stood on his head and walked blindfold causing shrieks from the audience when he professed to make a false step. His 4th trip along the rope involved carrying a man on his shoulders...'*.

BLUE ANCHOR pub existed in the early 18th century but its location is unknown.

BLUNDELL RULES The slide rule and scale manufacturers opened a factory at Lynch Lane industrial estate early in 1956.

BOAR'S HEAD tavern In 1588 there was a tavern called the Bore's Head in Melcombe Regis, but the location is unknown.

BOARD'S TYPING SCHOOL Board's Weymouth School of Shorthand and Typewriting, No. 51, St Mary Street was run by various members of the Board family from at least 1915 until 1958 when their premises behind the Guildhall were demolished.

BOGG family *see* BOGUE, Ida

BOGLE, Captain Harry, RE and his sister Miss Ethel Bogle of Wellington Lodge, Dorchester Road drowned in Weymouth Bay when their yacht capsized on 26th September 1910. Both had sailing experience and they had hired a boat and set out for a sail that afternoon.

BOGUE, Ida M. (1885-1972) *Amendment to the main entry in Bumper Book I.* Daughter of William and Mary Bogue who moved to Weymouth from the London area in the 1890s when he was appointed postmaster, living in a newly built house Sunnybrae, No. 1 Kirtleton Avenue (the move coincided with a change of spelling of the family's surname which had previously been BOGG).

Ida, who never married and remained in the family home until her death, was a talented artist and taught art at St Aubyn's School in Carlton Road. An unpublished children's book *Child Hazel*, which she wrote and illustrated, was highly praised when it was featured in the BBC-TV programme 'Antiques Roadshow' in 2004.

BOHAYES is an old Wyke place name. A large house called Bohays House stood on the site of Stonehill Court in Westhill Road and was pulled down in the 1970s. There was also farm known as Little Bohays Farm (but no farmhouse).

BOILING ROCK This was the name of the spring at Sutton Poyntz from which the first water supply to Melcombe Regis was obtained in 1797.

BOMBARDONS Trials of the giant hollow steel caissons which formed the breakwaters across the channel for the D-Day Mulberry Harbours took place in Weymouth Bay on 1st and 2nd April 1944.

BOOTH, General In addition to the Salvation Army leader's visits to Weymouth in 1890 and 1906, the eighty-one year old General was also here on 26th September 1910 and gave a lecture at the Sidney Hall.

BOOTS CIRCULATING LIBRARY opened in the St Mary Street shop in the summer of 1901. All Boots libraries closed at the end of January 1966.

BOTTLE BANKS came into use in Weymouth in Summer, 1981.

BOULTON VILLA A Victorian house off Buxton Road which was later known as Wyke Lodge. Now demolished, the houses of Lodge Way and Boulton Close fill the site. It was the home of Catherine Dowman (1878-1972) whose husband Captain Wilfred Dowman began the restoration of the tea clipper *Cutty Sark* which she later presented to the nation.

BOUNDARIES The extent of the borough's boundaries at various periods in its history are described in *Bumper Book I*, but the following are contemporary descriptions of the boundaries of Wyke Regis in 988 and Radipole in the 16th century.

Wyke Regis. A Saxon charter of the year 988 describes Wyke's boundaries. It contains some place names which are recognisable today, but others have been lost:
From the West Sea to Saggeloth-
from Saggeloth to Muleditch,
from Muleditch to Blackstone,
from Blackstone to Goldcroft,

From Goldcroft to Sorediche,
From Sorediche to Lodmore,
and from Lodmore to the East Sea.

Radipole's boundaries were perambulated in 1582 and described in the parish register as follows:

'*At Hockerhill* [formerly a farm near the village], *the Rector read in the hall, thence they went from the highway to the Brickworks* [possibly Bullworks or Bulwarks] *that turn on the left hand, and went to the Chesil* [the seashore], *to the end of a great dyke, where was a cross, the foot of which remained; which dyke parts the Manor of Sutton Points and Radipole. Thence they went to the Chesil, by the main sea, to a bound, where a gallows did stand, and a pirate was executed; which bound parts of the Manor of Radipole and the Borough of Melcomb and read again, over against Temswell* [Greenhill]'.

BOUNDARY STONES A count of Boundary Stones on a post-1933 Ordnance Survey map of the borough (the last major extension of the boundaries prior to the inclusion of Portland in 1974) reveals more than 30 stones marking the borough boundaries. A perambulation of the borough today would take some time. Other stones remain from earlier borough boundaries and may not now be on their original sites or even exist at all due to more recent building developments. Some have been saved – one from 1895 when the

Boulton Villa, later known as Wyke Lodge.

Weymouth boundary was extended to include parts of Wyke Regis has been re-sited on Buxton Road opposite the end of Rylands Lane. Another was re-positioned when Preston Beach wall was rebuilt in 1996. Boundary stones put in place in 1895 bear the name of Mayor T. H. Williams, those from 1933 that of Mayor F. W. Hamblin.

BOWLEAZE COVE TAVERN opened 8th April 1982. Stone used in the development came from Gloucester Street Congregational Church, demolished in 1980.

BOWLEAZE COVEWAY The roadway was completed in 1927, the start of the development of the area by the Weymouth Bay Estate Company.

BOWLS Weymouth Bowling Club was inaugurated on 1st June 1907. Having failed in their attempt to secure the exclusive use of the 1906 Greenhill Gardens bowling green for two days each week, the members established their HQ on a bowling green behind the Royal Oak Hotel on Dorchester Road at Lodmoor Hill. The club celebrated its first anniversary in 1908, which makes a photograph of Weymouth Bowling Club members, bearing a date of 12th May 1898 rather puzzling, especially since they are clearly assembled behind the Spa Hotel at Radipole. Greenhill Bowling Club was established in 1910. Melcombe Regis Bowling Club was formed in 1926 when a green was laid out and a Pavilion built on the newly reclaimed land of Melcombe Regis Gardens. In 1994 the Weymouth Bowling Club and Melcombe Regis Bowling Club amalgamated under the name Weymouth and Melcombe Regis Bowls Club, playing on the green in Melcombe Regis Gardens where a new Pavilion opened in 1995. Whitehead Bowling Club was formed in 1931, members initially using

Bowleaze Coveway overlooks the Cove – very little developed in this early view.

This picture of Weymouth Bowling Club is dated 12th May 1898 – although first mention of the club has only been traced back to 1907.

The Riviera Hotel at Bowleaze was not built until 1937.

Melcombe Regis green until their own was laid out in 1935-36 – now part of Wellworthy Sports and Social Club.

BOYLE, Percy, MBE (1869-1953) He started work with the GWR as a boy in 1883 and later in the same decade came to Weymouth to work for the company, eventually becoming GWR Marine Superintendent here. He was Mayor in 1928-29 and 1929-30, welcoming the Duke of York (later King George VI) on the occasion of the opening of the present Town Bridge on 4th June 1930.

Mayor Percy Boyle (on the left), with the Town Clerk and a building surveyor, is hoisted aloft and swung out over the harbour to view the 1930 Town Bridge construction works.

BRACKENDOWN AVENUE Built in the mid-1960s as naval married quarters, three blocks with eight properties in each went up for sale in October 1981 as surplus to requirements by the navy.

BRADDON, Miss (1837-1915) Mary Elizabeth Braddon was a prolific novelist. She is the author of *Dead Sea Fruit* in which she uses the name Bayham for Weymouth. Her best-known novel was *Lady Audley's Secret*.

BRANNON, Philip He produced guide books to towns in east Dorset – Corfe, Wareham, Poole, Bournemouth, Swanage etc. and Hampshire towns between 1845 and 1884. His illustrations also appeared as engravings accompanying articles in the Illustrated London News.

BREAKWATERS, Portland Harbour Royal assent was given on 11th May 1847 for the construction of the first two breakwaters to enclose Portland Roads. Convict labour was employed in the Portland quarries to hew out the enormous amount of stone required to build up the breakwater profile. The foundation stone of the massive project was laid on 25th July 1849 by Prince Albert and it continued to be newsworthy until the final stone was laid on 10th August 1872. The Prince Consort paid several visits to view the breakwaters' progress until his death in 1861. Initial fears that such intense building works would disturb the genteel and fashionable image that Weymouth had fostered since its balmy days as King George III's favourite resort were soon dispelled as visitors flocked to the Island to view the breakwaters under construction – strolling without a care along rail tracks among trains laden with huge blocks of stone. Engineer in chief of the breakwater project James Meadows Rendel died in 1856, when John Coode, his deputy, took control and remained in charge of the project until its completion in 1872. The final stone was laid by the Prince of Wales (later King Edward VII). The breakwaters are part of the south coast defence works known

Philip Brannon's view of the Nothe Fort under construction in the 1860s.

The great Nothe Fort, part of the defence scheme which included the Portland Breakwaters. It is now a tourist attraction and houses the Museum of Coastal Defence.

The fine monument at Portland which commemorates the completion of the Breakwaters project.

as 'Palmerston's follies' which in this area include the Nothe Fort and the Verne Citadel, forts on the breakwaters themselves, **Upton Fort** (part of the original plan but not completed until 1902) and gun emplacements on the Nothe headland and at Portland. As submarine and torpedo warfare developed it was realised that the two breakwaters stretching out from Portland were inadequate to protect shipping in Portland Harbour and between 1893 and 1905 two more breakwaters were added from the Weymouth side, closing the gap between Bincleaves and the original breakwaters.

BRENTRY VILLA also known as BRENTRY HOUSE was No. 1 Lansdowne Square, at one time owned by the Devenish family.

BREWERIES Apart from a selection of specialist beers brewed on a small scale at Brewer's Quay, no brewing is carried on at Weymouth now. The two major brewers, John Groves and Sons and J. A. Devenish amalgamated in 1960 and in 1985, by then under the Devenish name, all brewing was transferred to the company's other establishment at Redruth. In previous centuries there were numerous small breweries in and around Weymouth, those in the Hope area being gradually absorbed by the two larger breweries.
Further reading: *Old Dorset Brewers* by Jimmy Young (1986).

BRIARSWOOD was a large house on the corner of Rodwell Road and St Leonard's Road which in pre-WW2 years was in use as a hotel. It was probably bomb-damaged and certainly in a state of dereliction when it was demolished. Flats built on the site in 1964 retained the original Briarswood name.

BRICKLAYERS ARMS pub was in Great George Street.

BRIDES IN THE BATH MURDER CASE An account of the events leading up to the sensational murder trial in 1915 of George Joseph Smith who drowned three of his wives in the bath can be found in *Bumper Book I under* SMITH, George Joseph. One of the victims was Bessie Mundy, who married Smith and lived with him for a short time at No. 14 Rodwell Avenue, Weymouth.

BRIDGE CLOSE, Wyke Regis was the location of Sapsworth's Food Factory off Camp Road, before Mandeville Road was built. Now (2009) the site of Value House store.

BRIDGE FARM In 1867 the 59-acre Bridge Farm at Wyke Regis was owned by Colonel Steward of Nottington.

BRIDGES MEDICAL CENTRE on the corner of Commercial Road and Gloucester Street, was built in 2002. For the history of the site *see* **BETTS, George William.**

BRIDGING CAMP, Wyke Regis. *Update to the main entry in Bumper Book I:*
The tented summer camp for the Royal Engineers to train in bridge building was established on the shores of The Fleet in May 1928. Over the years more training facilities were added with new buildings, marshalling and storage areas and an extended bridge-launching hard. The tented camp area became redundant following the erection of purpose-built accommodation blocks at Chickerell Camp and it was sold in 2008 and awaits re-development.

BRIDLE, Eli He was a Master Gunner, born in Maiden Newton, who served through the Crimea, witnessed the Balaclava charge and was at the Battle of Inkerman and Alma, and the Siege of Sebastopol. Aged 92, he was admitted to Weymouth Workhouse on March 24th 1920, a temporary placement until somewhere more fitting could be found. He subsequently went to live in the Chelsea Hospital for pensioners but was knocked down by a car and killed about two years later.

BRIG INN was at No. 30 High Street in the 1870s.

BRISTOL'S INSTRUMENT COMPANY, Lynch Lane The instrument making company, manufacturers of gauges, thermometers, pyrometers and automatic controllers, ships logs and recording instruments, moved to Lynch Lane industrial estate in December 1948. It had been founded in 1889 by an American, Professor William H. Bristol. Sales of the products in the UK led to the setting up of a factory in London and a larger new factory in Willesden in 1936. After the war the London sites proved to be unsuitable for expansion and the firm relocated to Lynch Lane. The company was bought by Elliott Bros. (London) Ltd. in 1953 but they closed the factory on 14th November 1958 in order to concentrate work at their other factory in Rochester, Kent.

BRITANNIA was a racing yacht owned by the Prince of Wales (later King Edward VII). A dinghy belonging to the yacht overturned in a storm on 25th August 1894 and the three men on board were drowned in Portland Harbour — the first mate and crew's caterer and a crew member from another yacht. They had been attempting to reach their yachts from the Portland shore.

BRITANNIA COTTAGES were in High Street, Wyke Regis, as was the Britannia Inn.

BRITISH BOYS SCHOOL, Belle Vue This was in the building currently (2009) occupied by the Elim Church. It does not appear on the 1841 Census, but is listed in 1851. An 1857 guidebook states the school *'has been long in operation'*.

BRITISH LEGION *Update to the main entry in Bumper Book I:*

The former HQ of the Royal British Legion in King Street, Weymouth was sold in 2008 and converted to a free-house pub called 'Number Six' after its King Street address.

BRITISH RESTAURANTS were government-sponsored and set up in WW2 to provide inexpensive no-coupons meals in cafeteria-style surroundings. They proved invaluable for those bombed out of their homes as in the days of food rationing neighbouring families had no food to spare. There were four in Weymouth, known as 'Cookery Nooks', at the Wyke Hotel (now Wyke Smugglers pub), Christchurch (in King Street, demolished in the 1950s), the Rock Hotel and the Sidney Hall (demolished in the 1980s. Now the site of Asda supermarket and car park). The last British Restaurant closed in April 1949.

BRITISH UNION OF FASCISTS *see* FASCISTS, BRITISH UNION OF

BROADMEAD This land, described as an area of 5-6 acres immediately adjoining **Sandesfort House** on Buxton Road, was up for auction as building land on 16th June 1905.

BROADMEADOW ESTATE Part of this estate, 107 plots of land opposite the Wyke Hotel (now Wyke Smugglers), was up for sale in June 1898 and was acquired by Weymouth Land Syndicate, the firm having already developed sites on Rodwell Avenue. Williams Avenue was built by September 1900.

BROADMEADOW SUB POST OFFICE on the corner of Portland Road and Williams Avenue, opened in July 1901.

BROADWEY is almost certainly one of the eight places listed as Wai or Waia in the Domesday Survey but none have been identified with any certainty. As a place name Broadwey (or Broadway, both spellings were in use well into the twentieth century and Broadway is still favoured by some) was first used in 1242. The manor and a large part of the estate in the 18th century became the property George Gould of Upwey and Fleet who married Abigail, daughter of Robert Goodden. It passed down through various family members until in 1866 was in the possession of Henry Charles Goodden of Upwey. St Nicholas Church, originally dedicated to St Michael, was much altered in the 19th and early 20th centuries. *See also* Nicholson Monument

BROADWEY FARM, No. 625 Dorchester Road The building is of late 17th century origin, much altered and enlarged. Once thatched, it now has a slated gable and roof.

BROADWEY FARM'S BARN, Dorchester Road was later used as a stable and converted to a house in 1964.

The church at Broadwey, an engraving by John Upham, 1825.

Ballard Brown entertaining on the Sands in the early 1900s at the Sea View Concert Platform.

The then owner's wife was from Norway and the house was called 'Stallen', Norwegian for 'The Stable'.

BROADWEY GAS HOLDER A Gasholder for the supply of gas to Broadwey and Upwey was erected near Nottington Corner in May 1930. It was taken down in the 1960s.

BROADWEY MOTORS moved from Lower St Edmund Street to their other premises in Weston Street in 1982. The firm now operates from Wyke Regis Garage and Owermoigne. Spinnaker View flats were built on the Weston Street site in 2005.

BROADWEY RECTORY This large early 19th century building in Lorton Lane ceased to be used by the clergy in the first half of the 20th century.

BROADWEY. ROAD WIDENING Dorchester Road was widened near the Swan Inn, Broadwey in 1959 when old buildings opposite the pub were demolished.

BROADWEY SCHOOLS *see* ST NICHOLAS SCHOOL, Broadwey; WEY VALLEY SCHOOL AND SPORTS COLLEGE; WYVERN SCHOOL

BROOK COTTAGE, No. 160 Church Street, Upwey dates from the 18th century.

BROOK HOUSE, No. 162 Church Street, Upwey dates from the 18th century.

BROWN, Ballard The first appearance of Mr Ballard Brown's Company of Entertainers at Weymouth appears to have been on 10th June 1905 when they performed at the Seaview Concert Platform at the start of their season here. They must have been a popular troupe as in 1913 Mr Brown was congratulated on erecting *'a roomy and comfortable theatre on the site of the old Seaview concert platform'*.

BROWN, I. J. and Son The firm of opticians was founded in Weymouth in 1883 and continues today.

BROWN POTTER, Mrs (1857-1936) appeared at the Jubilee Hall in March 1903. She was the former Mary Cora Urquhart of New Orleans, who visited England in 1886 with her husband and caught the eye of the Prince of Wales (later King Edward VII). The American beauty was popular in high society and stayed behind when her husband returned home. She embarked on a successful theatrical career using her married name.

BROWNS COTTAGES were in High Street, Wyke Regis.

BRUNEL, Theodore On his death aged 39 in 1861, Corsican-born Theodore Brunel was described in one local newspaper as 'a photographer's assistant', in another as 'an eminent photographer' and the latter description is probably more accurate since earlier in his life he had photographed the royal family at Windsor. His later years in business at Weymouth cannot have been happy ones as he was frequently drunk and violent. On the night of his death, a local police constable found him noisily knocking on the door of a house in Turton Street, having previously caused a disturbance at the Albert Hotel (now the rebuilt Queens Hotel) nearby. Brunel, resisting arrest, had his arms strapped down and the constable escorted him to the police station at the Guildhall. Almost there, he promised to behave and was unstrapped, only to reach into his pocket and take out a bottle containing cyanide of potassium, which he drank. Death was almost immediate. The inquest verdict was 'Temporary Insanity', the deceased having threatened suicide before.

BRYMER ROOMS These Conservative club rooms opened on 8th October 1909 in the former St Martin's Mission Hall at the entrance to Weston Road, close to its junction with Boot Hill. They presumably take their name from Colonel William Ernest Brymer, Tory MP for South Dorset from 1891-1906. Since demolished.

BUCKINGHAM, James Silk (1786-1855) Cornish born author and traveller. He travelled extensively in Europe, America and the East. The author of numerous travel books, he also wrote on social and political subjects. Believed to be the author of '*A summer trip to Weymouth and Dorchester, including an Excursion to Portland, and a Visit to Maiden Castle, the Amphitheatre and other places of Interest. From the Note-book of an old Traveller*', published in 1842.

BUCKLAND RIPERS was originally held by the Frampton family of Moreton. The seat of the Framptons and the Church were destroyed by fire in 1655 and both were later rebuilt. In 1704 the family sold the estate to Mr Damer of Dorchester and took up residence at Rempston, Corfe Castle. The village's name is derived from that of the De Ripariis or Rivers family, ancient lords of the manor here.

BUCKLERS LANE 17th century records describe Bucklers Lane (Boot Hill) as being the 'Churchway' presumably the route the inhabitants of the Weymouth side of the harbour took to reach their parish church, All Saints, Wyke Regis, in the days before the they had a church of their own (Holy Trinity, built in the 1830s).

BUCKLIN, Joseph He has gone down in history as the man who fired the first shot which triggered the American Revolution and is said to have been a descendant of William Bucklin of Radipole who emigrated to the New World in 1630.

BUDMOUTH TECHNOLOGY COLLEGE On the introduction of comprehensive education in 1985, two schools which shared a site at Charlestown, Weymouth Grammar School and Westham Secondary School, amalgamated to become Budmouth School which is now known as Budmouth Technology College.

BUFFALO BILL'S WILD WEST EXHIBITION was at Weymouth on 4th August 1903 at **Goldcroft Farm**. It arrived in 4 special trains carrying 500 horses and 800 people. For those who missed the real thing, the show could be viewed in the Jubilee Hall in December 1904, a pictorial record made on the British Biograph Company's machines.

BUGLER, Reginald Ernest (died 1959) Son of Mr and Mrs W. R. Bugler, coach proprietors, whose premises were in Abbotsbury Road. He began driving coach and horses and then became the town's first motor car taxi driver. He was a former landlord of the Duke of Cornwall Inn. A founder member of Weymouth Swimming Club, he was one of the originators of the Christmas Day swim. Around 1948 he made a wager with Mr R. S. Laker, his successor at the Duke of Cornwall. Each bet against the other's ability to swim across Weymouth Harbour on Christmas Day. Both managed it and so began the traditional swim. *See also* CHRISTMAS

BULL INN in Melcombe Regis is referred to in 17th and 18th century deeds.

BURDEN'S TRANSPORT The firm began in Weymouth on 1st April 1922, located on Custom House Quay (not to be confused with Burdon's coal stores on Custom House Quay which were founded in the 19th century).

BURDON, William Wharton *Update to the main entry in Bumper Book I:*

Further research has shown that William Wharton Burdon, a prominent coal mine owner in Newcastle upon Tyne and the original proprietor of Weymouth Gasworks, also owned a considerable amount of property around Weymouth. Included in this was Burdon's Buildings and it is now certain that these were named after him. In the 1860s when he already owned several dwellings in this tenement building in Commercial Road (formerly **Puckett's Stores** and later converted to become the Queen's Barracks) he began adding more until he owned all 35

The only photograph so far discovered of Burdon's Buildings.

dwellings within the building, which by the 1870s had become known as Burdon's Buildings. Burdon died unmarried in 1870, when his not inconsiderable fortune passed to Augustus Edward de Butts, a cousin. Augustus de Butts subsequently changed his name to Augustus Burdon. He died in the 1880s and 'Burdon's Buildings' were afterwards owned by Sir Richard Nicholas Howard. The later history of the block is in *Bumper Book I* under BURDON'S BUILDINGS.

BURNING CLIFF, HOLWORTH *Update to the main entry in Bumper Book I:*

Generally considered to have been a phenomenon of 1826-27, the spontaneous ignition of the shale cliffs at Holworth actually continued to burst forth for a number of years and was still active in 1833, when, although there was no fire to be seen, clouds of sulphurous vapour were issuing out of the cliff.

BURTON BRADSTOCK Practically all of the village of Burton Bradstock, 1,700 acres in total, including West Bay golf course, stretches of private beach, farms etc., was up for auction on 31st July and 1st August 1958. It had been part of the Pitt Rivers estate for more than 300 years but was proving uneconomic to run.

BUS RALLIES These were organised by the now defunct Dorset Transport Circle from 1971-1981 and were well attended events at Lodmoor, some of the 100 or so historic vehicles making a run to Portland and back.

BUS SHELTER, King's Statue was erected 1930/31. It was removed in 1954 when work began on the construction of the present large traffic island at the Statue, which may itself be removed if plans for the redevelopment of the Statue area go ahead. *See* ESPLANADE REGENERATION PROJECT

BUTCHERS ARMS INN, West Street, on the Melcombe side of the harbour was demolished in 2003 when the area was redeveloped. There was also a Butchers Arms Inn at Sutton Poyntz in the 19th century.

BUTTS GROVE or QUAKERS GROVE led to The Lookout.

BUXTON, Sir Thomas Fowell (1786-1845)
Additions to the Buxton family main entry in Bumper Book I:

Thomas Fowell Buxton is much associated with Weymouth, being one of the town's MPs from 1818-1837 and a descendant of the Buxtons of Belfield House, the property he was to inherit on Buxton Road. He was involved in moves to abolish slavery and the slave trade, as well as the improvement of English prisons. He leased Belfield to his uncle, Charles Buxton, as the main family homes were in London and Northrepps Hall, near Overstrand in Norfolk, where he is buried in the churchyard. He was created a baronet in 1840. In addition to a statue of him by Frederick Thrupp in Westminster Abbey, there is a Buxton Memorial Fountain in London designed by Samuel Sanders Teulon. This commemorates Buxton and others involved in the abolition of the slave trade and was commissioned by Charles Buxton, his son. It originally stood in Parliament Square, but was removed in 1940 and later re-sited in Victoria Tower Gardens.

BUXTON ROAD FOOTBRIDGE The prefabricated steel footbridge alongside the bridge which crosses the former railway line (now the Rodwell Trail) was moved here from its previous location on Preston Road opposite the Bridge Inn.

BUXTON ROAD JUNCTION WITH RODWELL ROAD The sharp right angle bend at this junction was replaced by a sweeping bend in 1963 to improve visibility. At the same time, one of the last WW2 bomb sites in the town was cleared – No. 78 Rodwell Road, the home of local GP Dr William Scott until it was demolished in an air raid on the night of 15th April 1941, from which everyone was safely rescued. His house was also known as No.1 Clearmount.

BUXTON'S LANE was an early name for Cross Road and that part of Buxton Road between Cross Road and Foord's Corner.

BUXTON'S ROW is listed in the 1851 Census and appears to be in the Hope Square area.

The King's Statue bus shelter of the 1930s, removed in the 1950s.

Cactus Tea Rooms

CACTUS TEA ROOMS formerly stood on the Pier but moved out in 2008 due to the proposed development there. They are now relocated at Nos. 33/34 The Esplanade as the Cactus Tea Rooms and Bistro.

CADE, John A sea captain and Royalist supporter in the time of the Civil War and one of a group of men whose successful plotting enabled Royalist forces to mount a surprise attack on Parliamentary-held Weymouth and Melcombe Regis on 9th February 1645. At the end of the month and after fierce fighting Parliamentary forces regained control and on 3rd March Captain John Cade and fellow conspirator John Mills, a Town Constable, were tried, found guilty of treachery and hung on the Nothe headland. Another of the original group, Fabian Hodder, was imprisoned but somehow escaped further punishment, returning after the Restoration in 1660 to become a member of the Corporation. The fourth member of the original plotters, Philip Ashe, died in the fighting at the end of February.

CAE RHYS ESTATE was on Dorchester Road at Radipole, just before its junction with Spa Road. In 1902 it was described as a handsome residence and grounds and 10 choice freehold building plots.

CAESAR, George Julius Adelmare, MPS An analytical chemist who carried out considerable experimental work in connection with the medicinal wells and springs around Weymouth, and also on Dorset oil shale. Managing director of Stedmans Ltd., (retail chemists) 1921-30. His son, Julius Adelmare Caesar was a reporter on the *Southern Times* newspaper.

CALLAN, Jon Stained glass artist. Locally his work can be seen in the Church of St Francis of Assisi at Littlemoor and St Andrew's Church, Portland, where stunning windows dedicated in 1981 commemorate the *Avalanche* shipwreck disaster of 1877.

CAMBRIDGE COURT This apartment block in Verne Road replaced an older house called Whitecroft.

CAMDEN PLACE is now part of Chamberlaine Road, Wyke Regis.

CAMP ROAD was formerly known as Green Lane. Another Green Lane leads from St Martin's Road to Buxton Road.

CAP IN HAND RIOTERS In Kent in 1830 desperately poor agricultural workers demanding more wages burned hayricks, smashed agricultural machinery and threatened to destroy the houses of wealthy landowners. The riots spread across the south of England and although Dorset labourers were involved most of the unrest was outside the Weymouth farming area. The alarming reports of rioting in other areas of the county led to the men of the Revenue Cutters being sworn in as special constables, unnecessarily as it turned out, as the local press reported that *'in Abbotsbury and neighbourhood all was continuing as usual, no hint of unrest'*. In the north and east of the county 71 rioters were later tried: those found guilty received sentences of transportation or gaol. The riots are also known as the Captain Swing Riots after the assumed name of one of the Kent men.

CAPA, Robert The famous war photographer was pictured in Weymouth with war correspondent Ernest Hemingway shortly before embarking for the landings on Omaha Beach on D-Day, 6th June 1944. His memorable account of the slaughter on what he described as *'the ugliest beach in the whole world'* was not matched by the photographs he took that day: all but eight were accidentally destroyed during processing. *See also* HEMINGWAY, Ernest

'CAPTAIN PORTLAND BILL' was originally a small marionette who appeared in strip cartoons. Created by David Leech of Weymouth, he evolved into a 7' 6" puppet who entertained visitors at the Pavilion Theatre and was used to publicise the resort in the 1980s.

CAPTAIN SWING RIOTS *see* CAP IN HAND RIOTERS

CAR EXPORTS Sealink handled the first-ever train to carry cars for export to the Channel Islands. A 21-wagon car train from Birmingham brought 105 Minis and Metros to Weymouth in 1983, which were shipped out in two batches.

CAREY, George Saville (1743-1807) Author, among other publications, of *The Balnea: or an Impartial Description of all the Popular Watering Places in England* published in 1799. His description of Weymouth is less than flattering, *'This royal watering-place has nothing to recommend but its conveniency in respect to bathing; no ride, no object, but that sterile the Isle of Portland; no walk but the Esplanade, which has little variety in point of view, but is one straight line of rubbish, thrown up from the level as a kind of barrier, to prevent the town from being overwhelmed by a more than ordinary tide'*. His comments range from accommodation at the first Royal Hotel - *'The person who keeps it was for many years the master of the Bedford Arms, in Covent Garden, in London, a house that has been of great noto-*

riety, time out of mind' – to the library, the baths and the theatre - *'The theatre is on a contracted scale, built in the shape of a wig box and not much wider ; this thing (for it is difficult to give it a name) is managed by one of the principal proprietors of Sadler's Wells'.* One more unusual custom Carey refers to is the strewing of small beach pebbles on the pavements in advance of the Royal visits. Carey, feeling that straw would be a better alternative, complains bitterly about this custom as the horses hooves sent the pebbles about like pistol shots, breaking windows and endangering eyes.

CARLO ALBERTA The Italian battleship was in Weymouth in June 1902. *See also* MARCONI, Guglielmo and ROSEBERY, Lord

CARLTON HOUSE was in Lennox Street. There was also a Carlton House and adjacent Carlton Villa on the north side of Chickerell Road.

CARNIVAL *Update to the main entry in Bumper Book I:*

In 1958 Weymouth Round Table organised Weymouth Carnival for the first time and in 2007 celebrated their 50th anniversary of running the event – the last time they would do so. In 2008 a new organisation took over and changed the format of the Carnival's main evening event from a motorised procession to a walking one, which met with a mixed reception. The procession since 1966 has started and finished at Lodmoor Car Park. Prior to this the floats gathered at the Westham Gasworks car park for judging before setting off for the Esplanade, but this site had become rather congested so the move to the north end of town was made.

CARNIVAL QUEEN The first, when the title was 'Weymouth Hospitals Carnival Queen' was Miss Bessie 'Babs' Bartlett in 1932. There was something of a furore in 2009 when the carnival organisers announced that the traditional competition to select a Carnival Queen was to be abolished and that the choice of person to lead the procession would be made by some other means. Protests were many and the 'Carnival Queen' competition was re-instated.

CARTER, Cyril An eccentric local poet, known for his verse on topical subjects. Died following a fire at his Melcombe Avenue home (outside which he frequently posted his poetry) in October 1981.

CASSEA COURT, Dorchester Road, Broadwey was built in 1982.

CAT RACING Cat racing at Weymouth was a 1930s hoax reported in the national press. Similar cat-racing hoaxes have occurred elsewhere.

CAT'S WHISKERS nightclub closed in October 1988 due to town centre redevelopment. The club was in premises originally 'Arcadia' attached to the Jubilee Hall,

later becoming known as the Regent Dance Hall and later again occupied by Weyrad as a factory. The nightclub opened in 1979 as 'Nino's' changing its name to The Cat's Whiskers three years later.

CATACOMBS Holy Trinity Church, Weymouth has catacombs beneath it but these have not been used for burials since 1856. The area below the church was used as an air raid shelter during WW2 and was converted to a hall in 1979.

CATHKIN HOUSE, No. 13, Greenhill *see* GREYSTONES

CATHOLIC CHAPEL OF OUR LADY, Preston and Sutton Poyntz The chapel of ease in Sutton Road is now closed.

CATHOLIC CHURCHES In 2007 the Diocese of Plymouth was negotiating to build a new church to provide a single borough-wide church to replace St Augustine's, Dorchester Road, St Joseph's, Stavordale Road and Our Lady and St Andrew, The Grove, Portland. *See also* CATHOLIC CHAPEL OF OUR LADY, Preston & Sutton Poyntz; CHURCH OF THE HOLY FAMILY, Upwey; ST CHARLES RC CHURCH, Wyke Regis

CAUSEWAY, Radipole is thought to derive its name from John de Cauz, an owner in medieval times. Other well-known names which occur over the years in the history of Causeway manor and farm are Payne, Pitt, William Ferris, Warren Lisle, John Herbert Browne and the Balston and Thresher families. Perhaps the best-known residents, and the most unfortunate, were the Bucklers in the 16th century. They took in a stranger from France in 1563 who brought plague to the family, resulting in the deaths of the widow of Andrew Buckler, three of his sons and a daughter and several other family members. The present Causeway House dates in part from the late 17th century.

CEMETERY ROAD appears to have been a name in use in the 19th century for what became Shirecroft Road.

CENTRAL HOTEL was at No. 38 St Thomas Street in the late 19th century. Today's Central Hotel is at No. 17 Maiden Street.

CHADDOCKS appears to have been a yard or possibly a slipway off North Quay in the late 19th century.

CHAFEYS LAKE/CHAFFEYS LAKE Although today's spelling is usually the former, Chaffeys Lake seems to be the older spelling occurring in 18th and 19th century documents and publications. Who or what Chaffey was is yet to be discovered. An intriguing reference in the Corporation minutes of 7th March 1785 permits two local men to lay oysters in the backwater describing the area as *'...for as much of the lake above the Bridge as extends North from* *the end of the lower Rails to the mouth of Chaffey's Bridge Lake'.* A 1932 history of Weymouth College, the boys' public school, refers to it as 'Chaphays Lake'.

CHALGRAVE HOUSE/TERRACE and CHAL-GROVE TERRACE are alternative spellings for a house at No. 1 Walpole Street and the terrace which became Nos. 38-48 Ranelagh Road.

CHANNEL ISLANDS. WW2 EVACUEES *see* EVACUEES

CHANNEL SWIMMERS Linda Ashmore of Weymouth holds the record as the oldest female to have swum the English Channel at the age of 60 and 10 months in August 2007. *See also Bumper Book I*

CHAPEL COTTAGES are now part of Sutton Road, Sutton Poyntz.

CHAPEL FORT The 14th century Chapel of St Nicholas at Chapelhay was converted to a fort by Parliamentary forces in 1642 on the outbreak of the English Civil War. Very much damaged in a bout of intense fighting in 1645 it was never again used as a place of worship and was usually known after the war as 'Chapel Fort'. *See also* FORTS and ST NICHOLAS CHAPEL in *Bumper Book I*

CHARLESTOWN *see* EAST CHICKERELL

CHECKER, Chubby Despite singing 'Let's twist again…', the Twist being the dance craze of the mid-sixties, American star Chubby Checker performed only 10 minutes of a half hour slot before storming off the Pavilion Ballroom stage in August 1965, apparently annoyed by people dancing while he sang. He did give a second half-hour performance later.

CHEQUER or CHEQUERS FORT This is the alternative name for Breakwater Fort, the large fort with its own small harbour on the outer of the two breakwaters built out from Portland. It takes its name from the distinctive chequered pattern on its stonework. *See also* BREAKWATERS

CHESIL BEACH BOMBING RANGE Proposals in 1934 for the establishment of Chesil Beach Air Gunnery and Bombing Range were initially met with great opposition locally. The objects of the range were to provide gunnery practice from the air against ground targets fixed on Chesil Beach and against targets towed by other aircraft and also for bombing practice against moored targets and against a moving target (an armoured motor boat). Local fishermen, landowners and various organisations protested to no avail, as the Air Ministry announced in August 1935 that the establishment of the range was *'of vital importance for the efficiency of the Home Defence Air Force'*. The range opened on 1 September 1937. RAF Chesil Bank Support Unit,

usually known as RAF Chickerell, was based in huts and a canvas hangar on the south side of Radipole Lane.

CHESIL BEACH BOUNDARY STONE lies atop Chesil Beach opposite Littlesea and indicates Portland's boundary. Beating the bounds at this particular spot involves either a long, long walk along the pebbles or a trip to a spot near the bridging camp to be ferried across in trows, the flat bottomed boats used on the Fleet. After a short service, the bounds ceremonies are usually quite jolly affairs, with picnics, pop and ale.

CHESIL SEA DEFENCE SCHEME The first stage of the 1980s scheme to prevent flooding at Portland was the modification of Esplanade wall at Chiswell, followed by the construction of a massive culvert to divert flood water into Portland Harbour and the raising of the Weymouth-Portland Road at its Island end to bring it above the flood level of the severe storm of December 1978.

CHESTERFIELD PLACE is part of Prospect Place at Upwey. In Weymouth Chesterfield Place is now Nos. 58 and 59 The Esplanade, the other properties being numbered as St Mary Street.

CHICKERELL BRICKWORKS Crook Hill brickworks at Chickerell were originally owned by G. H. Crickmay and from 1858 his widow took over the running of the works. Towards the end of the century when John Bagg was much involved in building projects at Westham, he purchased Crook Hill. Next owner was Webb, Major & Co., the company probably taking over around the time of Bagg's bankruptcy in 1910 until 1935 when three companies – Southern United Brickworks Ltd., comprising West of England Brick and Tile Company Ltd (2 works in Wilts, 1 in Dorset); Verwood and Gotham Brick and Tile Company Ltd (2 works in Dorset); Webb Major & Co., Ltd. (works at Chickerell) amalgamated to form one company. At Putton Lane the brickworks by the 1940s were operating as the Weymouth Brick and Tile Company, owned by Charles Mitchell and Sons, Ltd. *See also* EAST CHICKERELL

CHICKERELL CARNIVAL Started in its present form in 1981. This was a revival of earlier celebratory village events at Chickerell such as the Putton Feast, the annual Foresters Friendly Society procession through the village with brass band accompaniment and sports days and flower shows.

CHICKERELL MAYOR Since 1974, Chickerell has elected a Town Mayor, as has Portland, but these are not posts which are represented on Weymouth and Portland Borough or West Dorset District Councils.

CHICKERELL PRIMARY SCHOOL, Rashley Road opened in 1995, replacing buildings of the early 1900s in East Street.

CHIMNEYS IN WEYMOUTH Today the tall brick chimney of the former John Groves brewery in Hope Square is a striking landmark but a glance at old photographs of the town reveals that there were once a number of buildings boasting similar tall chimneys. Close to the harbourside in Helen Lane Templeman's Flour Mill chimney survived a disastrous fire in 1917, but was taken down later. A foundry chimney in Quebec Place can be seen in 19th century photographs. Along Westwey Road there were once the chimneys of the Gasworks, the Electricity Generating Station and the Sewage Pumping Station. Not far away in Westham was the chimney of Padgett's Brickyard (now the site of Pottery Lane) and that of the Weymouth Sanitary Steam Laundry (the site now occupied by Swallow Court). Others chimneys long gone include Radipole Brickworks (demolished in 1933, the last surviving part of the brickyard); Barnes Yard (on the Weymouth-Portland Beach Road where a 50 feet high masonry works chimney disused since 1928 was demolished in 1955); Sutton Poyntz Waterworks (taken down in 1979); Chickerell Brickworks (2 chimneys, 100 feet and 50 feet high were demolished in 1980); Whitehead's Torpedo Factory at Wyke Regis (70 feet high, taken down in 1984). There are probably more to add to the list.

Brick by brick, due to the proximity of houses below it, the electricity generating station chimney was dismantled in 1974.

CHRISTIAN SCIENCE CHURCH, Melcombe Avenue *Additions to the main entry in Bumper Book I:*

The church closed in 2004 – its final service was held on Sunday 29th August 2004. The building was demolished in 2008 and Weymouth Bay Methodist Church (built to replace the fire-ravaged Maiden Street Methodist Church) now stands on the site. *See picture page 88*

CHRISTMAS A selection of events which have occurred locally at Christmas time:

Five persons were '*sate in the stocks*' for Christmas drunkenness on 27th December 1617.

On Christmas night 1839 there was a huge landslide near Lyme Regis, eight million tons of cliff subsiding, one of the biggest landslips ever on the British coastline.

Shownight originated in the late 19th century when Weymouth shopkeepers 'dressed up' their shops inside and out and stayed open late into the evening for the crowds who turned out to see what was on offer at Christmas time. The tradition's decline in the early 20th century was accelerated by World War I but it was revived in the 1980s. More details in *Bumper Book I.*

Sir Henry Edwards Dinner for the Aged Poor was one of the many gifts made to the town by Sir Henry Edwards. He set up a fund in the 1880s to provide an annual dinner for old people which usually took place around Christmas time or early January. 500 people attended in 1897 and the fare at the Jubilee Hall included 42 huge plum puddings. The event was held each year until 1939 when it was suspended during WW2, re-starting in 1949 with a dinner for 500 at the Sidney Hall.

Some vessels had their voyages unexpectedly and sometimes tragically cut short in local waters around Christmas. The barque *Heroine,* outward bound for Australia, was wrecked at Lyme Regis on Boxing Day, 1851. All on board

L'Arguenon ashore on Christmas Day 1930.

were rescued but a small craft involved in the rescue over-turned and four of the five rescuers were drowned. The GWR paddle steamer *South of Ireland* was wrecked in fog in the early hours of Christmas Day 1883 on the rocks at Worbarrow Bay. All on board were saved, but the vessel was a total loss. Christmas Day 1930 saw the French ketch *L'Arguenon* stranded on Weymouth Sands. Festive food parcels were delivered to the crew and the vessel, originally on voyage Poole-St Malo, was eventually refloated.

Ralph Wightman made a BBC radio broadcast from Bincombe in the 1940s describing Christmas in the little village community – he had a vast audience as his programme was broadcast just before King George VI's traditional Christmas Day message to the nation.

All the inhabitants of the Purbeck village of Tyneham received notices that they must quit their homes by 19th December 1943 so that military training could take place ahead of the D-Day invasion. Despite assurances that they would be able to return when war ended, they never went back and the area was retained by the military. Today, although much of Tyneham has suffered from the effects of gunfire and shelling and still lies within the Army ranges, it can be visited at specified times. The church is undam-aged, some restoration work has been carried out on the ruined buildings and the documented memories and displays of village life more than 60 years ago are a real step back in time.

Ralph Wightman broadcast the Sunday Postscript programme from his home in Puddletown on 26th December 1943, which was relayed by the Forces broad-casting network to all theatres of war and across the British Empire and North America.

On Christmas Eve 1944 the American troopship *SS Leopoldville* was sunk by enemy action in the English Channel with the loss of over 800 lives. The vessel, a converted Belgian liner, had sailed from Southampton and many of the US troops who died had been based at Piddlehinton Camp. The tragedy is commemorated by a plaque on the American Memorial on Weymouth Esplanade.

The Christmas Day Swim across Weymouth Harbour originated, probably in 1948, as a wager between local men as to which of them would be able to swim from one side of Weymouth Harbour to the other. It seems to have been a popular annual event until 1985 when it was cancelled as being too dangerous for competitors to plunge into icy waters. The ban lasted only two years and the Christmas Day Swim restarted in 1987.

The first Christmas Tree set up at the King's Statue by the council appeared in 1948.

The Pram Race was an annual Boxing Day event started in the 1950s. It was run over a two mile course from the Embassy Hotel to Chalbury Corner and back in Fancy Dress. Competitors had to consume three pints of beer and biscuits and cheese en route.

CHURCH OF THE HOLY FAMILY Chapel Lane, Upwey The Roman Catholic chapel of ease has closed. It opened 2nd May 1954 and the last service was held on 26th

November 2004. The building is now owned by Mercury Dance Studio and called The White House.

CHURCHILL CLOSE, Wyke Regis Houses built by the Admiralty in 1965, initially unpopular due to their 'barrack-like' appearance. *See also* BLACKDOWN HOUSE in *Bumper Book I*

CHURCHILL GARDENS, Cross Road These are apartments and houses built in the grounds of 'Blackdown', the house on the corner of Buxton Road and Cross Road, in 2004.

CIVIL DEFENCE and CIVIL DEFENCE CORPS The stand-down parade of the local wartime Civil Defence personnel was held at the Recreation Ground (Asda super-market now stands on the site) on 27th May 1945. Three of their number had been killed on duty exactly one year before. Recruiting for a Weymouth Civil Defence Corps to prepare for the dangers of chemical warfare, atomic bomb hazards and the detection of radioactivity began in November 1949. Local and county-wide exercises were held in the 1950s and 1960s but there was always a shortage of volunteers. Nationwide the Corps was disbanded in 1968 as it became more obvious that civilian volunteers could do little in the event of a nuclear attack.

CLARK, George T. Superintending Inspector of the General Board of Health. His damning *Report to the General Board of Health on a preliminary inquiry into the Sewerage, Drainage, and Supply of Water, and the Sanitary condition of the Inhabitants of the parish of Melcombe Regis in the County of Dorset*', was published in 1850 and provides a very detailed survey of the very unsanitary conditions the Victorian resi-dents of the town were living in.

CLARKS SHOES It was confidently expected in the late 1950s that Clarks would occupy a new factory on the Chickerell airfield site (to become the Granby Industrial Estate) but problems over the lease were not resolved and although the firm reconsidered opening here in 1965, the move was never made.

CLAVELL TOWER The Clavell Tower, observatory, folly and landmark, was erected on the Purbeck cliffs by the Reverend J. Clavell who had inherited the Clavell estate at Smedmore. It was designed by Weymouth man **Robert Vining**, a celebration dinner being held to mark its comple-tion on 15th July 1831. Over the next 175 years the tower gradually fell into decay and, more significantly, coastal erosion brought the cliff edge perilously close. In 2006 it was decided to move the tower stone by stone and re-erect it further inland, and today, restored, it can be hired as a holiday home.

The CLAVINIAN (originally Clivinian) was the school magazine of Weymouth College, the boys public school. The first issue was published 1st December 1883 as

Weymouth College Magazine. The second, in January 1884, was called The Clivinian, in error, from the name of the Roman settlement, actually Clavinio. The name was subsequently changed to The Clivinian, the only local connection being that Thomas Hardy used the name 'Clavinium' for the site of the Roman Temple at Jordan Hill.

CLAVINIO In earlier centuries the place name Clavinio, which appears in the Ravenna Cosmography, was erroneously believed to indicate the Weymouth/Preston area but it has no local connection.

CLAY, Charles Robert (1851-1902) First proprietor of the Springhead Hotel, Sutton Poyntz. *See* SPRINGHEAD HOTEL

CLAYLANDS *see* BAYLY, Edward (1810-1905)

CLEARMOUNT CORNER Nos. 1 and 2 Clearmount were destroyed during a WW2 air raid. They stood on the (since widened) corner of Rodwell Road/Buxton Road. *See also* BUXTON ROAD JUNCTION WITH RODWELL ROAD

CLEVELAND HOUSE, No. 118, Dorchester Road was a private school in the late 19th/early 20th century.

CLIFTON was a house originally No. 12 Bincleaves Road, It was built for Herbert John Groves of Groves Brewery. It was later renumbered as No. 26 Bincleaves Road but has since been demolished and replaced with bungalows for the elderly.

CLIFTON COTTAGE was on the Nothe.

CLIFTON TERRACE Two notices in the local press offer these houses in Franklin Road for sale in 1906. One adds the detail that Nos. 15-26 Franklin Road were formerly known as Nos. 11-22 Clifton Terrace.

CLINTON ARCADE *Additions to the main entry in Bumper Book I:*

It was announced in January 1962 that the Clinton Arcade would be closed to become part of the Edwin Jones store although the shop entrances in St Thomas Street and St Mary Street would still provide a 'short cut' between the two streets. The way through was later lost when individual shop premises took over the site.

CLOVELLY, Belle Vue Road *see* BEALE, John Elmes

COACHES, Horse-drawn
Some of the early 19th century coaches out of Weymouth:

From the Golden Lion in St Edmund Street
> THE ROYAL DORSET – Weymouth-Bristol 3 times a week (1828, 1829)
> THE MAGNET – Weymouth-London every day (1829)
> also a coach Weymouth- Southampton every day except Sunday and Weymouth-Bath three times a week.
> THE WEYMOUTH AND SOUTHAMPTON COACH – Weymouth-Southampton every day except Sundays (1830)
> TOMS'S DUKE OF WELLINGTON coach 3 times a week Weymouth- Bath (1831)
> THE INDEPENDENT Weymouth-Southampton 3 times a week (1831)
> also a coach to Exeter on alternate days and a planned coach to Cheltenham (1833)

Cleveland House has been altered but is still recognisable at No. 118, Dorchester Road.

From Luce's Hotel on the Esplanade

THE JOHN BULL -Weymouth-Bath 3 times a week (1829)

THE INDEPENDENT – Weymouth-Southampton 3 times a week (1829)

also a coach to Bristol 3 times a week

THE TALLY HO! 3 times a week Weymouth-London (1831)

THE EMERALD Weymouth -Southampton every day except Sunday (1831)

From the Crown Hotel, St Thomas Street

TOMS'S DUKE OF WELLINGTON COACH Weymouth-Bath 3 times a week (1829)

COACHES, Motor *see* RIDGEWAY DISASTER

COAL IMPORTS were an important part of Weymouth's harbour trade. Josiah or Joseph Tizard seems to have been the leading merchant in the early century 19th coal and stone trade but one of the largest importers of sea coal was **William Wharton Burdon** of Newcastle upon Tyne, owner of collieries in the north east. Coal was also brought in to supply the coal hulks in Portland Harbour. The GWR in the 1880s imported Welsh coal for their vessels on service here.

COBURG COTTAGE was in Barrack Lane.

COBURG TERRACE is Nos. 1-8, Ashton Road. In the 1901 Census the enumerator's sequence is as follows: Prince of Wales Road, Ilton Terrace, Selway Terrace, North View, Melrose Terrace, Chickerell Road, Lilac Cottage on the Marsh, Coburg Terrace, Fermain Terrace, Lulworth Terrace, Springfield Terrace and 16 houses at the back of Lulworth Terrace, Arch Terrace and cottages, south side of Town Lane.

COCKLES LANE takes its name from 'Cockle', an old field name.

COIN HOARD, Roman On July 21st 1928 near the top of Jordan Hill a hoard of over 4000 Roman bronze coins was found. Sets were distributed to museums and other institutions and some can be seen in Weymouth Museum. It was at that time the largest such coin hoard ever discovered. *See also* PRESTON ROMAN HISTORY

COIN HOARD, Town Bridge When the foundations were being dug in the early 1820s for the new Town Bridge of 1824, a large quantity of old silver coins was discovered in an earthen pot, dating from the 16th and 17th centuries. Around the same time when an old house in St Thomas Street was pulled down to make way for the bridge, the following inscription was found whitewashed-over on one of its walls:

God save our Queen Elizabeth
God sende her happie daies
God grant her grace to
Perform His most Holy wayes. 1577

COLDHARBOUR is a common English place name and its meaning is 'shelter from the cold'.

COLE, John Bennett A jeweller, watchmaker and optician with a shop at Nos. 14 and 15 Bond Street. He was one of the early developers of Westham, having acquired land in the Stavordale Road area to build houses, using bricks from the original Royal Hotel, demolished in 1891. His own house, Sunnybank, was built here a little earlier, dating to about 1886, and he sold the house and its grounds to the Corporation in 1901 to provide a site for Weymouth's new Electricity Generating Station. Died 1919.

Above: John B. Cole, Weymouth businessman and Westham developer.

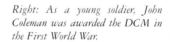
Right: As a young soldier, John Coleman was awarded the DCM in the First World War.

COLEMAN, Lance Corporal John William (Jack) (1887-1968) Of the 2nd Battalion The Border Regiment. Awarded the Distinguished Conduct Medal for his heroic actions at the Battle of Festubert in May 1915. The citation reads '*For gallantry and devotion to duty on 16th May 1915 at Festubert in helping to carry in a wounded officer from between the British and German lines under a very destructive fire. Later in the day, assisted by another man, he brought back over 50 wounded men under intermittent rifle and shell fire*'. It is thought that Jack Coleman (later Sergeant Coleman) received his decoration in Weymouth, but local newspaper searches have failed to provide any record of the event and many of the Border Regiment's records did not survive WW2.

COLWELL SHOPPING CENTRE, School Street opened 16th July 1984. The earlier history of this site can be found in *Bumper Book I under* COLWELL HOUSE.

COMMANDO UNIT Commando training in this area during WW2 is recorded on a plaque in the foyer of the Pavilion Theatre: '*No. 4 Commando. Lofoten Islands 1941, Boulogne 1942, Dieppe 1942, Normandy Landings D-Day 1944, Dives Crossing, Flushing, NW Europe 1944-45. This plaque commemorates the fiftieth anniversary of the founding of No. 4 (Army) Commando in Weymouth July 1940 and records with gratitude the hospitality of the townspeople with whom they*

Fine motor cars on display at Weymouth's Concours d'Elegance in 1934.

were billeted' An accompanying illustrated panel displays the history of the Commandos.

COMPTONS, No. 84a St Thomas Street Specialist stationery and art shop. Founded in 1853 as H. J. Butcher, No. 82 St Thomas Street and later F. L. Harwood, becoming Comptons in the early 1930s. In 1989 the business moved to No. 84a St Thomas Street when the original shop was demolished to reveal the early 19th century building which stood behind it (the 'Old Rectory', currently occupied by the Barracuda Bar). Comptons closed in 2008.

CONCERT HALL PUBLIC HOUSE, CONCERT HALL TAVERN, NEW CONCERT HALL PUBLIC HOUSE all appear to be names used for a pub at No. 12 St Nicholas Street which was also known as the Music Hall Tavern.

CONCOURS D'ELEGANCE was the name given to a motor rally held at Weymouth on Wednesday September 12th 1934.

CONDOR 7 The hydrofoil service to the Channel Islands began on 10th April 1987, the first vessel on the route being Condor 7.

CONIFERS PRIMARY SCHOOL opened on 29th September 2006. It replaced Westhaven School and was built on an adjacent site in Radipole Lane.

CONSERVATIVE CLUB, No. 13 Greenhill *see* GREYSTONES

CONTRABAND CONTROL was a wartime examination service to ensure that vessels entering the port were 'friendly' and not carrying anything likely to assist the enemy's war effort. Four of Cosens' paddle steamers were enlisted to assist the Navy in this work and HQ for the contraband service was in the former fire station building on the corner of St Edmund Street and Maiden Street, the new North Quay fire station having opened in 1939.

COOK, Bobby (1931-1981) Concert organiser and charity fund raiser. Born in Weymouth. After a career in professional theatre he returned to Weymouth where he organised shows and raised nearly half a million pounds for charity. A bronze bust of him was unveiled at the Pavilion Theatre in May 1982, sculpted by Marion Shoebridge of Owermoigne.

CO-OPERATIVE SOCIETY In 1865 a group of Weymouth GWR railwaymen met to consider the formation of a Co-operative Society and on 1st January 1867 The Weymouth Industrial and Provident Society was formed and registered, changing to Weymouth and District Co-operative Society in 1905. Portland started a society in 1901 which amalgamated with Weymouth in 1909. The first shop to open was a butcher's in Park Street and over the next hundred years the Co-op influence spread across all areas of the town. In the 1880s and 1890s more shops opened in the Park District and Chapelhay with premises in Park Street becoming the central store. Wyke Regis Co-op on Portland Road opened in July 1904 and replaced a small shop in Williams Avenue which had opened two years earlier. Drapery and boot and shoe departments opened at No. 25 Park Street in the early 1900s, drapery moving to No. 50 St Mary Street in 1916. Coal deliveries began in 1911. 1912 saw the opening of a shop at Westham and in 1914 a new Co-op Bakery opened in Lower Cromwell Road, replacing a 1905 bakery in the Park district. Later taken over by other Co-op departments, the 1914 bakery building has since been demolished. In 1919 the firm took more premises in the town's St Mary Street. 1926 brought the grand opening of new central premises in Westham Road. The 1930s saw great expansion with the opening in 1932 of the Franklin Road Dairy milk processing and bottling plant (closed in 1984), a butcher at No. 1 St Thomas Street in 1931, a pharmacy at the central premises in 1933, a grocer at Broadwey in 1933, more shops at Westham and the Co-op Hall in Caroline Place in 1937 (this building later housed the Co-op Bank and is now a snooker club). 1940 saw the opening of a shop in Sussex Road, and 1942 one on Preston Road plus a fish shop in St Thomas Street. 1957 brought a new Co-op shop to Chapelhay where two Co-ops had existed until the grocer at Franchise Street was bombed out in 1942. The Westham Road central store was enlarged in 1930, being extensively extended and modernised in 1961 and 1981. It closed in 1999 (now occupied by Wilkinsons store). Today the Co-op's shops are supermarkets and convenience stores on Portland and at Weymouth, Wyke Regis and Preston, with a funeral service at Westham.

Horse-drawn deliveries in the Co-op's early days.

CORFE HILL HOUSE is built on lands which were originally a farm. In 1820 the farmlands were purchased by Edward Balston who built Corfe Hill House, surrounded by extensive grounds, the following year. Sometime after the 1860s the Corfe Hill estate passed to Captain Thresher and it remained in the Thresher family until his son, Mr Edward Balston Thresher (born 1863) sold much of it in 1929, the estate including practically whole of the village, Manor House Farm, Causeway Farm, another large farm on the main road and Corfe Hill House.

Corfe Hill House hosting a local meet in the early 20th century.

CORINTHIAN CLUB was a yacht club which reformed in March 1902. Having flourished in the late 19th century it had lapsed in 1900.

CORK AND BOTTLE pub was renamed Moby Dick's, 2009.

CORN MARKET The lower end of St Thomas Street was referred to as the Corn Market in the early 18th century.

CORONATION FILM The film of the Coronation of Queen Elizabeth II '*A Queen is crowned*' was shown at local cinemas in the last week of July 1953.

CORONATION SEAT Broadwey. A seat at the junction of Weyview Crescent and Dorchester Road was unveiled on 29th November 1953.

COSENS PADDLE STEAMERS Once such a familiar sight in Weymouth: the last one left the town in 1967.

Cosens' Consul *in the days when a paddle steamer trip was very much part of a summer holiday in Weymouth. The last paddler left in 1967.*

COURT HOUSE, Sutton Poyntz *see* SUTTON POYNTZ. COURTHOUSE

COURTENAY, John Henry Lumley, JP (1860-1934) He was the nephew of **John B. Cole**, and eventually succeeded him in the business. He was also chief officer of

Heron Court fills this site in Ranelagh Road today.

the volunteer Weymouth Fire Brigade for more than 25 years. He was found drowned in Weymouth Harbour on 8th February 1934, following several weeks of illness.

COX'S FOUNDRY The foundry of R. Cox and Son was established in 1839 in Quebec Place off Park Street and moved later in the century to the northern end of Ranelagh Road. The business was sold to builder Theo Conway and was later known as the Paragon Engineering Co. and the Vixen Forge. All trace of the foundry has now gone and the flats of Heron Court stand on the site.

CRABB AND CO's extensive garage and car showroom in Crescent Street was built in 1929. It is now a bingo hall.

CRANES In the days when the port handled regular cargo trade, huge cranes were very much a feature of Weymouth harbourside. As the trade dwindled in the latter years of the twentieth century the cranes too began to disappear and none remain on the quay today.

The cranes seemed to disappear almost unnoticed in the latter half of the 20th century.

The pier cranes seen from the Nothe.

CRICHEL DOWN was compulsorily acquired in 1937 as a bombing site by the Ministry of Defence who held on to it afterwards, refusing to sell it back to Lord Alington's inheritee. The subsequent court case regarding the legality of the Ministry's actions brought down the Minister of Agriculture, Sir Thomas Dugdale.
Further reading: *The Battle of Crichel Down,* by Douglas Brown (Bodley Head, 1955).

CRICKET *see* WEYMOUTH CRICKET CLUB

CRICKETWAY was anciently a manor or small farm in the parish of Broadwey. The name may derive from the family of Cruket or Creket in Cricket, Somerset.

CRIME AND PUNISHMENT Punishment by way of a spell in the **stocks** or **pillory**, the **ducking stool** (usually for female offenders) and whippings were among the sentences handed out by the Borough Petty Sessions in dealing with petty crime in earlier times, most of these punishments being intended to publicly humiliate the offender. By the early 19th century they were seldom used.

CRISDYS is a name which appears frequently on old deeds, sometimes as Crisdy's Close and Crisdy's Gardens, and was a close of meadow on the Weymouth side of the harbour. May derive from the surname Crisdey which occurs in 17th and 18th century local leases.

CROFTON HOUSE was in Lennox Street.

CROOKED BILLET alehouse was in the Hope Square area in the first half of the 18th century.

CROWN AND SCEPTRE was an early 18th century inn in Melcombe Regis, its location unknown, although it has been suggested that this may have been an alternative name for the Crown Inn.

CROWN HOTEL, St Thomas Street stands on the site of the old Crown Inn. It is thought to have been built between the 1860s and 1880s. The Hotel was much enlarged in the late 1920s at the time the present Town Bridge was being constructed and the Victorian building in buff brick can clearly be seen between the newer red brick extensions on either side. The present hotel dining room on the corner of Lower St Edmund Street and St Nicholas Street stands on the site of a former warehouse, at one time used by banana importers.

CROWN INN, Osmington Mills was a former name of today's Smuggler's Inn, which was also known as the Picnic Inn. The town's Crown Inn (also known as the Crown Hotel in the early 1800s) stood on the site of the present Victorian Crown Hotel in St Thomas Street.

CROYDEN, Ratcliff Henry He was a stationer and auctioneer who moved his business from St Alban Street to **Statue House** in 1865. The large lettering on the building advertising his name and business led to this spot being known as 'Croyden's Corner'. He went out of business in 1887.

CUBITT family The names of at least two of the well-known Cubitt family of civil engineers occur in Weymouth's Victorian history and the firm appears to have had an office at No. 6 Great George Street. There are references to a Cubitt plan in 1840 regarding harbour improvements and in 1853 the opinion of Sir William Cubitt was sought regarding repairs to the Esplanade wall, damaged in gales the previous year. Early in 1860 the Town Council was *'to take into consideration communications and plans from Mr Cubitt with reference to the entrance gates and landing stages at the Pile Pier, and decide upon what steps to be taken thereon'* and in May that year it was Joseph Cubitt who signed off the completed Pile Pier works. *See also* STONE PIER

CUCKING STOOL *see* DUCKING STOOL

CURRYS opened a Cycle Shop at No. 64 St Mary Street in July 1919, but left Weymouth in 1924 when the shop was sold to Bon Marche (later part of Edwin Jones). The firm returned to Weymouth in 1959, to No. 80 St Mary Street – a shop they purchased from Edwin Jones, later also taking over Nos. 34-35. Currys store is now at the Jubilee Business Park.

Although the Currys main shop entrance was in St Mary Street, the premises extended back to St Thomas Street, as shown here.

CURTIS MARINE SERVICE STATION, Commercial Road was demolished July 1989.

CUSDYS was an area on the Weymouth side of the harbour, possibly a variation of CRISDYS.

CUSTOM HOUSE QUAY takes its name from the Custom Houses which have stood on the harbourside. The first was close to where Town Bridge steps are today and probably relocated when the 1824 Town Bridge was built. The Customs next occupied the fine building which is now the HQ of Portland Coastguard, probably built originally for one of the town's wealthy merchants. Rebuilding of the harbour wall and quays has altered this area over the centuries and commemorative stones have probably been lost during such works. After a two-year reconstruction in 1890 a final stone was laid bearing the following inscription: *'Custom House Quay. This stone, on the completion of the new Quay, was laid by Alfred Dennis, Esq., J.P., Mayor, October 9th, 1890. W. Barlow Morgan, A. M. Inst., C. E., I. Sanders, contractor.',* but it no longer exists.

CUSTOMS HALL, Weymouth Pier The current administration block of offices and accommodation for the Customs and other marine staff on the pier was built in 1963.

D-Day

D

D-DAY On 6th June 1944 of thousands of allied troops landed on the coast of occupied France in Operation Overlord, the massive amphibious assault on the beaches of Normandy. In the first wave, codenamed Operation Neptune, were 2 British, I Canadian and 2 US Divisions, part of a vast armada massing along the south coast. It was the men of the US 1st Division, known as the Big Red One from their distinctive shoulder flash, who embarked at Weymouth and Portland Harbours, moving down from the camps in the countryside around the town where they had been waiting for the signal to go. At Weymouth Pier in-

fantrymen were loaded into small personnel landing craft and ferried out to transports in the Bay. Portland Harbour was crammed with ships and landing craft loading transport, supplies and ammunition. A queasy 24 hours followed as the invasion plan was delayed due to worsening weather but on 5th June the fleets began moving out into the Channel to make the assault on the five beaches on the Cherbourg peninsula. For the men of the 'Big Red One', landing on the beach codenamed 'Omaha' it was to be a bloodbath as they struggled ashore from landing craft,

A line of DUKWs, American amphibious vehicles, assembled at Ferrybridge car park.

Notices in the Dorset countryside in the pre-invasion days.

The scene in Portland Harbour as vehicles are loaded aboard vessels in early June 1944.

A brief break at Greenhill for refreshments before the US troops embark at Weymouth Pier.

Entering the landing craft via the ferry steps close to Devonshire Buildings.

seasick, laden with equipment and under a relentless barrage of fire from enemy guns. It surely was 'The Longest Day' and by nightfall some 3000 of the American troops who left Weymouth and Portland were dead, wounded or missing. *See also* BIG RED ONE; POINTE DU HOC

DASHWOOD, Sir Francis (1701-1763) The politician who has gone down in history less for his parliamentary career than for his involvement in the 'Monks of Medmenham Abbey' a group famed for its debauchery, was the town's MP from 1761-1763.

DAVISON, (Margaret) Ann She and her husband (William) Frank Davison set sail in atrocious weather conditions and against advice in the ketch *Reliance* in 1949. Debt-ridden, they were attempting to start a new life far away from England. Off the Devon coast they refused help and eventually the yacht went ashore at Portland on 4th June 1949. They had taken to a raft, but her husband died from heart failure and exhaustion before reaching the shore. She survived and went on to be the first woman to make a solo crossing of the Atlantic in 1953.
Further reading:*Last voyage*, by Ann Davison. (Heinemann,1950).

DE GAULLE, Charles General De Gaulle is known to have made at least one visit to Weymouth during WW2, when he inspected Free French naval men operating motor torpedo boats out of Weymouth Harbour. His son is thought to have been among those based at Weymouth. Nothing was reported in the wartime press due to censorship restrictions.

DEBENHAM, Sir Piers Stood as Anti-Common Market candidate for the South Dorset constituency by-election in November 1962. He polled 5057 of the 41,137 votes cast and lost his deposit. Conservatives lost the seat to Labour by 704 votes, the first time a Labour MP had been elected for South Dorset.

DECONTAMINATION CENTRE A WW2 gas decontamination centre at the end of Westwey Road was converted for use as a Children's Library in 1959. It was later linked to the main building on the other side of the car park. All the buildings were demolished when Weymouth Library transferred to Great George Street in 1990 and the apartment blocks of Harbour View/Corscombe Close now fill the site.

DEEP SEA ADVENTURE, No. 9, Custom House Quay is a shipwreck and diving museum opened in the late 1980s in a converted building occupied in the 20th century by Burden's Transport then Deheers (stevedores, warehousemen and ships chandlers) and latterly by Hanney's fish warehouse.

DELAMOTTE, Peter His *'The Weymouth Guide: exhibiting the Ancient and Present State of Weymouth and Melcombe Regis; With a Description of Lulworth Castle, the Island of Portland And Other Places Worthy of the Attention of Strangers who visit Weymouth. To which is added, an Account of the Mineral Waters at Nottington, about two miles distant'* was published in 1785 and sold at his Library in St Thomas Street. His advertisement stated *'The following little work owes its appearance to the repeated enquiries of many persons, who, during a temporary visit to Weymouth, wished to know something of its history etc.'* This was the first real Guidebook of Weymouth, published four years before the visits of King George III to the town and forerunner of the numerous similar publications which followed, including updated versions of his own work. He was father of the artist William Delamotte. His library, demolished in 1865, stood on the site of the present No. 39 St Thomas Street.

'DESTINATION WEYMOUTH' South West Trains named one of their diesel locomotives *'Destination Weymouth'* on 6th July 2007 to mark the borough's involvement in the 2012 Olympic Games as host of the sailing events.

DEVON TERRACE (Nos 1-3) is in Abbotsbury Road.

DEVON AND CORNWALL BANK on the corner of St Thomas Street and Lower Bond Street (New Bond Street) was built in 1903 and later became Lloyds Bank. The premises are now occupied by NatWest, formerly the National Provincial Bank.

DEVONSHIRE BUILDINGS is now numbered from No. 1 ('the Round House') to No. 6 The Esplanade, but the numbering originally ran the reverse way (i.e. the Round House, also known as Devonshire House, was No. 6 Devonshire Buildings).

DEVONSHIRE HOUSE, No. 6, Devonshire Buildings, Esplanade Today this house, now No. 1 The Esplanade, is usually known as 'the Round House' but in the 19th century it was 'Devonshire House'. In the 1890s

William Daniel's view of Weymouth in 1826 shows Devonshire House, the 'round house' at the end of Devonshire Buildings.

and early 1900s royalty stayed here when it was occupied by **Montague John Guest**.

DIAMOND COTTAGES are part of High Street, Wyke Regis.

DICKENS, Charles One of the highlights of the 1889 programme of the **Weymouth Town Society** was an evening of Mr Charles Dickens reading from his father's works at the Burdon Hotel on 12th November.

DIGBY, A. J., Ltd. A fruit and vegetable wholesaler with premises in the Victoria Arcade, Crescent Street. The arcade was demolished in 2001 and flats were built on the site in 2006.

DISTORTER, or EVENING DISTORTER was the humorous rag-style paper produced by Dorset Evening Echo staff from the 1960s -1980s and sold at Carnival time to raise funds for charity.

DIVING RAFT The first diving raft at Greenhill (formerly used in connection with torpedo trials in Portland Harbour) was put in place for swimmers in the summer of 1922.

DIXONS LANE This was one of several alternative early names for St Leonard's Road.

DOCKSEY, William Long-serving Sergeant at Mace and caretaker of Weymouth Guildhall who took on the posts in the late 1930s. He retired in 1962.

DOLPHIN COURT, Bincleaves Road was built 1965-66.

DONKEYS The Weymouth beach donkeys owned by the Downton family retired in 2000 but since 2005 Maggie Aldridge's donkeys have provided the children's rides which are such a popular seaside feature.

DORCHESTER ROAD was widened near the Swan Inn, Broadwey in 1959 when old buildings opposite the pub were demolished.

DORCHESTER ROAD ESTATE was the name given to the houses being built to the north and south of the Radipole Lane/Dorchester Road junction in the 1930s.

Blackwell the builder, developer of the Dorchester Road Estate.

DORSET BREWERS ALE HOUSE was a name temporarily bestowed in the 1990s on the long-established Red Lion Inn in Hope Square. It has now reverted to its traditional name.

DORSET HISTORY CENTRE, Bridport Road, Dorchester was formerly the Dorset Record Office.

DORSET INDUSTRIAL EXHIBITION was held for two weeks in July and August 1878 in two local schools – St Mary's National Schools (in Great George Street, demolished in the 1980s and now the site of Weymouth Library) and Melcombe Regis School (later the Arts Centre in Commercial Road). This was set up as *'a movement originated for the purpose of promoting habits of industry and stimulating invention amongst the artisan section of the community in Dorset, as well as developing latent talent amongst all classes'*. The exhibition included arts, crafts and manufactures – an amazing and diverse array which included agricultural machinery, needlework, glove making, carving, straw work, pottery, fashions, photographs, biscuits, jewellery, Portland Stone, furniture, aerated water, plus a collection of loaned 'museum exhibits'- mounted butterflies, birds eggs, foreign curiosities etc. etc. Also known as the Dorset Industrial and Loan Exhibition and claimed to be the first of its kind held in the county, it was opened by Lord Eldon.

DORSET TRADES AND INDUSTRIES EXHIBITION was held at Lodmoor in July 1966. Claimed to be the biggest show ever held on the south coast.

DOUGLAS, Kirk The actor was at Weymouth in December 1964 filming *The Heroes of Telemark*. The local cargo steamer *Roebuck*, suitably disguised as a Norwegian coaster, the *Galtesund*, also starred, being filmed both in Weymouth and Poole.

DOWELL or DOWLE BROTHERS, Fred and Sherburne (or Sherborne) of Wyke Regis were drowned in a boating accident in May 1906.

DOWNTON, Henry (1818-1885) The hymn writer best known for *'Lord her watch thy Church is keeping'* was born at Radipole.

DRAKE, Charlie The comedian starred at Weymouth in 1958 at the Alexandra Gardens.

DREDGER The dredger which cleared the silt from Radipole Lake for many years between the wars had to be constructed at the lakeside in 1928-29 due to Westham Bridge preventing such a vessel accessing the Lake. When it was no longer required, it was dismantled in situ.

The Radipole Lake dredger.

DROMEMA *see* Y.M.C.A.

DU BOULAY, Hubert Houssemayne, JP. Surgeon at the Royal Hospital and the Eye Infirmary, Weymouth. He was granted the Freedom of the Borough in 1924, the year he left the town to live in Hampshire, where he died in 1955.

DUCK ALLEY is in Radipole village.

DUCKING STOOL This rather odd device, also known as a cucking stool, was devised for the punishment of *'scolds and unquiet women'* and was a chair on the end of a pole which ducked the miscreant, presumably at Weymouth in the waters of the harbour. In 1620 three women in the town (including the rather aptly-named Temperantia Strickland) were found guilty of being *'quarrelsome and disturbers of the peace .. vexers of their neighbours…and common troublers and sowers of strifes and discords among their neighbours…'* and a ducking was their punishment. In 1634 the wife of Richard Rich was ordered to be punished by the Cucking Stoole *'if she doe hereafter trouble her neighbours'*.

DUCKY STONES The name used for blackened 'stones' thrown up on Chesil Beach after storm and shipwreck, which were actually silver coins, earning their finders good money when sold to local jewellers.

DUKE OF CUMBERLAND public house It appears from old records that there may have been a Duke of Cumberland public house on the west side of Weymouth Town Bridge prior to the construction of the 1824 bridge, its licence being transferred to the Duke of Cumberland in St Edmund Street (now the Duke of Cornwall). After military man William Augustus, 3rd Duke of Cumberland became known as 'Butcher Cumberland' and was reviled for his cruelty, his became a less popular choice as a pub name.

DUKE OF ORMOND alehouse was next to the New Inn, on the south side of St Edmund Street in 1732.

DUKE OF WELLINGTON public house, St Alban Street In 1836 a 'rude funeral urn' containing ashes and burnt bones was found buried in shingle six feet below the surface of what was then 'Petticoat Lane' (now St Alban Street) near what is now the Wellington Arms pub.

DUNNINGS, Hope Square A bakery business founded by William Dunning in 1881. It stayed in the family until 1982 when the last Dunning retired, although the business continued to trade under the same name.

DUROTRIGES Descended from Iron Age stock, with the addition of elements derived from Gaulish invaders, the Durotriges tribe occupied the whole of Dorset, with their headquarters at Maiden Castle. Relics of their occupation of the Weymouth area were found at the Jordan Hill Cemetery site and are now in Dorset County Museum. One of their coins was found in 1962 after a landslip at Furzy Cliff.

Eacock, Frank

E

EACOCK, Frank Chief Constable of Weymouth and Melcombe Regis from 1891-1915. He died 9th October 1917.

EAST, Frances E. She started the East Memorial Sailors' and Soldiers' Home on the Quay and later at No. 8 King Street. Run on religious lines, the home was named in memory of her father Rear Admiral East, who died at Weymouth, and her late brother, also in the Royal Navy. She died in 1917 but the home remained open until 1929 when visits by the Atlantic Fleet were fewer and it was decided to close.

EAST CHICKERELL became known as Charlestown in the 19th century. It has been said that the area took its name from Charles Crickmay, son of George Hayter Crickmay who directed that Charles should carry on the family's brickworks business after his death in 1857. The brickworks were at Crook Hill, but there is so far no real evidence as to how Charlestown was so named.

EAST STREET COURT follows No. 16 East Street in the 1871 Census.

EAST WYLD ROAD derives its name from a large open field on which much of Westham would eventually be built – it was known as the Wyld.

EASTBROOK HOUSE, Upwey A mid-19th century house, one of an impressive group of four properties built around the junction of Stottingway and Church Street – Eastbrook, **Westbrook**, **Southbrook** and **Upwey Manor**.

EASTBURY, Tarrant Gunville This enormous house, designed by Sir John Vanbrugh, was being built for George Bubb Dodington's uncle, who died before it was completed and left it to his nephew. Dodington, the wheeler-dealer of 18th century local politics (*See Bumper Book I*) spent huge sums of money on the house where court painter Sir James Thornhill painted the ceilings. There he entertained the leading artistic and literary figures of the day in what became known as the 'Eastbury Circle'. When Dodington died in 1762, Lord Temple inherited the property, but it proved to be something of a white elephant as Temple

didn't want to live in it and was unable to find a tenant for it. The solution was to blow up the grand house, although one wing remained and still stands today.

EATON VILLAS Appear on the 1901 Census between Kingswood and Longfield House, Rodwell Road.

EBN MAGID Local inhabitants were able to witness this blazing ship on which an out-of-control fire raged in Portland Harbour at the end of January 1986. Efforts to contain the fire were initially hampered by uncertainty about the cargo of the Libyan registered vessel, but it was eventually extinguished.

EDWARD COURT *see* BANK HOUSE

EDWARD STREET BUS GARAGE was rebuilt in 1929 when the Southern National Company took over

The bus garage as rebuilt in 1955.

premises formerly occupied by **Weymouth Motor Company**. The garage had to be rebuilt again in 1955 following an air raid on 21st October 1940. *See also* SOUTHERN NATIONAL GARAGE, Chickerell Road

EDWARDS, Sir Henry (Biographical details are in *Bumper Book I*) His seafront statue, 8 feet high, is carved from a single block of Sicilian marble and stands on a 10 feet high block of grey Cornish granite, from Par. It is the work of Messrs. W. and T. Wills of 128 Gower Street, London. The figure weighs 2 tons, the pedestal 10 tons. A portrait of Sir Henry hangs in Weymouth Working Men's Club in Mitchell Street. His philanthropic works extended to another area – South Nutfield in Surrey, where he laid out residential estates, a pub and shops. His main home appears to have been 'Nutfield' in Redhill, Surrey.

EDWIN JONES STORE The department store arrived in Weymouth in the 1950s, taking over No. 80 St Mary Street as well as gradually acquiring most of the shops in the Clinton Arcade. By 1958 the company had refurbished the Clinton building and in 1962 it closed the Clinton Arcade, although still providing a walk-through ground floor. Edwin Jones left Weymouth early in the 1970s. The short cut between the two main streets disappeared in the early 1980s when the site ceased to be one large store and was divided up into individual business premises.

EISENHOWER, Dwight D. General Eisenhower was in the area during the build up of forces prior to D-Day, 1944. He is said to have stayed at the Embassy Hotel, Overcombe which had been taken over by the military and accommodated high ranking US Army officers.

ELDON, John Scott, JP, DL, 3rd Earl Eldon, of Encombe He succeeded to the title in 1854 and was one of the largest landowners in Dorset. He had links with Weymouth, and opened the **Dorset Industrial Exhibition** in 1878, so may have influenced the naming of Eldon House, Eldon Terrace and Eldon Villas at Westham.

ELECTRICITY On August 15th, 18th and 19th, 1815 a Mr Clarke gave a series of three evening lectures on the subject of electricity complete with experiments to enthral his audience. The subject was in the local news again in March 1833 when the Reverends Beale and Crump gave lectures. A history of the town's electricity supply can be found in *Bumper Book I*.

ELIOT, George The author is known to have stayed in Weymouth and it is thought that she considered Radipole Mill as a setting for *The Mill on the Floss* before basing her fictional village on a Lincolnshire location.

ELLIOTT, Colonel Thomas Gilbert L., 87 Buxton Road He was Commander of the Weymouth and Portland Garrison on D-Day. Died 17th February 1959.

ELLIOTT-LEES ROOM, Westham Appears to have been a Conservative club. It was in existence in 1921 when prizes for billiards, whist etc. were donated by leading local Tories. It may have been named after **Sir Elliott Lees, Bt., DSO, MA, JP.**

ELLIOTT'S instrument making factory, formerly **Bristol's**, at Lynch Lane was taken over by the Cheltenham firm of aerial manufacturers Telerection Ltd. in February 1959.

ELSADENE, Verne Road A residential home for adults with learning difficulties opened in February 1989 after being disused for some years.

EMPOOL, West Knighton Increasing demands on the Weymouth water supply led to the opening of a new borehole at Empool in 1938 and the building of Empool Pumping Station. *See also:* WATER SUPPLY in *Bumper Book I*.

EMPRESS OF INDIA HMS *Empress of India* was sunk about thirty miles west of Portland by some over-enthusiastic target practice by the Royal Navy on 4th November 1913. Experimental firing tests on the obsolete battleship were witnessed by naval and military experts including Mr Winston Churchill, First Lord of the Admiralty; Prince Louis of Battenberg, GCB, GCVO, KCMG, Second Sea Lord; and Admiral Dudley R S De Choeur, MVO, Naval Secretary to the First Lord. It had been intended to take the damaged vessel back to Portland to ascertain the effectiveness of the guns, but the old vessel was so badly holed that she turned turtle and sank to the bottom of the English Channel.

ENDERBY HOUSE, No. 10, Clarence Buildings (now part of the Alexandra Hotel) was acquired by the Corporation's Health Department on 1st April 1918, having previously been a school run by the Misses Tizard who had moved there from Netherton House in 1905. Sometime around 1930 No. 10 was acquired by the proprietor of the adjacent Alexandra Hotel at No. 11 for the enlargement of his establishment.

ESPLANADE REGENERATION PROJECT (for the earlier history of the Esplanade *see Bumper Book I*) Grand improvements of the Esplanade are planned (2009) and the restoration of the King's Statue has already taken place. It will eventually overlook a pedestrianised area and the large 1937 shelter on the Esplanade will be removed to provide a clear view over the Bay. Conservation of the smaller Victorian shelters is ongoing. On the site of the old Aquarium/Sundeck it is planned to provide a Beach Rescue Centre with new public toilets to replace those at the end of Bond Street. A new glass structure will house the Tourist Information Centre and there will be improvements in the Jubilee Clock area and at the Pier Bandstand, which will reflect the art deco style of the 1930s structure. Update: in June 2009 it was announced that £6.6 million funding for the regeneration had been axed.

ESSO PETROLEUM In 1962 the company was granted permission for a pontoon in the Backwater beside their premises in Commercial Road to supply petrol to craft using the harbour.

EVACUEES In June 1940 the Channel Islands were under the shadow of the German invasion and almost 23,000 Channel Islanders were evacuated. They passed through Weymouth, bearing baskets full of tomatoes which they had refused to abandon for the enemy to enjoy. Weymouth was also the entry port for the entire population of Alderney on 23rd June 1940. Refugees were also pouring in from the continent and May and June brought 10,000 Free French and Moroccan soldiers who had been lifted from the coast of France in Operation Dynamo, the evacuation of Allied troops from Dunkirk and the ports of northern France. *See* EVACUEES in *Bumper Book I* for the London children who came to Weymouth in 1939.

EVENING DISTORTER *see* **DISTORTER**

EXCELSIOR STORES This grocery business was at No. 10 St Mary Street, close to Blockhouse Lane, in the early 1900s.

EXERCISE FABIUS *see* EXERCISE TIGER

EXERCISE TIGER In April 1944 a full scale rehearsal for the D-Day invasion ended in disaster. Eight Tank Landing Ships (LSTs) moved out into the Channel from ports in Devon to simulate a landing on the beaches of Slapton Sands in the South Hams, an area with terrain similar to Normandy that had been requisitioned for training purposes. Missing one escort ship which had been damaged earlier and protected only by a corvette, the slow moving LSTs were an easy target for nine fast German E-boats which slipped out of Cherbourg to hunt for Allied prey. They struck the convoy in the early hours of April 28th, their torpedoes sinking two LSTs and damaging another. Blazing craft, explosions and LSTs firing on sister ships in the ensuing chaos all contributed to the deaths of more than 700 US servicemen, some of whom leapt into the sea only to die of hypothermia and the incorrect use of untried new-style lifejackets. With local seas littered with bodies and the remaining LSTs making for Portland, the attack had put the whole of the secret invasion plan at risk. Those who gathered up the bodies, the surviving LST crews, hospital staff at Blandford and Sherborne where the wounded were taken were all sworn to secrecy and it was maintained. A few days later, Exercise Fabius, a second planned practice landing went ahead at Slapton without hindrance from the enemy. The details of Exercise Tiger were not fully revealed until many years after the war ended and even today the accounts of what happened that night are disputed.

EXETER HOUSE appears to have been on the east side of New Street.

EYE INSTITUTION Free treatment for the poor was available twice a week in 1830 from **Mr Reeves**, Surgeon and Oculist of Portland, at Hope Square.

EYE VILLA follows No. 1 Royal Terrace and is followed by Melcombe Villa. in the 1891 Rate Book.

The latest in delivery vans in the early 1900s.

Faircross Estate

F

FAIRCROSS ESTATE 3½ acres of land adjoining **Nettlecombe** and opposite Belfield Park was up for sale in May, 1906. An earlier sale of building plots had taken place in 1896. A later development also known as Faircross Estate (Fairclose, Faircross Avenue, Everest Road etc.) was laid out by builders Smith and Lander in the early 1930s. Just prior to this Faircross House had been sold by Leonard Harris to Colonel E. W. C. Sandes, who bought some adjoining land to prevent dwellings being built too close to his house, although the sale by Mr Harris of adjacent land for the Faircross Estate took away much of the rural aspect of the old house. *See also* FAIRCROSS in *Bumper Book I*

FAIRVIEW Houses with this name appear in the 1901 Census in the Southview Road. There is a street of this name linking Williams Avenue and Sunnyside Road at Wyke Regis, Fairview Road being the original choice of name for Sunnyside Road.

FALKNER, Charles Gaskell (1863-1932) The brother of John Meade Falkner (See *Bumper Book I*). He was a pupil at Weymouth College, the boys' public school, and returned there as a Master from 1890-1901, later becoming Secretary to the firm of Sir W. G. Armstrong, Whitworth & Co. Ltd. He retired to Weymouth and was one of the founders of the College's Old Weymouthians Club and its President in 1903 and from 1919 until his death.

Further reading: *History of Weymouth College to 1901* by C. G. Falkner. (Old Weymouthians Club, 1932.)

FALKNER, Thomas Alexander, MA (1820-1887) Father of **Charles Gaskell Falkner** and John Meade Falkner. Curate at Holy Trinity, Dorchester and then at St Mary's, Melcombe Regis until 1880 when he became curate at Buckland Ripers Church, dying in 1887 when he was due to move to West Compton.

FANNER, William Tolden A Weymouth casualty of a horrific explosion in 1911 at the grinding mill of Bibby's oilcake factory in Liverpool, which killed all 31 people working there instantly. The mills caught fire and another 115 required hospital treatment. His brother was Frank Fanner, long-serving Sanitary Inspector of Weymouth.

FAR FROM THE MADDING CROWD Weymouth in the autumn of 1966 was transformed into Thomas Hardy's Budmouth of 1865 for filming of *Far from the Madding Crowd*. Many locals appeared as extras in the MGM film starring Julie Christie and Terence Stamp. This was the first sound version – silent films based on the book had been made in 1909 and 1915.

FASCISTS, BRITISH UNION OF At least one meeting of the British Union of Fascists was held in Weymouth in the 1930s. On 24th May 1937 at the Burdon Hotel, the Union's secretary, Bill Risden, outlined the history and aims of the movement.

FENOULHET, Andrew Chadwick (1820-1862) Surgeon. Lived at Wyke Regis where he built himself the slightly eccentric Wyke Castle in the 1850s.

Dr Fenhoulet's home, Wyke Castle, in Westhill Road, Wyke Regis.

FERMAIN TERRACE (6 houses) is Nos. 9-14 Ashton Road. In the 1901 Census the enumerator's sequence is as follows:Prince of Wales Road, Ilton Terrace, Selway Terrace, North View, Melrose Terrace, Chickerell Road, Lilac Cottage on the Marsh, Coburg Terrace, Fermain Terrace, Lulworth Terrace, Springfield Terrace and 16 houses at the back of Lulworth Terrace, Arch Terrace and cottages, south side of Town Lane.

FERN COTTAGE and THE FERNS were in Derby Street. Nos. 1-2, Fern Villas are in Prince of Wales Road.

FERRY BRIDGE INN, Wyke Regis has been known as the Ferry House Inn, the Victoria Inn and the Royal Victoria Hotel. It is now the Ferry Bridge Inn.

FERRYBRIDGE ROAD is an old name for the Portland Beach Road.

FIJI ISLANDERS In June 1902 some 20 Fijian islanders came to England to take part in the Coronation festivities (word would not have reached them that ceremony was postponed until August due to King Edwards VII's appendix operation). They were said to be the first Fijians ever to have visited England and they were entertained in July 1902 at Osmington. The reason for their visit to a small Dorset village was that they were under the command of Major Joske, brother-in-law of the Vicar of Osmington. They arrived by train at Weymouth for their three-day stay and marched all the way to Osmington in bare feet.

FILMS In February 1946 it was possible to book a table at The Pier Café for 5 shillings and be served dinner with a Weymouth movie for entertainment. The full length colour travel film of Weymouth and Portland (courtesy of Regent Studios) included *The visit of John G. Winant to Portland* [he had unveiled the D-Day memorial on the Island in 1945]; *Submarine on the rocks at Portland* [probably the Free French sub *Minerve* which went aground under tow for Cherbourg in 1945]; V-*Day in Weymouth – bonfires, children's parties, etc.*; *A trip round the Bay in an MTB*; *Greenhill Flower Gardens in all their colourful beauty*; *Views of Weymouth from many angles*; *The Fleet from the air*; and, the advert continued, *many other items too numerous to mention here…all in beautiful colour.* The film doesn't seem to be deposited in any local archives: does it still exist?

FILMS *Additions to the list in Bumper Book I:*
   Bulldog Drummond (scenes filmed on the steam yacht *Elettra* in Weymouth Bay, 1925); *The Goodies* (TV series scenes filmed in Weymouth and Portland in the 1970s); Two Bollywood films – *Will you marry me?* and *Babul Pyaare (2006 and 2007); The Boat that Rocked* (2008); scenes for the TV series *Eastenders* (2008).

FINE FARE This supermarket chain was due to open on the former Sidney Hall/Weymouth Football Ground site in Newstead Road in 1988 but by the time the store opened the chain had been taken over by Gateway. Since 1989 it has been Asda.

FIRE BRIGADE The future of the local fire service is currently under discussion (2009), and a move from the 1939 Fire Station on North Quay to the site of the former Westhaven School at Radipole Lane has been proposed for a Community Fire Station which would involve more public participation in education, demonstrations, home fire safety advice and such like.

FIRES The 17th century Town Fire which destroyed much of Melcombe Regis occurred in July 1665, not 1666 as in *Bumper Book I*.

FISHERMAN'S ARMS There have been pubs of this name in High Street, Weymouth; Lower Putton Lane, Chickerell and Wyke Regis.

FIVEWAYS GARAGE (previously Scource's) at the junction of Chickerell Road and Benville Road was demolished in October 2007. The site is being redeveloped as housing (Summer 2009).

FLEET, The The stretch of brackish water which separates Chesil Beach from the mainland for eight miles between Portland and Abbotsbury takes its name from the Saxon word 'fleet' – a bay or gulf where the tide comes up. The shores of The Fleet have provided evidence of very early occupation of the area, with Mesolithic and Iron Age finds. The possibility of draining The Fleet has been explored at various times and in 1630 there is evidence that a dam was actually constructed but the project failed due to percolation of water through the Chesil Beach at high tide. Local fishermen use **Trows** to cross The Fleet, flat-bottomed craft which have been used for centuries. Although this is a very beautiful area, it can be a dangerous place and in November 1958 a father and son drowned when returning from a fishing trip on Chesil Beach. Halfway across The Fleet their trow was hit by big waves. It was here, too, during a tempestuous storm along the south coast on the night of 22nd/23rd November 1824 that huge waves came over Chesil Beach, stormed up The Fleet and engulfed **Fleet** village.

FLEET The village takes it name from its nearness to the waters of the **The Fleet** and lies in two parts – East Fleet is the village and West Fleet the mansion house and farm. This tiny place has an extraordinary air of remoteness about

Fleet village church as it looked before the 1824 'Great Gale'.

All that remains of the church today.

Fleet House in the 19th century – now Moonfleet Manor Hotel.

it, despite being close to the B3157 coast road, and it was John Meade Falkner's setting for *Moonfleet* his classic tale of smuggling and shipwreck on the Dorset coast. Published in 1898 the book, which takes its title from the Mohun family, has since been both filmed and televised. Fleet, which is listed in Domesday, came into the possession of the Mohuns in the 16th century and Maximilian Mohun is thought to have built the original Fleet House at West Fleet.

In the 18th century the estate passed, by marriage, to the Gould family, of Upwey. When the village was over-whelmed by the flood waters of the Great Gale in 1824 and its cottages and church knocked down, it was George Gould, then the Vicar of Fleet, who was responsible for the speedy rebuilding of the present Holy Trinity Church at Fleet. It opened in 1829 on a site safely distant from the sea. The chancel of the old church has been restored and contains monuments to the Mohun family. Fleet House had several owners after the Goulds and in the 1930s was owned by Sir Saxton and Lady Noble, she being a grand-daughter of Isambard Kingdom Brunel. Like many other large houses in the Weymouth area it was requisitioned by the military in WW2 and in post-war years converted to a hotel, today the Moonfleet Manor Hotel. *See also*: John Meade FALKNER in *Bumper Book I*

FLOODS OF 1955 *Views of the locality following the record rainfall which fell on the night of 18/19th July 1955. See also* FLOODS 1955 in *Bumper Book I*

FLORA COTTAGE was in South Parade.

Park Street is under water but no-one seems to mind.

The floods at Radipole: Alma Place and Tumbledown Farmhouse, Radipole Lane.

Cheerful locals greet flooded neighbours still awaiting rescue in Newstead Road.

Marsh Road residents have milk delivered by the local bobbies, in the floods of 1955.

FLORESTON HOUSE was in Brownlow Street.

FLYING SCOTSMAN The famous LNER locomotive was saved from the scrap yard when bought by a railway enthusiast in 1963. Restored to her former LNER livery she made a run to Weymouth and was on show at Weymouth Station on the afternoon of Sunday, 12th September 1965.

Then, as now, crowds turn out to greet a steam locomotive, and the Flying Scotsman was a rather special engine.

FOLLY ROAD In 1901 building plots were being offered for sale with frontage to '*Buxton or Folly Road*'.

FOOKS, Charles Berjew One of the leading developers of the town in the 19th century but he became embroiled in what became known as the 'Park Scandal'. In 1842 as Alderman Fooks, he and William Lock purchased from the

Corporation for just £162.15s 0d the 26 acres of land at the northern end of the town which were originally intended to be laid out as a public park. The land had been enclosed in the 1830s at a cost of £2,300 and leased for grazing to the two men on the understanding that they would vacate it when work was due to begin on the new park. Unfortunately, despite frequent complaints from those in favour of the park proposals, years went by and nothing was done to implement them.

When it was discovered by a public-spirited councillor that the land had been quietly sold to the two men for such a paltry sum there was an outcry, a public meeting was held and it was found that the sale was too far advanced to be stopped. Local solicitor John Henning took up the cudgels, working tirelessly and at his own expense. He brought a Suit in Chancery which lasted seven years, by which time it had become obvious that the Railway Companies planning to run lines into Weymouth would have powers to take some of the park land and as everyone was tiring of lawyers expenses and court fees, the matter was settled. Fooks and Lock agreed to pay £4,200 for the land – almost 26 times the original sum of £162. 15s 0d. John Henning duly received a testimonial signed by many townspeople in recognition of getting proper payment for the Park lands, but there was yet more dissent within the Council when it was proposed to pay some of his expenses!

FOORD'S CORNER, Wyke Regis On the south side of Buxton Road at Foord's Corner once stood an old cottage, occupied in the mid-19th century by Henry Foord and his wife, who was the local midwife and known as 'Granny Foord'. The cottage was demolished in the 1950s, possibly when plans were being made to improve the sharp bend which existed here at the junction of Buxton Road and Portland Road. Work started on the road improvements in January 1960 and included the construction of a roundabout. More recent works at the Corner have included the provision in 1996 of a bench seat overlooking Portland Harbour in memory of the late Brenda Dench, Wyke Councillor, School Governor and former Mayor of Weymouth and Portland. Funds for the seat were raised by Wyke Junior and Wyke Infants Schools.

FOOT AND MOUTH DISEASE Occasional outbreaks in Dorset were not uncommon but there was a particularly bad occurrence in January 1935 when farms at Broadwey, Bincombe, Littlemoor, Preston and Sutton Poyntz were affected. Bincombe was especially hard hit, having all its livestock wiped out.

FORD'S CORNER *see* FOORD'S CORNER

FORREST, Aston Author of *The extraordinary islanders, being an authentic account of the cruise of the Asphodel'*, published in 1903. This was a nom de plume so the author's identity is uncertain, but he is believed to be from Weymouth.

FORSYTH, Bruce Topped the bill at the Alexandra Gardens Theatre in Bernard Delmont's 'Showtime' in 1959. He was then starring in TV's 'Sunday Night at the London Palladium'.

FORTY-NINE CLUB was on the Town Bridge (now The Rendezvous) Opened in 1965, closed in 1970.

FOWLER, Simon Jenkins, JP (died 1912) A native of Weymouth, he was a junior clerk in the solicitor's practice of Sir R. N. Howard until he joined Cosens' engineering and shipping company in 1863, ultimately being responsible for much of the company's growth. He stayed with Cosens for 48 years, rising to become secretary, then managing director until in 1897 he took control of the company. He was on the Council from 1877-1895 and died on 4th February 1912.

FOX The exploring ship was in Weymouth in November 1860, having been in the Faroe Islands, Iceland and Greenland surveying the proposed North Atlantic route.

FOX, George (1624-1691) Founder of the Quakers. He was in Melcombe *'where the Quakers had become fairly numerous'* probably shortly after the end of the Civil War as he was accompanied by a Parliamentary Captain. On another occasion, in 1655 *'Having left Dorchester…George Fox went to Weymouth and four score of people gathered in a priest's house to hear him, where his listeners were more receptive than those at Dorchester… afterwards to Honiton'*.

FREDERICK PLACE is a terrace of 12 three-storeyed houses with basements on the west side of St Thomas Street at its northern end and built on the former extensive gardens of **Gloucester Lodge**. It was completed around 1834. Some of the bow windows at street level have been replaced by shop fronts. No. 1 Frederick Place is probably best remembered for its long use in the 20th century as Forte's Ice Cream Parlor and Restaurant and its location at the junction of St Thomas Street and Westham Road was, and sometimes still is, known as 'Forte's Corner'. It became a pub in the Hogshead chain and in 2008 was taken over and refurbished by the Wetherspoons chain which gave it the new name 'William Henry', after the Duke of Gloucester, builder in 1780 of Gloucester Lodge. No. 1's first occupant was Richard Bower, Mayor of Weymouth in 1850-51 and 1851-52. Sometime in the mid-1870s dentist Walter Burt moved in, remaining in practice there until the 1920s when the premises became a café, taken over by Forte around 1929-30 Another house in the terrace, No. 11, bears a plaque on its exterior wall commemorating William Thompson, a local solicitor, who practised here and is famous in the annals of photography for having taken the first known underwater photograph in 1856. The spelling of Frederick Place and who the terrace is named after is a bit of a puzzle. Rate books of the time it was built in the 1830s list it as Frederic Place. An 1850 listing of the local properties which formed part of the Johnstone Estate also names it

This building is No. 1, Frederick Place, now the William Henry public house.

as Frederic Place. Since the Johnstone family often used the forename Frederic and always spelt it without the 'k' it seems likely that it was originally intended to be Frederic Place.

FREEDOM OF THE BOROUGH In addition to the local volunteers who served in the Boer War and are listed in *Bumper Book I*, the local press reported in June 1903 that an additional five men had been granted the Freedom of the Borough, which would be conferred on their return from South Africa. They were G. Hibbs, J.F. Horniblow, W. D. Poynter, A. Ware and F. Younghusband.

FREEMASONRY In addition to those listed in *Bumper Book I*, there were some short-lived Lodges in Weymouth in the 19th century. They were: Lodges attached to The King's Own Stafford Militia (1804-1827); The 11th Dragoon Guards (1807-1810) and the 7th Dragoon Guards (1810-1814). On the Weymouth side of the harbour Arimathea Lodge, White Lion Inn existed from 1809-1828. This is the only reference to a White Lion Inn in Weymouth, although there was one of this name in Melcombe. The Red Lion in Hope Square is sometimes referred to as 'The Lion' so perhaps they met there – or crossed the water for their meetings.

FREEMASONS ARMS There were pubs of this name in High Street, Weymouth, Upwey (which probably became the Masons Arms) and High Street, Wyke Regis.

FRIAR WADDON takes its name from belonging at one time to the Knights Templars. Waddon is a 'hill or down where woad grows'.

The FRONT is Weymouth's Sk8tepark, opened in July 2001. It stands on the site of a disused filling station at Lodmoor. It is a non-profit making community enterprise providing skateboard, rollerblade and BMX facilities, a social area and snack bar.

FRY, Jessie Mayor of Weymouth and Melcombe Regis 1978-79. Died February 2009.

FUSEE I and FUSEE II Two RASC general service launches which were a familiar sight for many years berthed in the Cove. In the early 19th century military stores for the Army were transported from Woolwich Arsenal to Weymouth in sailing cutters until 1886 when War Department steam coasting vessels took over. The first one on permanent detachment here was the *Stewart* in 1904, joined later that year by *Fusee I*, which remained here when *Stewart* left in 1922 and was joined in 1935 by *Fusee II*. Both carried out target towing tasks as well as working closely with the TA camps at Weymouth, Portland and Wyke.

Gas Supply

G

GAS SUPPLY An outline history of the gas supply to the town is contained in *Bumper Book 1. See also:* BROADWEY. GAS HOLDER

GASWORKS. ACCIDENTS *see* PALMER, George Joseph

GEORGE CROSS Boy Seaman **Alfred Lowe** was 17 and on board *HMS Illustrious's* liberty boat when it overturned in Portland Harbour in 1948. After he had reached a lifebelt he struck out for *Illustrious* when he spotted a man in difficulties. Instead of being hauled to safety by a rope from the ship, he turned back in an attempt to save the life of the unconscious man. He was awarded the George Cross.

GHOSTS The supposed haunting of a house in East Street caused some excitement in 1861. At the home of Thomas Talbot, an old boatman, knockings were heard, latches mysteriously lifted and walls trembled as if they had the ague. Such was the interest that crowds turned out in such numbers that the street became impassable. It transpired that the sounds were only heard when the old man's grand-daughter was staying with him -when she returned home the 'ghost' also disappeared. Other buildings in Weymouth where sightings of ghosts have been reported are the Boot Inn, the Duke of Cornwall pub and the Trinity Street Cottages. Waddon Manor is said to be haunted by a black-faced man. One of the manor's owners in the 17th century was Bullen Reymes, who shot and killed his negro servant, believing him to be an intruder.

GIMBLETTS, Ironmongers William Beadon Gimblett originally had shops at No. 14 Trinity Road and Nos. 34 and 79 Abbotsbury Road. Today (2009) the business operates from No. 79 Abbotsbury Road although the Gimblett family's ownership of it ceased in the latter half of the 20th century.

GIPSY WEDDING of Miss Priscilla Penfold took place at All Saints Church, Wyke Regis in June 1904. It was a fairly conventional affair but hundreds turned out to see the couple, both from travelling families. Celebrations followed at the gipsy camp.

GIRL GUIDES SUNDIAL A granite sundial in Greenhill Gardens was presented by the 1st Weymouth Girl Guides to commemorate the 21st year of the company in 1935.

GIRLS FRIENDLY SOCIETY LODGE was at No. 8, North Quay in the early 1900s and appears to have continued until the 1940s, when it became a branch of the YMCA for a short time, then Holy Trinity Youth HQ, then a guest house. The building was known as Sowter Lodge after Canon Sowter of Holy Trinity Church.

GLADSTONE, William Ewart The former Liberal Prime Minister (1868-1874, 1880-1885 and 1886) visited Weymouth on 8th June 1889. He addressed an election-eering meeting at the King's Statue but the crowd was reportedly not very large. He and Mrs Gladstone were after-wards driven by carriage to Portland where they embarked

Not too many Liberals turned out on a sunny summer's day to support William Ewart Gladstone in 1889.

on the yacht *Garland* for Devon and Cornwall. He served as Prime Minister again from 1892-1894.

GLADSTONE VILLA was in Lennox Street.

GLEBE CLOSE is part of a 1980s development on the site of Glebe House, a former vicarage of Holy Trinity Church, 'glebe lands' being those belonging to a church.

GLENCOE TERRACE became part of Franklin Road.

GLOUCESTER HOTEL *Additions to the main entry in Bumper Book I:*

When the former royal residence Gloucester Lodge was sold in 1820 it was purchased by Mr W. Young who occupied it as a private house, later lived in by his widow. It appears to have continued as a private residence until 1859 when it was converted into a 'first class hotel' by Thomas Luce, who also ran the adjacent Royal Hotel. The 'County Club' extension on the southern end was added in the 1860s. When the building was on the market again in 1900, the Council discussed the possibility of using the site for a proposed new Pavilion and Winter Gardens, but the debate about where to site a new theatre was to rumble on for years, eventually culminating in the opening of the first Pavilion Theatre on the Pier late in 1908. The Gloucester remained a hotel, redecorated and refurnished in 1901. In the 1920s it was bought by Lady Honywood, of the Honywood Hotels chain. Badly damaged by fire on 3rd March 1927, it was back in business by spring 1929. It survived the post-WW2 years and was bought by brewers Devenish in 1966, but the 1980s saw the failure of various ambitious schemes for its revival by individuals who leased it from the brewers and by 1984 it was occupied by DHSS tenants. Suggestions to turn the building into a library, museum and arts centre were not pursued and in 1988 the decision was taken to convert the Gloucester into offices and flats with a pub in the basement. The long glass verandah along the front of the building was removed in spring, 2009.

GLOUCESTER ROW At some time in the early 20th century the last house of Gloucester Row was demolished and rebuilt with curved end to widen the road at the Esplanade's junction with King Street.

GOAT CARTS were an alternative to the popular seaside

An unusual mode of transport on the Esplanade.

donkey rides in the 1920s and 1930s and one goat cart was still in use in the 1950s.

GOERING'S MOTOR CAR was on show in Channon's Garage on the Esplanade between 11th and 16th August 1952, admission charges going to the Soldiers, Sailors and Airmen's Families Association. Hermann Goering's bullet-proof touring car had been discovered by the British Army in a large enemy vehicle park at Lentforden, Schleswig-Holstein after the capitulation of the German forces. It was a Mercedes Benz weighing 5 tons, with an eight cylinder supercharged engine of 7.7 litre capacity and a body fitted with bullet-proof steel panels and bullet-proof glass windows – the glass 1¾ inches thick.

GOLDCROFT CRICKET CLUB was renamed Westham Cricket Club in 1902.

GOLDCROFT ESTATE Goldcroft Road and Goldcroft Avenue were built by local firm Bird and Cox in the late 1920s/early 1930s.

GOLDCROFT FARM seems to have been a popular venue for large-scale events in the early years of the 20th century. June 1914 saw Bronco Bill's Great Wild West Exhibition and Mammoth Two-Ring Circus performing there and July 1921 brought F. Ginnett's Circus and Hippodrome to Westham. The farmhouse in Goldcroft Road was demolished in 1970. Nos. 26-30 Goldcroft Road stand on the site.

GORDON BRIGADE FOOTBALL CLUB Formed at Holy Trinity Church, the footballers' ground was on the site of the present Marina Gardens, Wyke Road.

GORDON CLUB *Additions to the main entry in Bumper Book I*

The Gordon Club and Reading Room for men only, opened in 1885 in the former Nelson Inn on North Quay. A Junior Gordon Club started the same year in the former High Street Coffee Tavern. The North Quay property was up for sale in 1906 when it was described as being *until recently known as the Gordon Club*.

GORDON ESTATE at Rodwell commemorates General Charles Gordon and his death at Khartoum in 1884. Hence Khartoum Road and Sudan Road, built in the late 1890s.

GOSPEL HALL, Rock Assembly Rooms, Westham Known as the Rock Mission, it appears to have started in November 1904.

GOULD CHARITY, Broadwey William Gould in his will of 1624 gave a close of meadow in Nottington, Broadwey called the parish meadow to exempt the poor from statute labour on the highways. This land was let annually by candle auction: on the termination of the year of the previous tenant, an auction was held at which an inch of candle was lit and bidding commenced, continuing until the candle burnt out. Whoever had the bid as it was extinguished held the land for that year.

GOVERNOR'S LANE COURT was between Nos. 12 and 13 Governor's Lane.

GRAF ZEPPELIN Local people have reported seeing the German airship *Graf Zeppelin* over Weymouth in 1929 or 1930. In August 1929 the local press reported that the airship was over the English Channel but *'was not seen or heard at Portland Bill'*.

GRAHAME-WHITE, Claude The famous aviator gave demonstration flights in his Henri-Farman seaplane at Weymouth in 1912 when he was here with another aviation pioneer, Benny Hucks, to participate in the Home Fleet review in May that year.

GRAND HOTEL, No. 24, Greenhill *Amendments to main entry in Bumper Book I:*

When Greenhill House (later to become the Grand Hotel) was sold in 1906, the auctioneer provided a brief history of its ownership and the building appears to be of earlier date than 1850.

He stated it was built for Colonel Gordon – this would be Colonel John Gordon, MP for the town in the 1820s and 1830s. The next occupant was John Trenchard who was certainly there in 1851. The next owner was Sir Richard Nicholas Howard and it was his death in 1905 which was the reason for the 1906 sale. Around 1900 there were some alterations and internal remodelling of the building by Sir Aston Webb. The buyer in 1906 and next occupant was Vere L. Oliver who purchased the house for just 500 guineas. He died in 1942. Greenhill House was requisitioned during WW2 and the last owners of the house as a private residence seem to have been the Misses Leafe, although they may not have resided there as the house had been empty for some years before it was purchased by Edgar Wallis in 1959 and converted into a hotel. In 1989 it was converted to flats.

GRAND NAUTICAL EMPIRE BAZAAR AND NELSON 'VICTORY' EXHIBITION was held at the Hotel Burdon (now the Hotel Prince Regent) in November 1910, a prestigious two-day event held to raise funds for the local Sailors' Bethel and opened in fine style by Princess Henry of Battenberg, youngest daughter of the late Queen Victoria.

GRAND PIER is an alternative name for Weymouth's Stone Pier.

GRAY'S CORNER is the local name for the junction of Dorchester Road and Old Station Road, Broadwey. It derives from the former shop of J. E. Gray & Co., grocers at No. 624 Dorchester Road, currently (2009) a veterinary practice. Joseph Gray, the shop's original owner in 1909, died in 1969.

GREAT EASTERN see SUTTON POYNTZ. WATERWORKS

GREAT WESTERN RESTAURANT was in Trinity Street in the early 1900s.

GREEN, Hughie lived aboard his cabin cruiser *Rake's Retreat* in Weymouth Harbour while appearing in the summer show at the Pavilion Theatre, 1966.

GREEN DRAGON In 1694 there was a house called the Green Dragon on the west side of East Street. May have been an inn.

GREEN GODDESS Army fire engines were on duty in the local area during the 1977-78 firemen's strike.

GREEN LANE leads from St Martin's Road to Buxton Road. It is also an early name for Camp Road.

GREENHAM TERRACE is at Westham, possibly on Abbotsbury Road or Newstead Road.

The Army's Green Goddess fire appliances were pressed into service during the firemen's strike in 1977-78.

GREENHILL, No. 3 This building, recently converted to apartments, was the High School for Girls in the late-19th century. Now renumbered as No. 10, Greenhill.

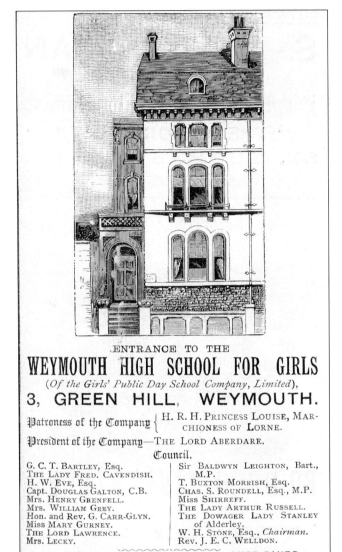

No. 3 Greenhill was one of many private schools in the borough in the 19th century.

put forward to rejuvenate the block and improve the gardens with a gallery, a new café to replace the 1958 structure and an outdoor exhibition space.

This was the open walkway before the second tier of chalets were added at Greenhill in the 1930s.

GREENHILL, No. 35 A substantial 1900s red brick house on the corner of Greenhill and Melcombe Avenue was demolished in 2007 and has made way for a large futuristic white house.

GREENHILL CHALETS The two tier chalets in Greenhill Gardens were originally a row at ground level with an open walkway above, built in the 1920s. Approval was given in November 1933 for the construction of the additional tier of chalets. Plans to demolish the chalets and build new ones on the site have been scrapped as the originals now have a Grade II listing. New proposals have been

GREENHILL HOUSE *see* GRAND HOTEL, No. 24, Greenhill

GREENHOUSES AND PALM HOUSE, Melcombe Regis Gardens were erected in 1927.

GREYFRIARS, No. 13 Greenhill *see* GREYSTONES

GREYHOUND INN was at No. 2 St Nicholas Street in the 1871 Census. It is sometimes listed as St Thomas Street.

GREYHOUND RACING at the Wessex Stadium commenced 5th August 1954.

GREYSTONES, No. 13 Greenhill (sometimes erroneously called Greyfriars) A Crickmay design, the house was built in 1890. WW2 saw it in use as a home for evacuee expectant mothers and in the 1950s the building was extended when it was the house and surgery of a local doctor. It was bought by the Tories in the late 1960s for use as Weymouth Conservative Club and reverted to use as a private house in 1998 when it was renamed Cathkin House. Another 'Greystones' was built in the 1960s at Southdown Avenue, Preston and a much older property adjacent to the Spa House at Nottington also bears the name *(see next entry)*.

GREYSTONES, Nottington Lane Originally two 18th century cottages which later provided accommodation for those visiting the adjacent Nottington Spa. The carved stone pelicans atop its wall and the Steward family crest were originally at Nottington House, home of the Steward family, which was demolished in 1967.

GRIFFITH, Tudor (Josiah Rees Tudor Griffith) (1914-1960) Solicitor, Town Councillor, Alderman and twice unsuccessful Labour candidate for South Dorset. An eloquent speaker who was never far from controversy.

GRIMALDI, Joe The famous clown appeared at the Theatre Royal in the days of King George III's visits 1789-1805. On one occasion he recited some light-hearted verse, believed to be his own work, extolling the virtues of Weymouth. Just a couple of samples from it to give a flavour of the work:

But the place of all places for me
Is Weymouth, so handsome and gay,
Where you sniff the salt air of the sea
And drive your complaints all away.
And he ends with
Can Weymouth be equalled? Oh no!
And here is the proof I will bring,
For beside these delights it can show
That it adds to the health of our King.

GROSSMITH, George Author, with his brother Weedon, of *The Diary of a Nobody.* Gave a performance at the Burdon Hotel on 25th August 1902 and appeared again in September 1905 on a farewell tour which he failed to complete due to illness.

GROSVENOR HOUSE was in Grosvenor Place, Esplanade. It was a private school in the early 1900s.

GROSVENOR VILLAS were at Radipole.

GROVE BUILDINGS were in Great George Street and included No. 22, the Phoenix Inn. There are also Grove Buildings at Broadwey.

GROVES, T. B. Chemist. Sold his business in St Mary Street to Mr J. R. Eyles in 1893. Well-known antiquarian who also established a meteorological station on the Nothe. Died 1st July 1902.

GUEST, Montague John, JP, DL (1839-1909) MP for Wareham from 1880-1885. In the 1890s he lived at **Devonshire House** on the Esplanade (the 'Round House', Devonshire Buildings) where he entertained royalty, including the future King George V in 1898. Member of the Royal Yacht Squadron. He was in Weymouth in the Royal Yacht in 1902 accompanying King Edward VII and at that time was Commodore of the Royal Dorset Yacht Club. There is a memorial tablet to him in Canford Magna Church.

Montague John Guest of Devonshire House.

GULLESHAYES A local place name dating back at least to the 17th century in the Gypsy Lane/Wyke Road area.

Haggard, Rider

HAGGARD, Rider He was in Dorset writing a piece on agriculture for a London journal in April 1901. He was a farmer as well as a novelist.

HAIGH, Captain Francis Evans Percy, RN (1873-1934) Lived at Wyke Castle from 1914-1919 after being posted to Whiteheads to work on torpedo design and development. He designed the War Memorial in Wyke Regis cemetery which commemorates 52 men of Wyke who sacrificed their lives during WW1. He left Wyke in 1919 to continue his work at the RN Torpedo Factory at Greenock.

HALF MOON ALEHOUSE in the 18th century stood on the east side of St Mary Street, near the Guildhall. Another Half Moon Public House was on the north side of King Street, at its junction with Crescent Street and has been converted to shop premises. The Half Moon public house at Portesham closed in September 1989 and has been converted to residential use.

HALF MOON COPSE was an alternative name for Horse Lynch Plantation (more recently Teddy Bear Woods).

HALFWAY HOUSE is an alternative name for the Tollhouse which once stood halfway along Preston Beach Road. Also popularly known as 'Sugar-em Shorey's'. *See* SHOREY, Sugar-em *and* PRESTON TOLL HOUSE in *Bumper Book I*.

The old tollhouse on Preston Beach Road, once home of 'Sugar-em Shorey', and demolished in 1959. Also known as Halfway House.

HALLETTS A long-established high class furniture shop at No. 73 St Thomas Street, which closed at the end of 1982. Founded in Coneygar Lane in 1837 by William Hallett, as cabinet makers, upholsterers and funeral furnishers. Subsequently moved to St Mary Street and then in 1937 to St Thomas Street.

HAM, Elizabeth Born in 1783 in Somerset, Elizabeth Ham spent the holidays of her childhood and teenage years at Weymouth and her account of those years when King George III and the royal family were also holidaying in the resort makes entertaining reading. The diary is retrospective. She began it in 1849 when she was sixty seven years old, having had moderate success with a novel in the 1840s and a book on English grammar many years earlier. The diary was not published until 1945, almost one hundred years after she began writing it.
Further reading: *Elizabeth Ham, by herself 1783-1820*, introduced and edited by Eric Gillett. (Faber & Faber Ltd., 1945.)

HAMBLIN. Francis Woodward, Engineer Captain, RN, Rtd., JP Mayor of Weymouth and Melcombe Regis 1930-31, 1931-1932 and 1932-33. His name can be found on some of the boundary stones around the borough which mark the extension of the boundaries during his mayoralty in 1933.

HAMBRO, Colonel Charles John Theophilus (1835-1891) Conservative MP for Weymouth in the 1860s and 1870s. Gave his name to the Hambro Rooms in New Street and probably also to Hambro Terrace, Bridge Inn Lane, Preston and Hambro Road, Portland.

HAMILTON, James *Correction to main entry in Bumper Book I:*
Bridport Town Hall was designed by William Tyler, not James Hamilton, although Hamilton worked on the building.

HAMILTON HOUSE was in Lennox Street but has no connection with architect James Hamilton. Hamilton House at Wyke Regis was designed by James Hamilton.

HANCOCK, Tony Appeared at the Ritz Theatre in September 1951.

HANDEL HOUSE, No. 25 St Thomas Street A sheet music seller and pianoforte warehouse run by William Rogers until his death in 1901 and then by his son Robert. Founded in the mid-19th century in St Alban Street.

HANNEYS FISH WAREHOUSE, Custom House Quay was converted to the **Deep Sea Adventure** in the late 1980s.

HANOVER TERRACE is now part of Hanover Road.

A train on the Weymouth Harbour Tramway passes the Custom House on its way to the Pier. Once the harbourmaster's office it is now HQ of Portland Coastguard.

HANSOM CAB The local press reported in April 1874 that *'The first Hansom Cab has made its appearance on our streets and is now plying for hire'*.

HARBOUR CLUB One of the many names that the building on the Town Bridge, now (2009) 'The Rendezvous', has gone under since it began life as a furnishing store. This club dates back to the 1970s and 1980s.

HARBOURMASTER'S OFFICE In the earlier part of the 20th century the harbourmaster occupied premises in a warehouse at the rear of the Guildhall (these later housed Board's Typing School until the warehouse was demolished in 1958). The harbourmaster moved to newly built offices at No. 20 Custom House Quay in 1935, transferring again to the Custom House and then in 1989 to the present building, formerly a warehouse.

HARDY, Thomas He attended the Pavilion Theatre, Weymouth for a performance of *Tess of the d'Urbervilles* by the Dorchester Hardy Players on 11th December 1924. The performance was to raise funds for the Mayor's Weymouth's Unemployed Christmas Fund. Hardy had attended a performance here by the Players once before when they produced *The Trumpet Major*.

HARDY COURT *see* POLICE STATION, Dorchester Road

HARDY'S MONUMENT commemorates Admiral Sir Thomas Masterman Hardy, Nelson's flag-captain at the Battle of Trafalgar 1805. The monument, erected in 1844 with stunning views across land and sea, has been said to look like a factory chimney, but much more appropriately it resembles a telescope, with the eyepiece at the top. When the monument was restored in 1900 it was placed in charge of the National Trust by the descendants of Sir Thomas Masterman Hardy, on whose land it stood.

The monument to Admiral Sir Thomas Hardy on Blackdown Hill above Portesham and visible for miles around.

HARLEY-DAVIDSON the annual motor cycle ride takes place in May, from Warmwell to Lodmoor Country Park, Weymouth.

HARMAN TERRACE is now in Sutton Road, Sutton Poyntz.

HAWK INN was the name originally chosen for the new post-war pub at Chapelhay but it was changed to The Prospect before the pub opened on 1st May 1959. The Prospect closed in 2008 and the building or the site will probably be converted to housing.

HEATH, Francis George The well-known Devonshire writer died in 1913 at his son Dr Rodier Heath's home in Abbotsbury Road.

HEATH, Ted and his band were here in the 1950s, a popular act at summer dances.

HELEN LANE The former Templeman's Mill building,

Helen Lane and Templeman's Mill, where the entire workforce has turned out for the photographer, some of them rather precariously perched.

which suffered a serious fire in 1917, later became the property of Weymouth Water Company and was converted into flats. The building was extended and a silver dome added in 2007. For the history of Templeman's Mill see *Bumper Book I* under TEMPLEMAN, Thomas John (1848-1919).

HELL A survey of 1732 lists '*A house called Hell on the west side of East Street, bounded to the south by Hell Lane*'. Today's Helen Lane.

HEMINGWAY, Ernest The American author and war correspondent embarked at Weymouth in June 1944 for the D-Day landings.

HICKEY, William The 18th century diarist was in Weymouth in July 1776 but made little reference to the town, apart from judging the unnamed tavern in which he stayed to be '*as good as any in England*' and finding '*a set of very tolerable actors*' appearing at the Theatre Royal on the Esplanade. Visits were made to Mr Sturt and to Mr Buxton -the latter at Portland, where Hickey commented that '*the want of trees made it, in my opinion, look dreary; in winter it must be dreadfully so*'.

HIGGS, Alfred Charles Auctioneer with premises in St Thomas Street. Successful in his early days in Weymouth in the 1890s and officiated at a number of major auction sales but was declared bankrupt in 1902.

HIGH CROSS/HIGH CROSSE this location occurs in 17th and 18th century deeds relating to property on the Weymouth side of the harbour and appears to have been near the Old Town Hall.

HIGH STREET, Weymouth is sometimes referred to as Weymouth Street in early documents.

The narrow winding High Street was picturesque but not easy to photograph. The top view looks towards Boot Hill, the lower one towards Holy Trinity Church.

HIGH STREET, Wyke Regis No. 109, High Street, Wyke Regis was pulled down in 1964 and was described as *'the last of the old fishermen's cottages'.*

HIGH WEST STREET TAVERN, High West Street, Weymouth closed in 1978.

HIGHLAND COTTAGES (Nos 1-2) are listed in the 1891 Census. At Westham.

HILL, Benny Was the star of the show on the opening night of the Pavilion Theatre, 15th July 1960, appearing with Cyril Stapleton and his Band.

HILL HOUSE is No. 117 Dorchester Road, at its junction with Alexandra Road.

HILL VIEW is a terrace of three houses on the west side of Boot Hill. There was another Hill View at Westham.

HILLCOURT is Nos. 53 and 55, Dorchester Road

HINDUSTAN, HMS The battleship arrived at Portland Monday 7th August 1911 with the Prince of Wales (later King Edward VIII) on board. He had just started his naval career as a midshipman. He came ashore and strolled on the Esplanade, apparently unrecognised. He left the ship at Weymouth in October that year and travelled by train to London to bid farewell to the King and Queen who were leaving on a tour of India.

HINTZE, Ed Performing as Elton John he appeared in the BBC-TV programme 'The one and only…' in 2008.

HOBBS, William Author of an early unpublished geological work *The earth generated and anatomized* written around 1715, the manuscript of which is now in the British Museum. He lived in Weymouth, where he kept a register of tides in the early 1700s -*Mr Hobbs of Weymouth's Tables of the Tides Observed By Him There*, a paper now in the Royal Greenwich Observatory Archives. He may have been the William Hobbs who was a schoolmaster in the town in 1723.

HOCKERHILL/HOCKERILL was originally a farm, part of Nottington on the boundary of the parishes of Radipole and Broadwey.

HOCKRIDGE, Edmund The singer appeared at the Alexandra Gardens in June 1957.

HODDER, Fabian *see* CADE, John

HOGSHEAD pub *see* WILLIAM HENRY pub

HOLLAND HOUSE Houses of this name in Hardwick Street and on the corner of Westham Road/Great George Street.

HOLLAND ROAD From the *Southern Times* issue dated 4th January 1936: *'A gift from the Weymouth Corporation: the imposing gates at the new entrance of the Grammar School. The gates were formerly at the old Royal Jubilee Hall, on the site of which the Regent Theatre now stands.'* The ornate gates still stand at the end of Holland Road, although the school buildings have since given way to a housing development.

HOLWELL was a farm in Buckland Ripers.

HOLY TRINITY CHURCH *see* main entry in *Bumper Book I*. Since publication a new history of the church has been produced: *The parish of The Holy Trinity, Weymouth: the church by the bridge*, by Geoff Pritchard (2006).

HOLY TRINITY CHURCH, Fleet The present church at Fleet was consecrated 25th August 1829. It replaced the original village church which was almost totally destroyed in the Great Gale of 1824. The old church and its graveyard on the Fleet shore can still be visited, the chancel having been restored after the gale. It contains monuments to the Mohun family of Fleet. *See also* FLEET

HOLY TRINITY SCHOOLS CofE Primary School and Community Nursery, Cross Road opened on 5th September 2007. Demolition of the old school buildings on the same site began that month.
Further reading: *Three into one will go: the story of Holy Trinity Schools, Weymouth* by Geoff Pritchard (2008).

HOLY TRINITY VICARAGE, Longfield Road The Portland stone Gothic-style building was erected around 1860. It has now been converted to private housing.

HOLZEWICKEDE COURT at Littlemoor is named after Weymouth and Portland's German twin town. A commemorative plaque marks its official opening on 12th June 2009.

HOME CLOSE GARDENS *see* WYKE REGIS. GARDENS

HONEST MAN INN was an early pub in Radipole village, certainly there in the 1780s. When the building was up for sale in 1833 it was described as *'late the Honest Man Inn'*.

HOOD, HMS the old battleship was deliberately sunk to block the South Ship Channel entrance to Portland Harbour on 4th November 1914, to prevent submarine and torpedo attacks. She still lies there, gradually sinking lower and breaking up.

HOOPER, Pelly Town Clerk of Weymouth and Melcombe Regis from 1879 until his death in March, 1894. He had been Acting Town Clerk for some months due to the illness of the previous postholder, F. C. Steggall who died in 1879. Since 1870 the two had been in partnership in a firm

Obsolete battleship HMS Hood, *stripped of her fittings, is positioned in the South Ship Channel between Portland Breakwaters just prior to being sunk in 1914.*

Ancient and attractive buildings in Maiden Street were swept away when Hurdle's Corner was redeveloped in the 1920s.

of solicitors known as Steggall and Hooper. Lived at Highclere, No. 21, Wyke Road, since demolished.

HOPE COVE *'It having been represented that the Cove, in Weymouth, was very offensive at low water, and that it was the wish of the neighbouring inhabitants to have the same inclosed and filled up, who (with others), have subscribed a sum of money for that purpose, and, it being supposed that no injury will accrue to the Harbour thereby; it is resolved that leave be given for building a wall across the said Cove, from the Quay opposite to Mr William Schollar's, to the Slip in Hope Street, and for filling up the said Cove'.* This was the infilling of 'Macsaunders Hole' in 1781, providing much of the land on which Hope Square now stands.

HORSE LYNCH PLANTATION (more recently known as Teddy Bear Woods) was also known as Half Moon Copse.

HORSFORD STREET probably takes its name from the Horsford family who were in Weymouth at least as far back as 1800. Joseph Horsford was Mayor in 1836.

HOVERCRAFT RALLY The British Hovercraft Club's first rally to be staged in other than inland waters was held in Weymouth at the beginning of April 1972.

HOWARD'S TERRACE was at Chickerell.

HUGIN This was a well-known replica Viking ship which visited Weymouth in August 1949.

'HUGO' Baptiste Hugo was advertised as a French 'giant' – a man 22 years old, 7 feet 6 inches tall and weighing 401 lbs. Billed as 'the biggest man in the world', he appeared in fairground sideshows and was in a marquee on the sands in

the summer of 1901. His visit was somewhat marred by troublesome crowds and a summons for assault was brought against him when children in the melee were slightly injured. It was dismissed.

HURDLE'S CORNER took its name from Hurdle & Co's shop, and is the junction of St Edmund Street and Maiden Street. Mr Hurdle rebuilt his shop after the demolition of some of Weymouth's oldest houses here in the 1920s, a great loss to the street scene.

HUTCHINSON, Leslie 'Hutch' West Indian cabaret singer and pianist. Born 7th March 1900 in Grenada. Reputed to have had an affair with Lady Edwina Mountbatten as well as many other society women and men. He appeared in Weymouth in the 1950s and may have been here in 1944 entertaining troops prior to the D-Day landings. He died on 18th August 1969.

HUXTABLE, Henry Anthony Town Clerk of Weymouth from 1905 until his death in 1915, having previously been Assistant Town Clerk. Although praised in his obituary notices, the choice of Dorchester resident Huxtable, who ran a solicitors practice in the county town, was not approved by all and at a Town Council meeting after his death it was resolved:
'That a Town Clerk be appointed who shall devote the whole of his time to the duties of the office, that the sum of £450 per annum, rising to £800 by annual increments of £25, be paid to a municipally trained solicitor, who shall reside within the borough'.

HYDROPATHIC BATHS A hydropathic baths establishment opened in June 1898 at No. 25 Dorchester Road (St John's Terrace). Hydropathic baths are also shown on Pierse Arthur's map of 1857, at the rear of Victoria Villa, Lennox Street.

Ice Show

I

ICE SHOW A rather unusual tented event for a seaside resort in summer was the staging of an ice show on the site of the burnt-out Ritz Theatre on the pier in July 1956. A big top was erected and 'Robin Hood on Ice' was the show.

ICE SKATING Winters in Weymouth were much chillier in the 19th and early 20th centuries and there are a number of reports of ice skating on a frozen Lodmoor in the 1860s and 1870s, continuing into the early 1900s. What a lovely evening it must have been in January 1861 when locals skated at Lodmoor by torchlight, accompanied by music provided by the bands of the Weymouth Volunteer Rifles.

ICEN VILLAS are on the east side of Roman Road.

IDA TERRACE was at Chapelhay, probably in the Love Lane area. There was a terrace of the same name in Gallwey Road, Wyke Regis.

IDEAL LAUNDRY was founded in 1928 in Waverley Road (then known as Reliable Drive). It later became part of South Dorset Laundries Ltd and these works closed in the early 1960s.

ILAM house was on Dorchester Road at Broadwey.

ILLUSTRIOUS, HMS Memorial seats overlooking the scene of the *ILLUSTRIOUS* tragedy in Portland Harbour were dedicated on Monday 23rd April 2007 on the Rodwell Trail near Ferrybridge. 29 young naval men returning to their ship from shore leave in Weymouth were drowned when their launch overturned in rough weather and sank just 60 yards from the aircraft carrier on 17th October 1948. *See also* MELVILLE, Commander Francis William, RN who drowned in 1904 when returning to an earlier *HMS Illustrious* in Portland Harbour, *and* GEORGE CROSS.

ILSINGTON HOUSE at Puddletown was the home in the 19th century of Major-General Thomas Garth, a royal equerry who was said to be the father of Princess Sophia's illegitimate baby boy born in 1800 – she being the daughter of King George III. The story has never been confirmed or denied, but the child, known as Tommy Garth, who in later life turned out to be a thoroughly bad lot, was brought up as Garth's son. Was Garth the father, or was he protecting the royal family from scandal? Some claimed the father was Sophia's own brother, Ernest, Duke of Cumberland. More than 200 years on, the truth will probably never be known.

ILTON TERRACE, (Nos. 1 – 8) was in Prince of Wales Road.

INVICTA HOUSE was in Lennox Street.

IT is my wish that every poor child in my dominions should be taught to read the Bible were words spoken at Weymouth by King George III to educationalist Joseph Lancaster. They were inscribed on a plaque once on the outside wall of St Mary's Schools in Great George Street. When the schools were demolished in 1988, the plaque was transferred to the main staircase of Weymouth Library, which opened on the site in 1990.

IVY BANK *see* POWELL VILLA

A snowy Dorchester Road close to its junction with Mill Street at Broadwey.

Jackson, Samuel H.

JACKSON Samuel H. (1845-1927) Architect. Founder of a firm of architects and surveyors at York Buildings. Lived in Westham where he also designed the Abbotsbury Road laundry and the Co-op Bakery in Cromwell Road (both since demolished). All his five sons trained as architects and on his death in 1927 two of them, Samuel Holyoak Jackson and Horace G. Jackson, carried on the business.

JAKEMAN family Long serving railwaymen with the GWR. George Thomas Jakeman had completed 50 years with the company when he retired in 1922, forty of those as a stationmaster. His brother and two sons were also GWR stationmasters, one son, Councillor T. F. E. Jakeman, being stationmaster at Weymouth.

JAMES AND CADDY, boat builders launched their first boat in 1947. Firm set up after WW2 by Mr F. James and Mr W. Caddy. By 1953 James was the sole owner.

JEANES GARAGE was at Nos. 114-116 Abbotsbury Road, the former **Westham Cinema** site. It was sold in 1951 to provide shop premises.

JEFFREYS DAIRY on the corner of Westham Road/Great George Street closed in January 1979.

JEHOVAH'S WITNESSES First met in the 1940s in a rented room at the Golden Lion Hotel. Many different locations were used over the years until the congregation purchased the Coffee Tavern in High Street in 1978.

JERVOISE, Edwyn An architect and author in the 1930s of books on ancient bridges. Born in Weymouth.

JESSAMINE COTTAGES are part of Old Station Road, Broadwey.

JESTY FAMILY Jesty Limited was formed in May 1901. The company was founded by Charles Jesty of Antwerp, Radipole, mayor in 1896-7 and 1897-8. He died in November 1901. His eldest son William Charles Jesty of East Chickerell Court ran a wholesale business in meat, poultry, game etc. Another son, Benjamin Jesty ran a

haulage business which he transferred to H. J. Carter in 1901, to concentrate on his farms and contractor's business, the newly formed firm of Jesty and Baker.

JETTY, Trinity Street The ferro-concrete jetty in Trinity Street was completed around 1930.

JOHNSON, Sir Edward, KCB, JP (for Dorchester), DL (1786-1862) Born in Ireland. Although he was a Deputy Lieutenant for Dorset, lived at his Greenhill, Weymouth address for more than ten years and seems to have represented and entertained Conservative MPs and parliamentary candidates locally, no local newspaper carried an obituary of him and even the brief notices in the 'Deaths' columns spell his surname incorrectly as Johnston. He left most of estate to his family, in particular to his nephew **William Johnson Smith, MD** the founder of the Weymouth Sanatorium.

JOHNSTONE, Sir Frederic John William, 8th Baronet, of Westerhall in Dumfriesshire (1841-1913) *Additions to the main entry in Bumper Book I:*

Although Sir Frederic Johnstone's life is outlined in the first *Bumper Book of Weymouth*, the extent of his property ownership in Weymouth and his extravagant lifestyle make him one of the most interesting characters in the town's later history. He was the first-born of twins, his father having predeceased him and he inherited enormous wealth and property when he came of age, the fortune having come down the family, being originally amassed by Sir William Pulteney (formerly Sir William Johnstone) in the 18th century, largely by his marriage to an heiress of the Pulteney family of Bath. It was Pulteney who acquired the Weymouth properties which were to become the 'Johnstone Estate'.

Although Sir Frederic was to become a benefactor of Weymouth in many ways – he was frequently asked to provide sites for buildings of a religious or charitable nature – some felt that he and his agents had too much influence in the town. This was demonstrated in 1884 when his ownership of land at Greenhill was disputed. He had laid out gardens on what many felt was common land and quite a large mob trampled down his fences and gates, leading to a protracted court case. Although Sir Frederic won, it soured his relationship with Weymouth and he rarely visited the town again. (He did, however, present the disputed Greenhill Gardens to the town as a Coronation gift in 1902). His lifestyle ate up his fortune. He was a great horse-racing man and a close friend of King Edward VII, who was a frequent visitor to Sir Frederic's home, the Hatch, at Windsor and had also stayed at his luxurious villa, Le Nid, at Monte Carlo. The sale of land he owned off Dorchester Road in 1890 may have recouped a little money (these building plots were in the Carlton Road, Glendinning Avenue, Kirtleton Avenue area) and in 1903 it was announced that he planned to dispose of his inherited lands in America – the Pulteney estate in the neighbourhood of Bath, New York State, which was already substantially smaller in size than it had been originally. Things had gone badly wrong by 1911 after he had executed a deed of assignment of his property for the benefit of his creditors, leaving himself with nothing, an assumption being made that he was of unsound mind. His affairs were finally settled in the Chancery Division in May, 1912, when a case was brought to set aside the deed, Mr Henry Chaplin having been appointed receiver of Sir Frederic's estate under Section 116 of the Lunacy Act 1890. The proposed settlement was that the furniture, clothes etc. of Sir Frederic at the Hatch, Windsor would not be sold or removed during his life and he would be allowed to remain in possession of the Hatch for life. He would also receive an income of £2,500 a year for life. In Mr Chaplin's view there would be a surplus of about £41,000 worth of assets over liabilities and as the

Sir Frederic Johnstone aboard his luxury yacht Zenaida.

order was being made by consent he thought it only fair that costs should be provided for. The judge decided it was a fair settlement and the matter then ended. Sir Frederic died at the Hatch on 20th June 1913, his twin brother having died the previous year. His Weymouth property devolved to his widow, Laura, Lady Wilton and became known as the Wilton Estate which was finally sold off in the 1930s. The estate office in New Street still stands, now converted to a fast food outlet. The estate's agents in the 20th century were Henry Nagle, followed by H. A. L. Young and finally A. W. Burch.

JOLLY SAILOR INN was at No. 30 Park Street in the 1870s, having also been called the Friendship Inn, a name it reverted to later.

JORDAN HILL *see* PRESTON. ROMAN HISTORY

JORDAN HOUSE, Preston Road dates from around 1800 and is a former farmhouse.

JOY'S CONVENIENCE STORE at Overcombe Corner celebrated its 50th anniversary in 2007 – began in 1957 when Betty and Bunny Joy bought the business from Mr and Mrs Price. It was originally H. Joy, newsagent.

JUBILEE CLOCK *Additional information – the Clock's history is contained in Bumper Book I:*
In June 1960 an electrical mechanism replaced clockwork which required frequent winding.

JUBILEE HALL *(update: the Hall's history is contained in Bumper Book I)*
During demolition in 1989, some parts of the Jubilee Hall's structure were rescued and taken to a Portland quarry for storage. There they stayed until January 2007 when they were transferred to the Poundbury development at Dorchester where it is hoped they may be used in a new structure. This would be on a much smaller scale than the original Jubilee Hall's dimensions of 140 feet in length, 90 feet in breadth and 65 feet in height. Although the timbers did not survive, some of the ornate columns were still sound and stonework, although eroded and damaged, was thought to be repairable.

A pair of very imposing and decorative iron gates which lead into the housing development at the end of Holland Road at Westham were originally at the entrance to Weymouth Grammar School, which previously stood on the site. The gates were formerly at the Jubilee Hall and were probably removed during its 1926 transformation into the Regent Theatre and Dance Hall. They were presented to the Grammar School in 1936 by Weymouth Corporation following the addition of a new wing to the original school buildings. *See page 152 for a photograph of the gates*

JUBILEE TERRACE As well as Jubilee Terraces at Nos. 27-39 Newstead Road and Dorchester Road, Broadwey, there was also one in Lennox Street.

THE VICTORIA JUBILEE HALL

WEYMOUTH.

(Erected by the Weymouth and Melcombe Regis Baths, Public Entertainment and Recreation Company, Limited.)
Chairman, Sir Richard Howard; Secretary, Mr. Henry Nangle.

The interior of the newly built Jubilee Hall in 1887.

JUBILEE VILLAS, Nos. 2-3 are in the 1891 Census and appear to be in Abbotsbury Road.

JUBILEE WOOD, Radipole Lane The Civic Society's Jubilee Wood off Radipole Lane, opposite the Church and Manor House, celebrates the Society's 50th Anniversary in 1994 and there is a commemorative stone at the site. It was created by Weymouth Civic Society in partnership with the borough council and a Friends group regularly undertakes enhancement of the wood, planting and caring for it.

JURADO, Steven Painted the murals on the subways at the Swannery, Esplanade and Manor Roundabout. He was presented with an award by Weymouth Civic Society, offered to young people for original public art, in 2008.

JURASSIC COUNTDOWN by June Vernau. A children's adventure novel published in the Legendworld Adventure series in 2005, featuring children in a race against time to save Weymouth and Portland being taken over by giant sea dragons and a fierce megalosaurus.

Kayes Lane and Kayes Close

K

KAYES LANE and KAYES CLOSE at Wyke Regis were renumbered in 1962.

KEAST COURT, Overcombe takes its name from the builder, Geoff Keast.

KENNEDYS STORE, Lower Bond Street Kennedy's builders' merchants were the last occupants of the site on the corner of Bond Street and Commercial Road before its redevelopment as Debenhams store. Kennedys opened in 1955, replacing Bell's Garage which had taken over the Regent Garage in 1946. The Regent Garage replaced a tenement block, Burdon's Buildings, pulled down in the late 1920s. The tenements were in a former Georgian barracks which were themselves a conversion of **Puckett's Stores.** *See also* REGENT GARAGE.

KING STREET ROUNDABOUT is part of the Weymouth Way Relief Road works and its construction began in February 1984.

KING'S ARMS pub is in Trinity Road today, but early 18th century deeds refer to a King's Arms Inn on the west side of St Thomas Street.

KING'S HEAD INN, Maiden Street was demolished in the 1860s to make way for Maiden Street Methodist Church.

KING'S STATUE *Update. The history of the King's Statue is in Bumper Book I:*

The work of restoring and repainting the statue of King George III began in 2007 and was completed in May 2008. The removal of some 20 layers of old paint revealed that the ironwork framework within the statue had rusted and was fracturing the Coade stone of which it is made. It was replaced by a new stainless steel frame and the statue was repaired, as were the magnificent lion and unicorn and the plinth. Complete repainting followed, including the use of real gold leaf for the gilding details and the whole of the lion. The front face of the plinth was re-lettered. The conservation project was part of the Melcombe Regis and Esplanade Townscape Heritage Initiative (THI) co-funded by Weymouth and Portland Borough Council and the Heritage Lottery Fund. The work was carried out by Poole-based firm Osirion Conservation.

In the background of this early photograph stands the King's Head Inn, demolished in the 1860s.

KING'S STEPS In June 1802 five-feet wide stone steps with iron stanchions and iron railings were built for the use of the Royal Family when they went on board the royal barge. They were near Devonshire Buildings, the location usually known as Ferry Steps today.

The early 1900s, when only a few shrubs and low railings surrounded the King's Statue.

KINGS WINE AND ALE HOUSE opened in 1986 in the former Sun Inn, King Street, but the pub has since reverted to its original name.

KINGSBURY COURT, Stavordale Road is an apartment block which replaced No. 5, the Kenora Hotel.

KINGSWOOD HOTEL *see* LONGHILL COTTAGE

KIRTLETON AVENUE was once tree-lined. Large trees were felled in December 1962.

KNIGHT'S COTTAGES (Nos. 1-8) Probably part of Knightsdale Road, taking their name from local landowner Emmanuel Knight.

Kirtleton Avenue, one of several streets to have lost many of its trees over the years.

L

Labour Club

LABOUR CLUB, No. 42 Southview Road The Club closed early in 2008 and was put up for sale in May that year. The building also houses the constituency office of the Labour Party, the Weymouth Labour Club having rented the premises from them for more than 30 years.

LAKE'S PASSAGE is mentioned in 18th and 19th century documents but is only described as *'leading off'* or *'leading out of'* St Mary Street.

LAMB AND FLAG pub was in Radipole village. On the 1861 Census it is included in the list of properties in Duck Alley, beyond Westend Cottages. Another Lamb and Flag pub was in Lower Bond Street. It closed in 1958 and was converted to a Royal Sailors Rest, later becoming a probation hostel, but was demolished in the 1990s to make way for a new shopping development.

LANDSCAPE VIEW, Nos 1 and 2 These properties were at Chapelhay, possibly at the eastern end of Chapelhay Street.

LANEHOUSE ROCKS ESTATE construction of the council houses at Lanehouse by builder R. V. Curtis began in the late 1940s. The private sector housing on the opposite side of Lanehouse Rocks Road was by the Littlesea Estate Company and began in 1956/7.

LANEHOUSE ROCKS FARM Fire at the old farm on 16th December 1987 led to the death of its only occupant, Mr Victor Charles Vine, aged 90. The derelict site was redeveloped as housing in 2005 when stone from the old building was used in some of the new properties in Vines Place.

LANGDALE VILLAS (Nos. 1-2) were on Abbotsbury Road in the vicinity of St Paul's Church.

LANGTON HERRING Langton is derived from 'Long town' and the village is strung out along a long street. Herring is from its ancient lords of the manor. It was once held by the family of the 'Butcher of England' John Tiptoft, Earl of Worcester who was executed in 1470.

LANSDOWNE HOUSE *see* LANSDOWNE TERRACE

LANSDOWNE TERRACE (Nos. 1-8) is now Nos. 3-17 Wyke Road. Lansdowne House is No. 17.

LARKWORTHY, Ambrose An Exeter surgeon who opened the town's first Chemist's shop in Bond Street around 1830, later moving to No. 53 St Thomas Street. Father of Falconer Larkworthy, banker in the Australian gold fields in the 1850s and 1860s.

LARLING VILLAS are in Old Parish Lane.

LAUREL LANE, Upwey includes Laurel Cottages and Laurel Terrace.

LAURISTINE TERRACE became Nos. 103-117 Abbotsbury Road. It had formerly been Rose Terrace or Rose Cottages.

LAVINIA COTTAGE was in Hardwick Street.

LAW, C. Orlando He was the architect of the present Royal Hotel, Esplanade.

LAWN HOUSE was in Lennox Street.

The LAWNS, Fernhill Avenue One of Weymouth's grander houses, at one time the home of **V. H. Bennett**, department store owner and mayor in 1919. Converted in 1949 to become a Dorset County Council Social Services home for the elderly.

LEA HOUSE was in Lennox Street.

LECTURE SOCIETY was in existence in 1883 under the guidance of architect Mr Crickmay. It was disbanded or absorbed into the **Weymouth Town Society** which began in 1883.

LEE, Ruby The stage name of Mrs Jenny Whitehouse-Vaux. She appeared in the shows at the Vaudeville Pavilion on Weymouth sands between the wars with her husband Val Vaux and the Vaudesques.

LEES, Sir Elliott, Bt., DSO, MA (1860-1908) Of South Lytchett Manor. Soldier, sportsman and politician. As Commander of the Queens Own Dorset Imperial Yeomanry, he fought in the South African War for which he was decorated and awarded the Distinguished Service Order. He had served as a Conservative Member of Parliament for non-local constituencies (Oldham, Birkenhead) in the period 1886 -1906 and in 1907 was chosen as the prospective candidate for South Dorset, but on 16th October 1908 he died of pneumonia at the Royal Hotel Weymouth, where he was staying. *See also* ELLIOTT-LEES ROOM, Westham

The Wyke lerret Agnes, *setting out not on a fishing trip but to recover the body of an Army balloonist who drowned with a fellow officer when their balloon* Thrasher *was blown off course in 1907.*

LENNOX HOUSE is No. 47 Lennox Street and was originally known as Victoria Villa.

LEONARD TERRACE is now Nos. 144-154 Abbotsbury Road. The five houses were advertised to let in 1906, so were probably newly built then.

LERRETS These are the sturdy clinker-built craft, canoe shaped and very broad, which were once a common sight on Chesil Beach. Being double ended and very strong they could be hauled up and down the beach easily. Four or six-oared, they are some 16 feet in length with a 5-6 feet beam. The name is said to have been inspired by the *Lady of Loretto*, an Italian boat of similar design. Traditionally, no boat put to sea unless it had tied to it a lucky pebble – one with a natural hole in it. As well as being used for fishing, lerrets and their crews from Portland and the villages along the Chesil coast took part in many heroic rescues at sea.

LETTER BOX COTTAGE, Radipole Lane was once known as Pillar Box Cottage.

LIDO see TAR BOAT

LINDEN TERRACE (Nos. 1-6) was at Westham in the Newstead Road/Milton Road area.

LINDEN VILLAS (Nos. 1 and 2) became Nos. 7-9 Stavordale Road. **John B. Cole** lived at No. 1.

LION pub This was in Hope Street in the 1820s so is probably an alternative name for the present Red Lion.

LISLE, Warren (1699-1788) was a Dorset Customs man who waged war on smugglers in the days when many customs officials were in league with them. He was based in Weymouth as Supervisor of the Riding Officers which covered an area from Wareham to Bridport and lived in St Edmund Street. He advanced rapidly up the career ladder and eventually bought an estate at Upwey, living in **Upwey Manor**.

LITTLE TERNS Dorset's only Little Tern colony nest on Chesil Beach close to Ferrybridge.

LITTLEFIELD LEVEL CROSSING was at Abbotsbury Road, Westham on the Weymouth and Portland Railway. This is now the start of the Rodwell Trail, along the former line, which closed to passengers in 1952 and all traffic in 1965.

LITTLEMOOR COMMUNITY ASSOCIATION'S community centre on the west side of Canberra Road opened in 1965.

LITTLEMOOR PRIMARY SCHOOL was renamed Bincombe Valley Primary School in January 1999.

LLOYD TERRACE *see* SOUTHERN NATIONAL GARAGE, Chickerell Road, Charlestown

LODMOOR HIGH SCHOOL, No. 66 Dorchester Road A school was established around 1860 for boarders and day pupils at Lodmoor House, when the building was quite new. (It was built on the site of the Union Arms pub). Unless the premises were shared, the school appears to have lapsed in the 1880s as one of the masters at Weymouth College, the nearby public school, was using the house for boy boarders, which continued into the 1890s. It seems to have started up again as a girls' school sometime after WW1, the Misses Batt transferring their school from Grosvenor Road and initially calling it Westbourne School but later Lodmoor High School. As such it continued until 1955, apart from a short wartime break in temporary accommodation when boarding pupil numbers dropped. When the school closed in 1955 the building was taken over by the Convent of the Sacred Hearts until 1960 when the lease expired. Lodmoor House was then converted into holiday flats, with a club and casino being installed in 1966.

A period of disuse was to follow later and by the 1980s the building was dilapidated and dangerous. It was rebuilt with the condition that the façade of the new Lodmoor House had to replicate the old. Today (2009) the Avonlea Residential Home occupies Lodmoor House.

LODMOOR ROW (Nos 1-6) was the terrace on Dorchester Road at Lodmoor Hill, now partly rebuilt, which includes the Royal Oak pub.

LOG ROLLER Billed as a 'unique entertainment' which it certainly must have been, Tom Barton, the champion log roller of the world, gave two aquatic displays at Weymouth in June 1904. Sponsored by Bovril, his 'log' comprised soldered-together Bovril tins and was 1 foot in diameter and 9 feet long. He performed a selection of balancing tricks on the log in the Backwater, including spinning it with his feet and sitting on it at a table and chair drinking Bovril (never missing an advertising opportunity, the firm also dispensed Bovril drinks among the spectators, which the *Weymouth Telegram* estimated as a crowd of thousands). In the evening he performed similar stunts (in the rain) in the Bay. He'd won his extraordinary title at the Antwerp Exhibition in 1894.

The 'Bovril' log roller.

Lodmoor High School and Kindergarten

DORCHESTER ROAD, WEYMOUTH

TELEPHONE 819

Boarding and Day School for Girls   *Preparatory for Boys*

THE House, which has been modernised, is situated on the brow of a hill, near the Sea.

The Junior School (Boys and Girls) and Senior School (Girls), under the direction of a fully qualified and trained Staff, provide a course based on the requirements of the Board of Education.

Pupils are prepared for all examinations to University Entrance, the Associated Board of the Royal Schools of Music, the Royal Drawing Society and the London Institute of Plain Needlework Examinations. Special attention is paid to Physical Culture and Speech Training.

Boarders receive Home Care and Individual attention

Principal : Mrs. BAYLISS

A 1930s' advertisement for Lodmoor High School.

LONG SAND BARGE went aground in Weymouth Bay on 25th October 2007. Recovery work started in mid-November 2007. It was finally removed in July 2008.

LONGCROFT VILLAS (Nos. 1-4) follow No. 39 Longcroft Road.

LONGHILL COTTAGE was built in the early 1820s on a field known as Longhill Field. In 1885 the cottage was lived in by John Bradbury who rebuilt it or added to it and called it Kingswood. He leased it to Dr Eugene Victor De Meric who eventually bought the property. It remained in the family until 1930 or 1931 and was then converted to the Kingswood Hotel, No. 55 Rodwell Road.

Chickerell's Lugger Inn shortly after the fire.

LONGHILL ROAD was renamed Rodwell Road in 1872.

LONSDALE TERRACE was in Grange Road or Avenue Road.

LOOKERS LANE appears in early deeds. As it was on the south side of the harbour it might be an alternative to Hooker's Lane (as in Hooker's Dock).

LORRY DRIVER OF THE YEAR Weymouth was selected as an eliminating centre in the competition in 1958.

LORTON FARMHOUSE, No. 541 Dorchester Road. Was built c.1830 in a style with Gothic influence.

LORTON HOUSE was built for the Bridge family in 1857.

LOWE, Alfred *see* GEORGE CROSS

LUCE, Thomas Dorney 19th century hotel proprietor who ran, at various times, the Victoria and Great Western Hotel, the Gloucester Hotel and the Royal Hotel.

LUGGER INN, Chickerell The once-thatched pub caught fire on 21st February 1912, the fire spreading to an adjacent cottage. It was later rebuilt. In the 20th century its landlords were long-serving – Albert Parker (who was due to leave the week after the fire) had been there for 20 years and his successor's widow 'Auntie' Rosa Mowlem stayed on to become the pub's landlady, having clocked up 50 years when she retired in 1962. The Lugger closed in 1995 but re-opened on 6th August 2003.

LULWORTH TERRACE (Nos 1-22) is now Nos. 93-135 Chickerell Road.

LUSH, William Vawdrey MD, FRCP, FRCS (1831-1904) Dr Lush lived in Weymouth where he had a practice at No. 12 Frederick Place and for 32 years he was physician of the Dorset County Hospital in Dorchester.

LYDWELL COURT off Buxton Road was converted to flats in 1986.

LYNCH ESTATE Lynch Farm was up for sale in June 1852, 67 acres of highly cultivated arable, meadow and pasture land with cottage, dwelling house, outbuildings, orchard, garden and two labourer's cottages. Said to be excellent for wild fowl and shooting, it was purchased by Mr W. Schollar Ferris.

LYNDALE was a piece of ground opposite Ferrybridge Cottages at Wyke Regis, hence the street name Lyndale Road.

LYNES is an old Wyke Regis place name and was intended to be used for Lynes Close but an 'm' was substituted for 'n' and the road is now known as Lymes Close.

LYNN VILLAS (Nos. 1-2) are in Prince of Wales Road.

LYON'S WHELP This was one of the vessels which set sail from Gravesend for the New World in April 1629, a number of her passengers being from Weymouth and Dorchester, including three brothers of Upwey's Sprague family, although other sources state they sailed on the *Abigail* in 1628.

Mabel Cottage

M

MABEL COTTAGE was in Chelmsford Street.

MACINNES, Gurney *see* ALEXANDER TECHNIQUE

MCLEAN, J. Allan, MD, JP (died 1900) A surgeon, who lived at the since-demolished Bincleaves House in Bincleaves Road.

McMAHON, Laurance Born in Ireland. A builder, of No. 17 Charles Street. Died 25th December 1915. It is thought that he named Charles Street after Father John Charles, the priest at St Augustine's RC Church in the latter half of the 19th century.

MCSAUNDERS HOLE (now Hope Square) was infilled in 1781 – *'It having been represented that the Cove, in Weymouth, was very offensive at low water, and that it was the wish of the neighbouring inhabitants to have the same inclosed and filled up, who (with others), have subscribed a sum of money for that purpose, and, it being supposed that no injury will accrue to the Harbour thereby; it is resolved that leave be given for building a wall across the said Cove, from the Quay opposite to Mr William Schollar's, to the Slip in Hope Street, and for filling up the said Cove'* [Corporation Records]

MAGGADOR TERRACE is now in High Street, Wyke.

MAGNIFICENT, HMS This 74-gun ship of the line stood by for royal protection when King George III and his family were visiting Weymouth. Ever vigilant, when an American packet failed to lower her top gallant sails – the usual mark of respect – when she saw the royal pennant on the *Southampton*, the *Magnificent* was immediately on to her, firing a shot across her bows, whereupon the American vessel lowered most of her sails. The *Southampton* was a naval frigate on which the King enjoyed frequent boisterous trips in the Channel, insisting on the company of various family members, possibly not to their joy. Diarist Elizabeth Ham recorded that she had seen the Queen and Princesses *'looking very wet and bedraggled on their return'*.

MALT TERRACE was in Bridge Inn Lane, Preston.

MAN IN THE IRON MASK *see* BENSLEY, Harry

MANOR COTTAGE, Preston *see* PRESTON. MANOR COTTAGE. There was also a Manor Cottage in High Street, Wyke Regis.

MANOR FARM, Wyke Regis was up for sale in 1988. Its restoration and redevelopment as housing was completed in the early 1990s. The farmhouse itself dates in part from the 16th century.

Looking down on Wyke from Lanehouse, Manor Farm can just be seen on the right.

MANOR FARMHOUSE, Preston No. 2, Church Road, east side. Only one wing remains of the original 17th century building.

MANOR HOUSE, Melcombe Regis This is frequently referred to in early documents and deeds. The house is described as a *'Mansion house, outhouses, stables and garden in St Thomas Street, west side...'*, but its location has not been established. It was owned by the **Steward family**. Late 19th-century historian William Bowles Barrett suggested two possible sites – the present No. 67 St Thomas Street, where the Post Office is today, or a larger site, the present Nos. 73-76, a site adjacent to and including the present Natwest Bank, buildings all of much later date.

MANOR HOUSE ESTATE, Radipole The first sale of this land at Radipole took place on 5th May 1890. It was owned by the Eliot Brothers. (They were later to fall from grace in the great Old Weymouth Bank Crash of 1897. Although no-one suspected it at the time it is likely their personal funds were already running low. For details of the crash see Eliot, Pearce and Co's Bank in *Bumper Book I*). Richard ffolliot Eliot owned Radipole Manor, built in the Victorian period, also known as Westmead and not to be confused with Radipole Old Manor beside the St Ann's Church. The Manor House estate was land off the Dorchester Road in the Spa Road/Manor Road/Radipole Lane area and the first sale, held on 5th May 1890 comprised 117 plots of freehold building land. It included a hotel site (where the Spa Hotel would be built on land purchased at the sale by brewers Devenish) and shop and cottage plots. Special trains from London were laid on for important auction sales such as this and as well as free transport a luncheon was laid on for buyers. It was a very successful sale and a second part of the estate was auctioned in similar fashion a few weeks later on 14th July 1890, which included lots in Roman Road and Icen Road,

MARCONI, Guglielmo (1874-1937) The famous Italian inventor and electrical engineer was at Weymouth in June 1902 attending a concert at the Alexandra Gardens given by the band of the Italian battleship *Carlo Alberto*, from which he'd come ashore. He had also been in the town in August 1900, staying at the Burdon Hotel, and engaged in work with the Admiralty. A Dr Marconi, an Italian chemist, was here in 1935. He was carrying out shale oil experiments at a farm at Sutton Poyntz and set up a laboratory for extracting oil from shale, but his hopes of producing petrol at less than 4d a gallon were abandoned and no new industry was forthcoming. The oil-bearing Kimmeridge shales extending from Abbotsbury to Purbeck have frequently been the subject of such experiments.

MARINE TERRACE (Nos. 1-6) is in Old Castle Road.

MARKET HOUSE ARCADE is the way through from St Mary Street to Maiden Street (The Market House, a post-

The arcade runs through the centre of this block of shops at the lower end of St Mary Street.

WW2 replacement of an 1855 Market House, is now known as Brenda Dench House).

MARKET HOUSE INN/TAVERN In the late 19th century there appear to be two public houses with the same name – one in St Edmund Street and one in Maiden Street.

MARKHAM AND LITTLE FRANCIS Francis Farm, between Wyke Road and Chickerell Road was owned in the 17th century by Arnold De Sella Nova (or De Sallanove), who left it to his nephew Peter de Sella Nova. By the 1860s it was in the possession of the Swaffield family, owners Wyke House and extensive lands in the Wyke area, and, later, Markham House (which is now divided into flats, Nos. 140-144, Wyke Road). In 1952 part of the Markham House Estate was developed when 45 houses were built in the Markham Avenue/Hardy Avenue area but an application for further housing development was refused. In 1954 Mr R. L. Robbins, the owner of the estate, lost his appeal against the Council's tree preservation order on 415 trees which he wanted to fell because he thought they were dangerous. It was stated that area was included in the Development Plan as forming a green belt between Wyke Regis and Westham and was bordered on three sides by main roads. It contained over 2500 trees which were a prominent feature of the landscape and could be seen from most of Weymouth, the trees also acting as a screen for residences on Wyke Road.

MARQUIS TERRACE is now in Lanehouse Rocks Road.

MARRIED QUARTERS on the Nothe. The Army Married Quarters on the Nothe are remembered by many, especially those who grew up there, but the only photograph traced so far is from a newspaper published shortly before they were demolished in 1963.

MARRYAT, Ellen (died 1906) She lived at No. 4 Brunswick Terrace and was the youngest sister of children's author Captain Frederick Marryat.

The Army Married Quarters on the Nothe, 1963.

MARS, HMS On 14th April 1902 there was a massive explosion on board the battleship *HMS Mars*, attached to the Channel Squadron. The ship was off the south coast of Ireland carrying out gun firing practice. In one of the forward barbettes a party of twelve officers and men were engaged at a 12-inch, 50-ton gun which missed fire. The breech block then blew out with terrible results in the confined space, killing eleven men almost outright, the force of the explosion rendering identification of several of those who died impossible. One of the two dead officers in charge of the gun party was Lieutenant Tom Miller, of

The monument in Cobh, Ireland to those lost on HMS Mars *in 1902.*

Weymouth. He was the son of Commander Thomas Edward Miller of Glendinning Avenue, and had joined the Navy as a cadet in July 1894. All twelve who died in the explosion, apart from Tom Miller, were buried in Cobh (then Cork), their graves marked by a fine monument, on which his name appears. Tom's remains were brought back home and he was buried in Radipole churchyard.

MARSHALLSAY ROAD, Chickerell Homes for the elderly here were officially opened on 22nd November 1966. The development had been completed in four stages between 1956 and 1966.

MARWELL, James and Richard In 1606 James Marwell was Rector of Radipole-cum-Melcombe Regis and was not at all in favour of being appointed Rector of Melcombe Regis-cum-Radipole when the town's new church, St Mary's (originally known as Christchurch) opened in St Mary Street. He was a countryman who enjoyed living at Radipole where he farmed (a cottage there 'Marwells' or 'Marvels' still bears his name). He found his new rectory in East Street, Melcombe Regis *'unwholesome and beaten with every storm when the wynd is at sea'* and also felt that his extra responsibility should result in extra payment. His son Richard later became Rector of Melcombe and Radipole but he was a Royalist sympathiser and disapproved of the Presbyterian rule in the Church of England and was sequestrated from his living in 1645.

MARWELLS COTTAGE, West End, Radipole *see* MARWELL, James and Richard

MASONS ARMS pub was in Corney Terrace, Newstead Road. It *may*, at some point, have been known as the Quarryman's Arms. There was also a Masons Arms in High Street, Wyke Regis and another at No. 54 Church Street, Upwey, currently known as the Riverhouse Inn.

MAY QUEEN Electing a May Queen is an annual tradition at Lanehouse Methodist Church. First ever was in May 1954 – 11 year old Margaret Ford.

MAY TERRACE was in South Road, Wyke Regis.

MAYNARD, Bill was the star of Bernard Delfont's summer show at the Alexandra Gardens in 1956.

MAYPOLE Ltd was Weymouth's first supermarket, opened 28th May 1963 at Nos. 72/73, St Mary Street. In the same street three years later smaller grocers Pearks and Liptons closed, transferring business to the Maypole store, all three being owned by the same company.

MEDHURST, James *see* PRESTON. ROMAN HISTORY

MEDICAL OFFICER OF HEALTH (the post was

made mandatory for all local government authorities by legislation in 1872. Weymouth's MoH became a county responsibility on the reorganisation of local government in 1974):

    1873-1890 Dr Henry Tizard
    1891-1902 Dr Benjamin Browning
    1902-1905 Dr T. Henry Jones
    1905-1930 Dr W. B. Barclay (Dr W Bowden DSO
        served as deputy during the WW1 period)
    1931-1936 Dr F. W. Oldershaw (he died in 1936 and Dr
        T Gibson was Acting Medical Officer of Health until
        Dr Wallace was appointed in 1937)
    1937-1971 Dr E. J. Gordon Wallace. 1st Deputy Dr
        Charlotte Ward 1943-1964. Went on active service in
        1945 and Dr Ward carried out his duties assisted by
        Dr Kathleen Barnes).
    1972 -1974 Dr G. E. Thomas

MEDLYCOTT, Sir William Coles Paget, Bt. (1831-1887) Dorset-born, he travelled widely and drew and described the birds, animals and plants of the places he visited. His sketchbooks of Malta and North America are now in the Natural History Museum. Although frequently abroad, he had a house in Pulteney Buildings, Weymouth and died there on 8th January 1887, having accidentally taken an overdose of chloral.

MEECHERS LANE appears on a deed of 1627 and is possibly an alternative spelling of Michers Lane or Mitchers Lane, on the south side of Weymouth Harbour.

MELBOURNE TERRACE was at Westham and pre-dated the use of Australian street names commemorating the Anzac troops of WW1.

MELBURY ROAD Westham was once tree-lined. The tall chestnut trees were felled in January 1962.

MELCOMBE COURT was to be the name of a planned town centre shopping development in the early 1990s, but Speyhawk Developers went into liquidation in 1993. (The eventual name was New Bond Street, which officially opened 25th May 2000).

MELCOMBE REGIS WORKING MEN'S READING ROOM AND LIBRARY, No. 14 Great George Street was established in 1868. A reading room for the young men of the town opened in November, 1870.

MELROSE TERRACE (Nos. 1-19) is now Nos. 55-91 Chickerell Road. In the 1901 Census the enumerator's sequence is: Prince of Wales Road, Ilton Terrace, Selway Terrace, North View, Melrose Terrace, Chickerell Road, Lilac Cottage on the Marsh, Coburg Terrace, Fermain Terrace, Lulworth Terrace, Springfield Terrace and 16 houses at the back of Lulworth Terrace, Arch Terrace and cottages, south side of Town Lane.

MELVILLE, Commander Francis William, RN of *HMS Illustrious,* aged 36, was drowned when returning to the ship from Weymouth on 2nd October 1904. It was a wild night and Commander Melville had taken the helm of the picket boat from the coxswain when he fell overboard. He is buried in the Naval and Military Cemetery at Portland.

MEMBERS OF PARLIAMENT Because Weymouth was one of the 'pocket boroughs' and able to send four representatives to Parliament until 1832 and two from 1832 until 1885, its parliamentary history is a very involved one, filled with the corrupt election practices common in all the 'rotten' and 'pocket' boroughs. These are of particular note in the eighteenth century when, until his death in 1762, the notorious political 'wheeler dealer' and social climber George Bubb Dodington virtually controlled the elections together with his allies in the town and in parliament. In 1885 the town lost its right to send any members at all and became part of the South Dorset parliamentary constituency. In *Bumper Book I* are listed the South Dorset Parliamentary MPs to the present day. As those of the 18th century are a bunch of interesting characters they are listed below. This is not to say that earlier MPs are of any less interest. Names of men who represented Weymouth and Melcombe Regis are known from the 14th century and biographies of them, the election results of each particular period and an overview of local politics can be found in the various volumes of the *History of Parliament: House of Commons,* publication of which began in the 1960s and continues today. In 1998 the text of the all the volumes then available was also made available on CD-ROM. The compilers of the work have discovered much of local interest as many of the early MPs were men actually from Weymouth and Melcombe Regis, and as the *History of Parliament* is probably the only source of detailed information on them, it provides fascinating glimpses into their lives and occupations.

1715
Daniel Harvey
John Baker (died 1717, replaced by Edward Harrison)
William Betts
Thomas Littleton

1722
William Betts
Sir James Thornhill
Thomas Pearse (appointed to office, replaced by Edward
    Tucker)
John Ward (expelled 1726, replaced by John Willes)

1727
William Betts (election declared void 1730 replaced by
    George Dodington)
Edward Tucker
Thomas Pearse

Sir James Thornhill

1734
George Bubb Dodington (chose to sit for Bridgewater, replaced by John Tucker)
George Dodington
Thomas Pearse
Edward Tucker (appointed to office 1737, replaced by John Olmius)

1741
Joseph Damer
John Tucker
John Raymond
James Steuart

1747
Welbore Ellis
Richard Plumer (died 1751, replaced by Lord George Augustus Cavendish)
George Dodington
Edmund Hungate Beaghan

1754
Lord John Cavendish
George Bubb Dodington
Welbore Ellis
John Tucker

1761
Sir Francis Dashwood (1763 called to upper house, replaced by Charles Walcott)
John Tucker
John Olmius (later Baron Waltham died 1762, replaced by Richard Jackson)
Richard Glover

1768
Drigue Billiers Olmius, Baron Waltham
Sir Charles Davers
Jeremiah Dyson
John Tucker

1774
Welbore Ellis
William Chaffin Grove
John Purling
John Tucker (1778 vacated his seat, replaced by Gabriel Steward)

1780
Welbore Ellis
William Chaffin Grove (1781 vacated his seat, replaced by William Richard Rumbold)
John Purling
Warren Lisle (1780 vacated his seat replaced by Gabriel Steward)

1784
Welbore Ellis
John Purling
Gabriel Steward (1786 vacated his seat, replaced by George Jackson: Jackson vacated his seat 1788, replaced by Gabriel Steward)
Sir Thomas Rumbold

1790
Sir James Murray, Bart.
Richard Bempde Johnstone
Andrew Stuart
Thomas Jones (1791 vacated his seat, replaced by Sir James Johnstone: 1794 Sir James Johnstone died, replaced by Gabriel Tucker Steward)

1796
Sir James Pulteney (formerly Murray), Bt.
Andrew Stuart (died 1801, replaced by Charles Adams)
Gabriel Tucker Steward
William Garthshore

1802
Gabriel Tucker Steward
Sir James Pulteney, Bt.
William Garthshore (died 1806, replaced by Richard Augustus Tucker Steward)
Charles Adams

1806
Sir James Pulteney, Bt.
Richard Augustus Tucker Steward
Gabriel Tucker Steward
Charles Adams

1807
Sir James Pulteney, Bt (died 1811, replaced by Sir John Murray, Bt.)
Gabriel Tucker Steward (1810 vacated his seat, replaced by Sir John Lowther Johnstone, Bt. He died 1812, replaced by Joseph Hume)
Richard Augustus Tucker Steward
Charles Adams

1812
Sir John Murray, Bt.
Thomas Wallace*
John Broadhurst*
Henry Trail*
*their elections declared void Feb 1813

1813
Masterton Ure
Christopher Idle
James Brownlow William Cecil, Viscount Camborne (1817 vacated his seat, replaced by Adolphus John Dalrymple)

1818
William Williams
Thomas Fowell Buxton
Thomas Wallace
Masterton Ure

1826
Thomas Fowell Buxton
John Gordon
Thomas Wallace
Masterton Ure

1830
John Gordon
Masterman Ure
Thomas Fowell Buxton
Sir Edward Sugden.

1831
Charles Baring Wall
Masterton Ure
Thomas Fowell Buxton
John Gordon

1832
Thomas Fowell Buxton
Sir Frederic George Johnstone

1835
Thomas Fowell Buxton
William Wharton Burdon

1837
Lord Villiers
George W. Hope

1841
Ralph Bernal
William Dougal Christie

1847
William Lockyer Freestun
William Dougal Christie (by-election Dec 1847, replaced
   by Frederick William Child Villiers)

1852
George Mead Butt
William Lockyer Freestun

1857
William Lockyer Freestun
Robert James Roy Campbell

1859
Robert Brooks
Viscount Grey de Wilton

1865
Robert Brooks
Henry Gillett Gridley (by-election 1867, replaced by Henry

Edwards)

1868
Charles Joseph Theophilus Hambro
Henry Edwards

1874
Henry Edwards
Sir Frederic John William Johnstone

1880
Henry Edwards
Sir Frederic John William Johnstone

MENZIES, John, No. 88 St Mary Street In 1983 the newsagent and stationer was the first to occupy the former Debenhams store after extensive rebuilding and also had a branch in St Thomas Street near the Town Bridge (now the Swan pub). The firm amalgamated with W. H. Smith in 1998.

MERMAID INN, High Street, Wyke Regis closed in the late 1980s.

MERMAID TERRACE is now part of High Street, Wyke Regis.

METHODIST CHURCH, Bond Street The little Wesleyan Chapel of 1805 closed when Maiden Street Methodist Church opened in 1867. Locals will remember its use as a builder's store before demolition in 1975.

The little chapel stood near the White Hart in Lower Bond Street. It was demolished in the 1970s after being used as a store for many years. Behind it lay Bury Street burial ground.

METHODIST CHURCH, Elwell Street, Upwey
The Wesleyan chapel opened in 1870 and closed in 1971.

METHODIST CHURCH, Melcombe Avenue
Weymouth Bay Methodist Church stands on the site of the demolished Christian Science Church. It was built to replace the fire-gutted Maiden Street Methodist Church, which was too costly to restore. The new church is a multi-purpose building and as well as serving as a church it will be available as a performance and exhibition space and a meeting place for local groups. It seats up to 240 people. It held an open weekend 4th and 5th April 2009. Current plans are to turn Maiden Street Church into a restaurant and flats when the current economic climate improves.

The demolished Christian Science Church, Melcombe Avenue, now the site of a new Methodist Church.

METHODIST CHURCH, Wyke Regis The Gallwey Road chapel opened 22nd May 1901.

METHODISTS There was a Society of Methodists in Weymouth in 1791 and until the first Chapel was built, they held services in a variety of locations – the King's Head Inn Assembly Rooms, the Friends Meeting House in St Thomas Street and members' houses. The first Wesleyan Chapel opened in Lower Bond Street in 1805. History turned full circle when Maiden Street Methodist Church was built in the 1860s – when the King's Head Inn, their former meeting place, was demolished to provide a site for the new Maiden Street Methodist Church, opened in 1867. Sadly, the building was gutted by fire in 2002 and awaits redevelopment. The Methodists new meeting church is at Melcombe Avenue. *See* METHODIST CHURCH, MELCOMBE AVENUE

Maiden Street Methodist Church. Perhaps the shell of this formerly fine church will one day be restored to look like this once again.

METHODIST CHURCH, Newstead Road On the opening of Weymouth Bay Methodist Church in Melcombe Avenue, services ceased to be held at Westham Methodist Church on 15th March 2009, the congregation dispersing to other Methodist churches in the area. The building is still in use, hired out to local organisations for meetings.

METHODIST CHURCH, United Free The local press stated that the new United Free Methodist Chapel opened 18th March 1860 *'in an increasing part of the town'*. This was the building in Caroline Place, which has previously been dated to 1869. The United Free Methodists had been meeting in various rooms from 1850.

MICHERS LANE was on the Weymouth side of the harbour.

MICO TRUST OF JAMAICA (not to be confused with the Weymouth Mico Charity) Lady Jane Mico's will when she died in 1670 stated that if her dead husband's nephew Samuel married one of her six nieces he would inherit £2000. If he didn't, one of the £1000s was to be given to redeem poor slaves. He didn't, so the interest on the £1000 was given annually for the redemption of Christian slaves. These were crews and passengers on ships captured by Moorish pirates in the Mediterranean and forced into slavery. In 1680 a wharf and premises in London were purchased with the legacy, the rents to be used as instructed in the will, but the demands on it were not great and an action against the Moors in 1816 had forced them to free more than 2000 slaves. The money mounted up and at that time the movement for the emancipation of slaves in the British colonies was gathering momentum under William Wilberforce. The Government compensated slave owners and it was agreed that the Mico money would be used to assist in the education of 300,000 negro slaves. Weymouth MP Thomas Fowell Buxton was responsible for carrying out the scheme. A teacher training college in Jamaica is called the Mico College. For details of the Weymouth Mico Charity, which is quite separate from this one, *see under* MICO, Sir Samuel in *Bumper Book I*.

MIGHTY HOOD public house *see* RODWELL HOTEL

MILL HOUSE, Upwey was the setting for a lengthy inquest in January 1935 into the death of Mr Jeffreys Charles Allen, an 86 year old Somerset JP who died in a fire there in November 1934. A seven day inquest, with 34 hours of evidence including that by Home Office pathologist Sir Bernard Spilsbury led to a verdict of Accidental Death, in which neither of the women who had been in the house with Mr Allen were in any way implicated in his death.

MILLEDGE & SON A firm of auctioneers and estate agents at No. 74 St Thomas Street which was acquired by Henry Duke and Son at the beginning of 1958. Although it bore the Milledge name, the family, once prominent in local affairs, were no longer connected with it. The firm was established in 1823 by James Milledge (1801-1884) and carried on by his son his son Sidny Spark Milledge, who was instrumental in getting the borough boundaries enlarged in 1895. Another son, Zillwood, produced a history of freemasonry in Weymouth.

Further reading: *Historic Notes of All Souls' Lodge, No. 170, Weymouth, with illustrations,* by Zillwood Milledge, J.P., C.A., F.R.Hist. S. Preface and introduction by W. Bro. Wm Jas. Hughan, P.S.G.D.ENG (Sherren and Son, Weymouth, 1896).

MILLENNIUM 2000 Amidst all the razzmatazz, fireworks and threatened computer meltdown of the Millennium, the question as to whether the new Millennium and 21st century actually started in 2000 or 2001 remained a subject for debate. There were similar doubts about the beginning of the 20th century. In January 1900 the Rector of St Mary's Church, attending a local function, sidestepped the issue by saying *'People were very much perplexed as to whether they had entered the twentieth century or not...'* but said he wasn't going to discuss that question, but wished them a Happy New Year. It was the following year, on 1st January 1901 that Weymouth Town Council assembled *'to commemorate the first day of a new century'*. It was not a time of great celebration and the *Southern Times* editorial looked back rather gloomily, remarking that *'We have passed by this great landmark in time's history with far less emotion than might be imagined...'*, celebrations not being the order of the day while the Boer War continued and Queen Victoria was in failing health (she died later that month). In local matters comparisons were being made between the town's stagnation in the first half of the 19th century and its revival and progress in the latter half. Little else was made of the new century, apart from traditional New Year Watch Night services in the local churches and the ringing of church bells at midnight.

MILLER, Max The famous 'Cheeky Chappie' comedian appeared on stage in Weymouth in the summer of 1959.

MILLER, Tom *see* MARS, HMS

MILLS, Freddie The boxer fought his first professional fight at Weymouth's Alexandra Gardens on March 18th 1936. He drew with George Haskett.

MILLS, John, Town Constable *see* CADE, John

MINX During a gale in the late 1920s, the coal barge *Minx,* laden with some 500 tons of coal, broke from her moorings in Portland Harbour and went aground at Osmington Mills. Efforts to refloat her failed and what remains of the wreck can still be seen there, just offshore.

MITCHELL CHARITY Bernard Mitchell's will proved in 1647 left money to be paid annually for the relief of the poor in a number of local parishes. Plus 10 bushels of sea coals annually to the poor of Weymouth and Wyke Regis and 6 bushels of coal annually to six poor widows in Melcombe Regis.

MITCHER'S LANE *see* MICHER'S LANE

MIXED BATHING Many resorts were very disapproving of mixed bathing in the early 1900s and Weymouth seems to have been quite early in allowing it. A guidebook published for Weymouth Corporation with a title page date of 1906 states *'Mixed bathing is permitted'*.

MOBY DICK'S pub was formerly the Cork and Bottle.

MODEL VILLAGE formerly by the entrance to Lodmoor Country Park became a miniature 'Adventure Golf Course' with a pirate theme in 1994.

MOFFAT HOUSE was built on part of Radipole Farm. It appears to have been a private house, later purchased by the adjacent Weymouth and District Hospital as a nursing home for paying patients.

MOGG, Ronald (died 1982) A reporter on the *Echo* pre-WW2. Incarcerated in a prisoner of war camp, he operated a clandestine radio almost every night from winter 1941, receiving BBC news. He wrote *Sergeant Escapers,* the story of the RAF NCO's persistent efforts to escape, under the name John Dominy. Left Weymouth after the war and worked in Fleet Street and at Shell-Mex.

MONTEVIDEO HOUSE, Chickerell Is sometimes said to have belonged to Queen Charlotte, wife of King George III but this statement seems to be lacking in documentary evidence. In 1986 it was sold with planning permission for conversion to a home for the elderly, which it is today (2009).

MOONFLEET *see* FLEET

MOORE, Patrick The astronomer was in Weymouth in October 1982, to open extensions to Weymouth Boys Club on Chickerell Road.

MOORE'S HANDBAGS The shop, at No. 2 Westham Road closed 31st March 2007. With it went the attractive art deco shop fascia and the shop front is now bland plate glass.

MOORHEAD, John, MA, MD, JP (Born 1835) One of the main promoters of Queen Victoria's Jubilee Memorial at Weymouth. Honorary physician to Weymouth Royal Hospital for 43 years. Lived at No. 1 Royal Terrace.

MORRIS, Benjamin A draper, hosier and outfitter with rather fine premises in St Mary Street currently (2009) occupied by Boots. The business started in 1876 as a partnership, Evans and Morris, until he bought out Evans in 1889, later selling out to a Southampton firm when faced with mounting debts which led to eventual bankruptcy in 1911. He was Mayor in 1899-1900.

MORRIS, Mrs *'On the Weymouth side... Mrs Morris's Ladies French and English Boarding School has been established some years...the fair pupils are educated in every branch of useful and polite literature, its reputation is still rapidly increasing'.* These contemporary notes accompany the *'View of Weymouth Harbour'* in John Love's *'Collection of prints...'* published in 1790. Peter Delamotte's guidebook of Weymouth published in 1787/8 describes a house *'...formerly the residence of Ralph Allen esq., which is now converted by Mrs Morris into a French and English school...'* and presumably both refer to No. 2 Trinity Street.

MORTUARY The town mortuary was in Commercial Road, at its southern end, the site now redeveloped as flats. Three emergency wartime mortuaries were established at Weymouth College Chapel, Dorchester Road; No. 80 Elwell Street, Upwey and a garage at Kellaway Terrace, Westham, formerly used by the Weymouth Bathing Machine Company, the site now developed as housing.

MOSQUITO NUISANCE Still, shallow waters and reedy areas are good breeding grounds for mosquitoes and midges. Real problems on Radipole Lake began after the construction of the 1921 Westham Bridge, when the lake ceased to be tidal. After 1928 the Council employed a small dredger on the lake to keep the waterways clear of reed growth and insecticidal dust was used, although it had little effect. In more recent years little has been heard of the problem and it probably ceased when new efficient sluices were installed at Westham Bridge in the late 1970s. Electronic sluice gates were installed in June 2008 further improving water levels in the Lake, preventing flooding and stopping salt water entering the lake. The sluices are protected by a lakeside boom, which keeps rubbish away from them. These modern sluices have main-

Radipole Lake at Radipole in its tidal days.

tained a slightly higher level of water in the lake, which formerly fluctuated and often left large areas of mudflats, the ideal midge breeding grounds. It is odd to think that this area, now a very beautiful nature reserve, was in earlier years considered to be more of a hindrance to the town than an asset. *See also* DREDGER

MOSS, Stirling The motor racing ace was water skiing at Weymouth in September 1955, promoting a Bridport boat firm.

MOTO SAILS The firm closed in 1997. Its premises at Nos. 18-19 St Edmund Street, had been a military post office for Australian troops in WW1, a bakery, a tool and DIY shop, and now (2009) a convenience store.

MOTOR CARS *see* CONCOURS D'ELEGANCE

MOUNTWAY TERRACE (Nos 1-21) appears to be in the Old Borough Arms area of Chickerell Road.

MULBERRY CENTRE, Commercial Road is a department of Weymouth College. It opened on 7th June 2008 on the first floor of the former Weymouth Arts Centre building. A slightly confusing choice of name as the...

MULBERRY GALLERY opened in 1990 on the first floor of the adjacent Weymouth Library, Great George Street and is a venue for art exhibitions and arts events.

MUNICIPAL OFFICES Although the Guildhall in St Edmund Street was for centuries the centre of local government for Weymouth and Melcombe Regis, by the late 19th century the officers of the Corporation were occupying a number of buildings as office space and at a time when not all officials were full time, administration must have been extremely difficult. Just prior to 1904 when the Municipal Offices took over No. 1 Clarence Buildings, there were 'Municipal Offices' in East Street, Market Street and New Street, some of these addresses being the business premises of part-time posts such as Town Clerk and Borough Treasurer, a solicitor in practice and a bank manager respectively. The Clarence Buildings offices were already outgrown by the late 1920s and post-WW2 other sites were under consideration, including, in 1945, the bombed Radipole House off Dorchester Road at Lodmoor Hill. The present North Quay site was proposed in the 1950s and plans for new Municipal Offices and Library were finally approved in 1964, only to be halted in September 1965 due to government restrictions on all capital works except housing and school building. It was 1st June 1971 before the North Quay Municipal Offices were opened by HRH Princess Anne, the Library having been dropped from the plans. Weymouth had to wait until 1990 for its new Library in Great George Street, the service having been transferred to Dorset County Council on local government re-organisation in 1974.

MURDERS *Additions to the pre-1900s list in Bumper Book I:*

September 1619 Three men, named Maynard, Allen and Parmiter were involved in a drunken quarrel and came to blows, which resulted in Parmiter slugging Maynard over the head with a stone pot. Maynard then drew a knife and stabbed Parmiter, who collapsed and died shortly afterwards.

September 1622 *'Thomas Smale, the son of Jonathan or John Smale, slaine 9th September by James Scriven, was buried the Tuesdaie being the 20th September 1622'.*

December 1644 *'Elinor Knott, a married woman, whose husband was abroad, murdered her newly-born child, the father of which was one of the soldiers in the Town, apparently belonging to the Earl of Essex's forces'.*

August 1701 Winston Williams, a Customs House officer and William Freke, described as 'a gentleman of Upwey' drank punch 'to a greate height' one evening at the house of Customs official Thomas Bower in Governor's Lane. A quarrel broke out between Williams and Freke and they stormed off to fetch their swords. Williams, as he waited, began stamping around and swearing on one of the town's ropewalks, where he was angered even more by being reminded that he could be fined for the language he was using. By the time Freke arrived a crowd had gathered, excited at the prospect of witnessing a drunken duel. The two men rushed at each other with drawn swords and both fell to the ground. Williams suffered a fatal wound and died early the next morning. Freke went to the Crown Inn, told the ostler there that he very much regretted what he had done, mounted his horse and rode away. Although a hue and cry was raised it is not known

whether Freke ever stood trial.

October 1724 Murder at The Ship Aground beerhouse in East Street, where John Chick, a local labourer, was drinking flip (ale, brandy and sugar) for several hours. He and his friends began arguing and then wrestling. Landlord Stuckey tried to separate them and Chick knocked him down on the stone floor and either stamped on or beat his head on the stones. Stuckey died a few hours later and Chick was subsequently arrested.

1744 a Dutchman was buried 28th November 1744 *'murdered in the harbour'.*

April 1753 Grace Popplar, murdered by her husband was buried on the 24th April.

August 1906 Mrs Barbara Sophia Gregory Adams Devonshire was a Weymouth woman, but as the wife of the superintendent of the Indian Railway locomotive department, lived in Lahore. On a long visit to England in 1906 she was staying with her mother at 'Belgrando', No. 157 Dorchester Road. She went to London in July 1906 and subsequently to the Charing Cross Hotel, where she and her 10-year old daughter were found on 11th August, shot through the head. The inquest verdict was that she killed the child and then shot herself whilst of unsound mind. Mrs Devonshire had been upset over local gossip which appeared to have little foundation and had apparently been severely affected by either sunstroke or malaria during her time in India.

MUSGRAVE'S... In the early 19th century Musgrave's fashionable linen drapery warehouse was in Charlotte Row at the southern end of the Esplanade. A tiny unnamed street which links the Esplanade and Crescent Street at the prom's northern end was given the name Musgrave Place a few years ago, but it is uncertain whether the two names are connected.

'MUSIC BARROWS' Tradition has it that at two Bronze Age Round Barrows in the locality music can be heard at mid-day. One is the tree-crowned bowl barrow at Culliford Tree (SY 6990/8548), an important meeting place of the Saxon 'Hundred', another is a barrow on Bincombe Down.

MYRTLE COTTAGES The town abounds in 'Myrtle' house and terrace names some of which are listed in *Bumper Book I.* Additions are Myrtle Cottages at Nos. 611-613 Dorchester Road, Old Station Road, Broadwcy; Chamberlaine Road, Wyke Regis and Radipole.

Napoli

N

NAPOLI The container ship *Napoli* was en route for South Africa when her hull was breached during severe storms. The vessel attempted to make Portland Port for repairs but worsening weather and its deteriorating condition led to the decision to deliberately run the ship aground in Lyme Bay off the east Devon coast at Branscombe on the night of 18th January 2007. The incident was in the headlines for days as hundreds of looters descended on the beach collecting goods from the broken containers as they were washed ashore. The vessel was eventually refloated and broken up with explosives to facilitate removal and part remains (early in 2009) awaiting disposal. Some broken containers still deposit flotsam on Chesil Beach after storms.

NAVAL COLLEGE Despite representations in 1875 to the Admiralty in London and the First Sea Lord by Mr Henry Edwards, MP, Sir Frederic Johnstone, MP and the Mayor and Corporation of Weymouth regarding the advan-tages and suitability of Weymouth as a the site for a new naval college, Dartmouth was the town selected for the Britannia Royal Naval College.

NAVY DAYS Navy Days developed from Navy Weeks, the first of which was held at Portsmouth in August 1927. It was a chance for the public to see the Royal Navy at work and benefit naval charities, but proved somewhat disruptive in a normal working week. Instead, Navy Days were intro-duced, when naval dockyards were opened on Bank Holiday weekends. Portland Navy Days were hugely popular in the 1950s and 1960s but by the 1980s heightened security meant they were scaled down and they ceased altogether in the 1990s when the Royal Navy left Portland.

NEEBE, Frederick (1843-1897) was manager of the Theatre Royal, St Nicholas Street in 1870. An actor who progressed to theatre management in 1869, he was the lessee of various theatres in the south west. He was declared bankrupt in November 1884 and went to Australian later that decade, returning in 1891.

Further reading: *Frederick Neebe: Theatre Manager* by Tony Joseph (Bunthorne Books, 2000).

NELSON INN was on North Quay. *See also* GORDON CLUB

NETTLECOMBE, No. 74, Wyke Road was the home of Richard Caines Watts, Mayor of Weymouth, 1910-11. The house is now the Convent of Mercy.

New Close Farm, Wyke Regis taken before the building's restoration.

NEW CLOSE FARM, Wyke Regis A late 18th century building with Victorian alterations but with some 17th century structural remains. Originally a dairy farm but all its land was sold off for building and only the farmhouse remains. It was in a dilapidated state until extensively restored in the 1980s.

Detail of New Close Farm, Westhill Road, Wyke Regis.

NEW COVENANT CHURCH, Newstead Road was founded c.1991.

NEW INN Melcombe Regis once had a New Inn in St Edmund Street, Weymouth's was in High Street. Wyke Regis also had a New Inn and there is still a New Inn at Littlemoor.

NEW LOOK In 2009 it was announced that 250 jobs in the company's buying, merchandising and design sections would move to London from the local Mercery Road premises, to be phased in over the next year. The distribution centre move four years ago lost 500 jobs in Weymouth. The firm was founded here by Tom Singh.

NEW ROAD leads off North Quay by the Boot Inn. In the early 1920s Highland Road at Westham appeared in directories as 'New Road'.

NEW STREET today leads from the northern end of York Buildings on the Esplanade to St Alban Street. Old documents and deeds frequently refer to recently built areas as 'New Street' or 'the New Street' so may not indicate the present street. *See also* PEARSES STREET

NEWBERRY CLOSE In 1827 new houses were for sale in Wellington Place *'on a piece of ground formerly known as Newberry Close'*. Just over one hundred years later they were to be demolished under a slum clearance order in the 1930s. These houses in Wellington Place were known locally as the 'Twelve Apostles' although there were actually fifteen properties.

NEWBERRY HOUSE was in St Leonard's Road.

NEWBERRY TERRACE ROMAN PAVEMENT was discovered in the first week of February 1902 in what is now Newberry Road. This section of a tessellated pavement is now in Weymouth Museum and is thought to be part of a villa floor. More information can be found in *Bumper Book I* under ROMAN SETTLEMENT.

NEWNHAM TERRACE, or NUNEHAM TERRACE is in Ranelagh Road.

NEWSTEAD ROAD RAIL BRIDGE was demolished in the early months of 1987 but there are currently (2009) suggestions that some form of bridge should replace it to enable the Rodwell Trail to be a continuous walk without the necessity of crossing a busy road. The Rodwell Trail runs along the trackbed of the old Weymouth and Portland Railway from Abbotsbury Road (Westham Halt) to Ferrybridge. *See page 57 for a picture of the bridge*

NEWTONS ROAD FOOTBRIDGE The footbridge over Newton's Road, itself a 1934 concrete replacement of an earlier bridge, was demolished 28th/29th March 2009 and a new steel bridge with stainless steel handrails and a curved ramp at the Nothe Gardens end will replace it.

NEXT clothing shop, No. 86 St Mary Street. For previous occupants of this shop *see* BENSON & BARLING

NICHOLSON MONUMENT, St Nicholas Church, Broadwey. A headstone carved by Victorian sculptor N. N. Burnard to Thomas Henry Nicholson and his niece, who was Burnard's daughter. A sad story. In 1870 Nicholson was ill and his sister came to nurse him, bringing her small daughter with her. Sadly the child was taken ill and died just a day before her uncle, so they were buried together.

NORMANS FAMILY WAREHOUSE The Budleigh Salterton based chain took over the buildings at the end of Mandeville Road, Wyke Regis in March 1984 after Cashman's store closed, re-opening on 30th October 1984. Current occupant is a similar chain, Value House. The original buildings housed **Sapsworths** meat factory.

No. 4, North Quay, demolished in 1961.

NORTH QUAY'S TUDOR HOUSE, NO. 4 was demolished in 1961.

NORTH VIEW(Nos. 1-6) was in Prince of Wales Road or Chickerell Road. In the 1901 Census the enumerator's sequence was: Prince of Wales Road, Ilton Terrace, Selway Terrace, North View, Melrose Terrace, Chickerell Road, Lilac Cottage on the Marsh, Coburg Terrace, Fermain Terrace, Lulworth Terrace, Springfield Terrace and 16 houses at the back of Lulworth Terrace, Arch Terrace and cottages, south side of Town Lane.

NORTHDOWN FARMHOUSE, No. 106 Sutton Road, Sutton Poyntz. Early 19th century with barn and outbuildings. The cottages beside the millpond which were in a ruinous condition in the 1950s belonged to the farm – they have since been rebuilt.

NORTON'S FOLLY seems to have existed in the 19th century and was referred to in the 1860s as the *'remains of a refreshment place known as Norton's Folly'*. It was in the area of today's Sluice Gardens, and is shown in Arthur's map of 1857 as *'The Ice House or Norton's Folly (in ruins)'*.

NOTHE STEPS Late 19th and early 20th century maps indicate some form of steps leading from Nothe Parade to the gardens above but it was not until 1930 that the borough obtained the freehold of the Nothe Gardens and in 1931 an amount of £1,130 was approved for the building of the present handsome stone steps, construction of which began in 1931 and was completed in 1932.

NOTTINGTON HOUSE *see* STEWARD FAMILY

NOTTINGTON MALTHOUSE was used by a commercial mushroom grower in 1956.

'NURSERY' on the Sands, opposite York Buildings. This was a 'day nursery' set up in August 1913 where parents could leave their children to be looked after while they enjoyed an hour or two in the town. It seems to have been the forerunner of the Lost Children's Hut as six children were brought in as lost during the 1913 August Bank Holiday and reunited with their parents.

O. W. Budget

O

O. W. BUDGET is the magazine of Old Weymouthians, old boys of Weymouth College, the boys' public school.

OAKLEY PLACE may take its name from Okeley Close which occurs in 17th century deeds.

OAR HOUSE This suggested name for a public house which opened in the former Portland Railway Hotel at the junction of King Street and Commercial Road was firmly rejected and it was called the Dog House when it opened in 1989. It is no longer a pub.

'OBSERVER OF THE TIMES' was the author of *A Diary of the Royal Tour In June, July, August and September, 1789.* [An account of the first visit of King George III to Weymouth, 1789.]

OCEAN ROOM was the new name given to the Pavilion Theatre Ballroom in 1982.

ODDFELLOWS The Excelsior Lodge of Oddfellows began in 1861 at the Park Street Temperance Hall. Other Lodges which appear to have started in Weymouth around the same time were the Loyal Great Eastern and the United Brothers.

OIL TANKS The twenty oil tanks of Mere Tank Farm, formerly part of Portland Naval Base, were a familiar site on the Portland Harbour side of the Portland Beach Road. The last one was demolished on 1st May 2008. The cleared site will allow various improvements to be made at Osprey Quay in the run up to the sailing events of the 2012 Olympics and the expansion of commerce and industry in the vicinity. Construction of the oil tanks began in 1907, and although redundant, the steel recovered from them paid for their demolition costs. They were given concrete over-coats to protect them from WW2 bombs and although work on removing them began in 1950, it was not completed until 1963.

OLD SPA pub, Dorchester Road, Radipole was built in the 1890s as the Spa Hotel.

OLD TOWN HALL *Update of main entry in Bumper Book I* In March 2009 it was announced that the Old Town Hall in High Street had been leased to the Chapelhay Community Partnership for use as an art heritage centre focusing on the Siege and the Battle of Weymouth during the English Civil

Nothing is left of the oil tanks shown here.

War. The partnership aims to restore the building and make it available to the community.

OLD WEYMOUTHIANS are the old boys of Weymouth College, the boys public school. Their magazine is the O.W.Budget.

OLIVE TERRACE (Nos. 1-12) These houses were available for rent in September 1904, their location is given as 'near the Gas Works', probably Newstead Road.

OLIVERS BROS, Fish Merchants The business was started by William Oliver, continued by his son John and then his five grandsons James William, Herbert John, Percy Albion, Leonard and Joseph. Premises were originally in High Street, where they also had fruit stores.

OLYMPICS 2012 Celebrations of the choice of Weymouth and Portland for the sailing events of the 2012 Olympics began in 2008 with the staging of a Cultural Olympiad on 26th-28th September. Theatre and Arts productions included displays of pyrotechnics, acrobatics, multimedia installations, short films, brass bands, African drumming and contemporary dance at venues all around the borough. Weymouth and Portland Sailing Academy is launching a new flag to commemorate Weymouth's Olympic sailors and also the life of the Academy chairman, the late Bill Ludlow. *See also* PORTLAND MARINA

OMAHA BEACH *see* D-DAY

OPERA HOUSE is a 2004 apartment development in Derby Street.

OPERATION OVERLORD *see* D-DAY

OSBORNE VILLAS are in Prince of Wales Road.

OSMINGTON The place name Osmyntone or Osmentone predates the Saint Osmund of the church dedication and the Osmington spelling of today appears as early as 1291.

A big auction sale was held in September 1911 of property of the late Mrs L. M. Rice-Edwards and included Grove Farm, 246 and a half acres and farmhouse; South East Dairy Farm 81 acres with house etc.; East Farm with picturesque old stone and thatched house and 16¼ acres of meadow; Hitts Cottage, a bijou residence and acres of garden; Sandybarrow Farm, 72 acres with no house, plus land at Osmington Mills.

OSMINGTON BAY HOLIDAY CAMP, Shortlake Lane *see* PONTINS

OSMINGTON. BUS SHELTER is a memorial to Lieutenant David Edward Parry-Jones, son of local dentist H. Parry-Jones of No. 6 Frederick Place. He was killed in action with the Rifle Brigade in August 1944, having been overseas only a week. He was 20 years old.

OSMINGTON. CHARITY In 1839 Mrs Susanna Toogood bequeathed £200 the interest on which was to provide warm cloaks, coats, etc. for the deserving old men and women of the parish.

OSMINGTON. SCHOOL The village school, founded in 1835, closed in the summer of 1963.

OSMINGTON. TEA ROOMS were at the Fermoy Guest House and run by Reg and Winifred Smith, ex-stage acrobats who appeared as Renaldi and Katrina. At a farewell performance in 1988 at a Pavilion Theatre charity show (Reg was 79, Win 72) he could still lift her above his head on one hand and she could do handstands on his arms.

OSMINGTON MILLS. SHIPWRECKS *see* **MINX**

Osmington Fall in John Upham's engraving of 1825.

OSMINGTON MILLS. WATERFALL 'Osmington Fall' today is not quite as dramatic as that in John Upham's 1825 engraving. Coastal erosion over almost two hundred years has lessened the cascade.

OVERCOMBE was the name Thomas Hardy used in his novels for Sutton Poyntz.

OVERCOMBE At the far end of Preston Beach development of Mediterranean-style houses began in summer of 1987. *See also* BEACH COURT

OYSTERS An intriguing reference in the Corporation minutes of 7th March 1785 permits two local men to lay oysters in the Backwater describing the area as '...*for as much of the lake above the Bridge as extends North from the end of the lower Rails to the mouth of Chaffey's Bridge Lake*'. The use of The Fleet as another site of oyster beds goes back centuries but seems to have ceased in the 19th century, being restarted in the 20th by Abbotsbury Oysters Ltd, the company which currently owns the Fleet oyster beds. In 2001 Weymouth hosted an Oyster Festival for the first time and it is held annually in July.

Palm House

P

PALM HOUSE, Melcombe Regis Gardens was erected in 1927 and it is now part of a garden centre. Formerly part of Weymouth and Portland Borough Council's Parks Department, which relocated in December 1997 to nurseries in Lynch Lane.

PALM TREES on the promenade were treated as something of a joke in the late 1950s as the first two attempts to grow them were beaten by bitter winds and snow. They were initially known as Perry's Follies, after Albert Perry, the borough's Entertainments Manager whose idea it was to plant them, but he was proved right as palm trees now flourish on the Esplanade and in many gardens around the town.

PALMER, George Joseph Only one serious accident seems to have occurred in the 120-plus years that the gasworks was operating in Weymouth and this resulted in the death of 25-year old George Joseph Palmer on 18th June 1912. He was oiling machinery when he caught his head in it and received a fatal blow before the machine could be stopped. The inquest verdict of Accidental Death added a rider that a guard should be placed on the machine to prevent such an accident happening again, although witnesses were at a loss to explain why the manoeuvre was being carried out when the machine was not switched off. A popular local footballer, Palmer, of Valonia Place (Weston Road) left a wife and two young children. His funeral was held with full military honours as he was a member of the volunteer artillery.

PANDA CROSSING Weymouth was chosen as one of 45 sites in England and Wales for experimental Panda Crossings. It was installed outside Lodmoor Car Park and first used in April 1962 (although initially faulty).

PANKHURST'S MOTOR CYCLE SHOWROOMS were on the Town Bridge, in the building currently (2009) The Rendezvous pub, from the 1940s, when the firm replaced a wartime Services Club, until the mid-1960s.

PARDNES LAND was described as being in Helen Lane at its junction with East Street in a 1732 Rental.

PARK CHURCH, Chelmsford Street *see* St JOHN'S MISSION HOUSE

PARK DISTRICT *see* FOOKS, Charles Berjew; PARK ESTATE; PARK WALL and *Bumper Book I*

PARK ESTATE The Conservative Land Society at a public meeting on 28th August 1860 told Weymouth resi-

George Palmer's funeral cortege passes through Westham's Abbotsbury Road.

dents that *'great advantage will accrue to Weymouth by the construction of the roads and the drainage of the Park Estate and the conversion of the land into allotments for building purposes'*. The locals had long been resigned to the loss of their promised public park, weary of the litigation which followed its sale (*see* FOOKS, Charles Berjew) and possibly glad the railway to Weymouth had finally opened, albeit on land intended for their park. The first house in the 'Park Estate' seems to have been nearing completion towards the end of February 1861 as the *Weymouth and Portland Telegram* of 28th February 1861 reported *'During the gale on Thursday night the first house in course of erection on the Conservative Land Society's estate near the Railway Station was blown down'*, the Liberal newspaper adding rather sourly *'If the old adage prove true, that "a bad beginning has a good ending" the shareholders may look forward to a successful termination of their efforts to turn a swamp into a paradise. At present the prospects are that the expenses will far outweigh the profits'*.

PARK ESTATE COTTAGES (Nos. 2-4) were in Lennox Street.

PARK ESTATE HOTEL/INN was No. 22, Lennox Street.

PARK LANE runs between Carlton Road South and Carlton Road North.

PARK STORES, Augusta Place, Walpole Street is listed as licensed premises in the late 1890s/early 1900s.

PARK VIEW (Nos. 1-3) was in Queen Street, between the pubs now known as the Railway Hotel and the Giant Pot, formerly the Clifton Hotel and the Terminus Hotel.

PARK WALL This foundation stone of the Park Wall, behind which a large area of the Backwater was to be reclaimed for a proposed public park, was laid with great Masonic ceremony on 4th June 1834. *See also* FOOKS, **Charles Berjew** *and* PARK ESTATE

PARKMEAD FARM, Wyke Regis In the 1860s the farm comprised some 90 acres and belonged to Edward Bailey of Weymouth.

PARRY-JONES, David Edward *see* OSMINGTON. BUS SHELTER

PAVILION THEATRE AND FERRY TERMINAL SITE *Update of the main entry in Bumper Book I:*
   In the summer of 2008 Howard Holdings plc put forward plans for the site's redevelopment which included – 'renewed and strengthened sea defences; remodelling and refurbishment of the Pavilion Theatre including a new community performance space; space for a new World Heritage Visitor Centre; a new and improved ferry terminal facility; construction of a 4-star 140 bedroom hotel; new outdoor beachside performance space; a dynamic new 'entertainment quarter' featuring shops, restaurants, café/bars and public open spaces; contemporary new office and commercial spaces; approximately 340 private residential apartments; covered car parking with 400 public spaces; 110-plus new affordable homes for local people on this and other sites around the town, a new public pier extending into the bay and a new 290-berth marina'. By early 2009 the company had not put in a planning application and by March, having failed to progress the scheme, was officially out of the picture. Weymouth Council then took insolvency action to wind up its local operation and sought a new developer.

PAVLOVA, Anna The ballerina performed in a matinee at the Jubilee Hall on 19th July 1921, partnered by Alexandre Volinine and supporting dance company. It was a single performance and the huge hall was, according to the local press 'comfortably filled' (how comfortably is doubtful as the temperature that day was 90F in the shade).

PAWNBROKER Probably the best known pawnbroker in the town was Sargeant's at No. 9 St Mary Street. The shop, also a jeweller's, extended back along Blockhouse Lane to New Street. The traditional three golden balls sign was a familiar site on the corner of St Mary Street. It disappeared on occasion and in 1948 turned up on a warship in Portland Harbour, no doubt the result of a good night out for some naval ratings. Sargeants closed in the late 1950s. In 1960 the shop was bought by Woolworths, with expansion plans, their store at that time being on the opposite side of Blockhouse Lane. Permission to block or extend over the lane was refused and Sargeants was pulled down. The building which replaced it is now a building society.

PEARSES STREET/ PEERSES STREET/ PIERCE'S STREET/ PERCIE'S STREET appear, in the 1700s, to have been alternative names for New Street.

PELICAN of London. A Weymouth-based tall ship and former arctic trawler, the *Pelican* is a triple-masted square rigger, restored at Portland in 2007. She sails for the 'Adventure under Sail' charity.

PENGILLY, Sir Alexander A solicitor, knighted for political and public services in 1929. He purchased the local practices of D'Angibau and Malin and also Steggal, Hooper and Chave. His name continues in the firm of Pengillys today.

PENGOVER HOUSE is No. 1 Bincleaves Road.

PERKINS, R. M. *'An analysis of a compound gas evolved from the sea and lately discovered at the new pier, Weymouth'* was the title of a lecture he gave at Weymouth Institute on 13th November 1838.

PERKINS, Samuel (1877-1939) The Master of Weymouth Workhouse for 20 years before his retirement in 1939 due to ill health. His wife was Workhouse Matron for the same period.

PETO, Sir Henry, MA, DL (1840-1938) A barrister. He purchased the Chedington estate (Chedington Court, Misterton) in 1893 and greatly improved the village and the church and provided a reading and recreation room for the locals. He had provided the same facility at Chickerell in 1881 – the building known as the Peto Reading Room, which now houses a branch library, and paid for improvements at Holy Trinity Church, Fleet, these in memory of his late father. Sir Henry lived at Fleet House in the late 19th century.

PHOENIX or OLD PHOENIX on the Weymouth side of the harbour was built as a warehouse.

PHOENIX INN was in Great George Street (Grove Buildings) in the late 19th century.

PHOTOGRAPHERS This list of Weymouth and Portland photographers may be helpful in dating old photographs, either commercial picture postcards or family portraits. It has been compiled mainly from local directories which were often only published at three or five year intervals so the dates given are only those of the first and last directories in which the photographer's name appears – the photographers may have been working several years on

either side of these dates. Kelly's Dorset Directories were published from 1848 until 1939, Kelly's Weymouth Directories from 1929 until 1974.

ABRAHAMS, S. T., St Mary Street. 1915-1923
ABRAHAMS & Son, 55 St Mary Street. 1927-1955
ANGEL PHOTOGRAPHY, 85 St Mary Street. 1972-1974, currently in St Nicholas Street
BATEMAN, George & Son, 28 Abbotsbury Road. 1915
BELL, Mildred *see* Rosenau Studio
BILLINGHURST & DOVEY, 13 St Thomas Street & Fortuneswell, Portland. 1890
BREALEY, William, 33 Abbotsbury Road. 1915
BRIDGEMAN, Joseph, 2 Radnor Villas, 23 Milton Road. 1907-1920
BRUNEL, Theodore 1850s to 1861
BULL, John, 3 Melcombe Villas. 1865-1875
BULLOCK, F., Coburg Place. c.1899-1901
CHAMBERS, John E., 2 Royal Terrace. 1948-1955
CHAMBERS PHOTOGRAPHIC SERVICE, 2 Royal Tce/83 The Esplanade 1958-1974
COBURG or COBOURG STUDIO, Coburg Place. c.1899-1901
COLE, Geoffrey G *see* EXPRESS PHOTOGRAPHIC STUDIOS

The Phoenix building is on the far left of this picture of North Quay, adjacent to the garage. It was demolished in 1965.

COOMBE, John S., Fortuneswell, Portland. 1923-1955

COX, Edgar, 1a and 2 St Mary Street. 1859-1875

COX, W. G., St Mary Street. 1895-1907

CUMMING, Henry, 88 St Thomas Street. 1898-1907 succeeded by his son-

CUMMING, W. H., 88 St Thomas Street/ 2 Great George Street 1923-1974 (he only ran it until the 1940s – succeeded by Guy Woollatt, who kept the Cumming name)

DEBENHAM, E & Co., 88 St Thomas Street. 1885-1895 (taken over by Cumming)

DEE, William, Royal Arcade. 1915-1923

DOVEY, Walter J., 13 St Thomas Street. 1895-1907 (firm originally Billinghurst & Dovey. Dovey moved to Bournemouth c.1920 and died 1922)

EDWARDS, Miss M., 4 Gloucester Row/28 Avenue Road. 1915-1927

EXPRESS PHOTOGRAPHIC SERVICES/STUDIO (prop. Geoffrey G. Cole), Lower St Edmund Street. 1951

FAIREY, F., 96 St Mary Street, 1867

FELLOWS, A.

FIELD, David Taylor, Queen Street. 1907

FORCE, J. W. & Son, Church Passage. 1920

FORCE, James William 1923

FOX, W. H.

GEE, Charles Palmer, Lower Bond St/Turton Street/ 80 St Thomas St. 1874-1880

GEE, Louisa, 4 Newnham Terrace, Ranelagh Road 1895-1907

GEE, W. Burmain

GEORGE, Edgar. R., Ivy Bank Villas, Chickerell Road/ 264 Chickerell Road. 1923-1941

GEORGE, Frederick William, Fortuneswell, Portland. 1898-1903

GEORGE & LEE, 5 Abbotsbury Road. 1907-1920

GIMBLETT *see* WEEKS & GIMBLETT

GLOBE PHOTO COMPANY, Queen Street. 1903

GRAHAM, R., Kiosk, Westham Road. 1960

GRIFFIN, C. N., Kiosk, Westham Road. 1963

GUY, Henry F., Kiosk, Westham Road. 1955-1958

HARVEY, George, Fortuneswell, Portland. 1859-1865

HERBERT, S. J., 9 Coburg Place. 1923-1935

HERBERT, S. J. & Sons, 9 Coburg Place 1936-1967

HERBERT of Weymouth, 9 Coburg Place & Dorchester Road until G. V. Herbert's death in 1983

HEWITT, Charles F., 80 St Thomas Street. 1885-1898

HUGHES, H., 3 Bridge Terrace, Radipole. 1885

JACKSON, G. H., 42 Park Street/Turton Street. 1927-1931

JARVIS AND BREALEY, Queen Street. 1911 16

KESTIN, C. and Son, 55 St Mary Street. 1929- 1955

KESTINS, 55 St Mary Street. 1958-1960

KESTINS Ltd, 55 St Mary Street. 1963-1974

KING, Frederick William, Fortuneswell, Portland. 1907

LEE *see* GEORGE AND LEE

LESTON STUDIO (L. and A. A. Spencer), 157 Fortuneswell, Portland. 1948-1955

LLOYD, Harris H., Fernleigh Studio, 28 Avenue Road.

Known for Navy and battleship photographs. 1907-1908. Died July 1908.

MACKLIN, J., Fortuneswell, Portland. 1867

MARCUS, 11 Bond St. 1955-1967 and STUDIO MARCUS 17 St Mary Street 1948-1951

MASTERS

MEECH, R., 11 Gloucester Row. 1960-1963

MEECH, Ronald, 17a Wyke Road/ 45 East Street 1948-1951

MEECH'S, 25 St Thomas Street. 1958

MOORE, William J. 18 Queen Street. 1920-1933

MYERS, J. C. R., 36 Maiden Street. 1958

NICHOLLS, John, Clifton Place. 1875

O'ROURKE, William, 47 Lennox Street. 1915-1935

PEARSON, F. R., St Thomas Street. 1880-1888

PHOTOMASTERS (Prop. Colin Rogers) Derby Street. 1969-1974

PHOTOMATON LTD., Clinton Arcade. 1929-1931

PRICE, Alfred George, 44 Avenue Road. 1903-1907

RANDOLPH, R.

ROGERS, Colin R. *see* PHOTOMASTERS, SOUTH DORSET PHOTOGRAPHIC SERVICES

ROSENAU STUDIO (prop. Mildred Bell), Mount Pleasant, Radipole. 1927-1931

SEWARD, Edwin Henry, 13 Turton St/5 York Bldgs. 1907-1954 (died 16th June 1954)

SIMMONS, Leonard John. 1935

SMITH & BILLINGHURST, Lower Bond Street. 1885

SOUTH DORSET PHOTOGRAPHIC SERVICES (Prop. Colin R. Rogers) Derby Street 1958.

SPENCER L & A. A. *see* LESTON STUDIO

STONE, A. R., St Alban's Chambers, St Alban Street. 1973

STONE, Robert A. 1974

STUDIO MARCUS, 17 St Mary St. 1948-1951 and MARCUS, 11 Bond St. 1955-1967

THOMPSON, W. 19 St Leonards Road. 1907-1923

THOMPSON W.W., Chesil, Portland. 1927

THOMPSON, William. 1903-1923

THOMPSON, William 1840s -1879 (of underwater photography fame)

THORNE, Sidney Leslie, 131 Abbotsbury Road/9 Coburg Place. 1903-1920

THREDDER, William, Royal Baths (St Mary Street).1859-1865

VAN DYCK STUDIO *see* WHEELER, Harry

VINCENT, R., 151 Fortuneswell, Portland. 1967-1972

WALLIS, Thomas Samuel, 2 St Mary St./65 St Thomas Street. 1859-1875

WARE, Albert, Queen Street. 1898

WARREN & ROD LTD., 105 Fortuneswell, Portland. 1963-1974

WAVERLEY STUDIO *see* HERBERT (the firm used the Waverley name)

WEEKS BROS., 29 St Thomas Street. 1903

WEEKS & GIMBLETT, 29 St Thomas Street. 1907

WELCH, Clifford Donald, 31 Easton Street, Portland. 1948-1960

WEYMOUTH PHOTOGRAPHIC LTD., 39 Maiden

Street. 1971-1974

WHEELER, Harry 20/21 St Mary Street. 1880- 1927 (Van Dyck Studio)

WILKINSON, Thomas, 106 St Mary Street. 1867-1875

WINGETT, G., Fortuneswell, Portland. 1867

WOOLLATT, G. H., School Street and 2 Great George Street. He took over the business of H. Cumming in the late 1940s, in premises in School Street adjoining No. 88 St Thomas Street which had once been part of the Cumming business (now (2009) Mann, Estate Agent). Moved to Great George Street in 1968.

WYVERN PHOTOS, 7a New Street. 1951

PICKFORDS BEC Furnishings relocated to Southill from Lower St Alban Street and their former store was demolished in February 2008 to make way for Nautica, an apartment block currently (2009) under construction. Pre-WW2 this site had been occupied by the Hawkes, Freeman furniture depository which was bombed. The new building which went up in 1960 was occupied from then until the mid-1980s by Pickfords.

PICNIC INN at Osmington is now known as the Smugglers Inn. It was known in earlier times as the Crown Inn.

PIERROTS One of the earliest and best known of the seaside pierrot performers was Edwin Adeler who was performing at Weymouth in the mid-1890s. Pierrot troupes became a popular attraction in their baggy white costumes with black pompoms, conical matching hats and 'whiteface', usually a mixture of zinc and lard, appearing regularly at the Sea View Concert Platform on the sands in the early years of the 20th century.

PIGEONS on WW2 service Ted Hardy of the Victoria Inn, Knights in the Bottom bred homing pigeons which were flown in aircraft to France where the Resistance movement workers put vital information attached to their legs and sent them home again where a dispatch rider collected the info and took it to Whitehall.

PILLAR BOX COTTAGE is a former name of Letter Box Cottage, Radipole Lane.

PILLORY This was a much feared form of punishment as death or serious injury might result if a prisoner was unpopular. At the very least it was an unpleasant experience, especially on market days when the captive might be pelted with rotten fruit and veg. On the other hand, if he had been found guilty of an offence against authority he might well be cheered or freed. By the early 19th century the pillory was rarely used and in 1837 it was abolished altogether. The town's pillory was outside the Guildhall. *See also* DUCKING STOOL; STOCKS

PIRATES LANE, Wyke Regis This seems to be a name of relatively recent origin, the lane apparently once being known as Red Lane. Pirates Lane is not very apt as the lane leads down to the Fleet lagoon and no pirate would choose a stretch of water without escape route. As Red Lane led to Red Lane Cove the name may possibly derive from a small reed bed there.

PITT, William (the Younger) was Prime Minister from 1783-1801 and 1804-1806 and is known to have visited King George III when he was holidaying in Weymouth. William Pitt (the Elder) also stayed in the town, the Pitts being a Dorset family.

PLIOSAURUS found at Chickerell This fossilised giant marine reptile, which lived about 12 million years ago, was exposed after floods in 1955.

PLOUGH INN, Osmington On Osmington Hill, the pub building closed in the latter part of the 20th century and has now been converted to residential use.

POINTE DU HOC It was essential that a German Coast Defence Battery on the clifftop of Pointe de Hoc to the west of Omaha Beach was put out of action before American troops made their landings on the beach on D-Day, 6th June 1944. First ashore after embarking at Weymouth was the 2nd Battalion US Rangers and these men managed the seemingly impossible task of scaling the cliff with ropes and ladders, all the while under heavy fire. They destroyed the German position, but 70% of the American Rangers were dead or injured by the time the enemy guns were silenced.

POLICE STATION, Dorchester Road The building opened on 1st July 1955. It closed when a new police station for east Weymouth was built on an adjacent site in 2002, the same year that new Dorset Police Divisional Headquarters opened on 22nd February near the Wessex Stadium. The 1955 Dorchester Road police station was demolished and the housing development called Hardy Court now fills the site.

PONTINS, Shortlake Lane, Osmington Opened in 1946 as an 'adults only' holiday camp – no under-12s were allowed. The camp closed in 1999 and is now a Children's Activities Holidays Centre.

PONTOONS, Weymouth Harbour In the Inner Harbour, the first pontoons, accessed from Westwey Road, date from 1970. A second set was installed in 1973, accessed from North Quay. In the Outer Harbour those in the Cove and alongside the quays date from the late 1980s and 1990s.

PONY RACING was introduced at the Wessex Stadium on 30th June 1955, but was not a success, with only 500 turning up at the meeting. Pony races were held on the sands in the late 19th century.

POPE'S CLOSE was in the Chickerell Road area.

PORCELAIN HOUSE No. 84, St Mary Street. The shop of a china dealer in the 19th century.

PORTESHAM STATION on the Abbotsbury Branch railway was sold in 1962 and converted to a residence in 1963-4.

PORTLAND, Margaret Cavendish, Duchess of Portland (1714-1785) Owned famous shell collections. An early 19th century Weymouth guidebook noted that *'The cabinet of the late Duchess of Portland was considerably augmented from this shore'*.

PORTLAND HOUSE, Belle Vue Road The 'Hollywood Spanish-style villa' was built in 1935 for Geoffrey Bushby and was left to the National Trust by his sister, Dorothy Bushby, in 1985. She wanted people to enjoy it, but the property has always been rented out and has never been open to the public. She was a staunch supporter of the Scout movement and scouts camped in the house's grounds. It is considered an important 20th century building of its type and is Grade II listed.

PORTLAND MARINA Within Portland Harbour stone tipped during 2008-9 formed two breakwaters enclosing the new Portland Marina, as well as providing reclaimed land for the new facilities. A 600-berth Dean and Reddyhoff development, it will form part of the venue for the sailing events of the London 2012 Olympic and Paralympic Games. The Marina was officially opened on 1st April 2009.

PORTWEY is a coaling tug, once owned by the Portland and Weymouth Coaling Company. Newly built in 1927 by Harland and Wolff at Govan, she worked in Portland Harbour on the coal hulks (which included the former liners *Himalaya* and *Haytian)* and was kept busy delivering stores, assisting vessels in distress, ferrying pilots and a host of other duties in local waters. *Portwey* was transferred to Dartmouth in WW2 by her owners G. H. Collins & Co. (also owners of the Portland and Weymouth Coaling Co.), where she stayed post-war. Portland's coaling trade dwindled as coal-fired ships were phased out but *Portwey* reappeared briefly in 1948, when she towed a hulk from Dartmouth. Sold in 1952 to a Falmouth company it seemed by the 1960s that she was destined for the breaker's yard until a Dartmouth man bought and restored her and presented her to the Maritime Trust. *Portwey* paid a final visit to Weymouth at the end of May 1982 prior becoming a Maritime Trust exhibit on the River Thames in London.

POST HOUSE According to a 1732 Rental the Post House appears to have been both Inn and Post Office. It was at the junction of Maiden Street and Helen Lane.

POST OFFICE moved from No. 62 St Thomas Street to No. 72 St Thomas Street in the late 19th century. The present Post Office on the corner of St Thomas Street and Lower St Alban Street was opened on 18th March 1907, at that time occupying the site of Nos 64, 65 and 66 St Thomas Street, and later, in 1921, No. 67, the northern extent of the building today. In 2009 there was shock when the Post Offices in St Thomas Street, Weymouth and Trinity Street, Dorchester closed without warning on the afternoon of Tuesday 6th January when Counter Management Ltd called in the receivers, but both were back in action the next day.

POTTER, Beatrix (1866-1943) In April 1895 the author holidayed in Weymouth with her parents, staying at the Imperial Burdon Hotel (now the Hotel Prince Regent). Her diary entries concluded that although a fair-sized town, Weymouth was *'very old fashioned and empty'*. She explored, with her father, Preston and Sutton Poyntz (*'most quaint stone villages with heavy thatch roofs up and down in orchards and little gardens')*, Portland, Dorchester, and Abbotsbury. The family enjoyed other Dorset holidays, including Swanage and Lyme Regis.

Further reading: *The Journal of Beatrix Potter*, transcribed by Leslie Linder (published by F. Warne & Co., 1966).

POUND The Town Pound was at the northern end of St Thomas Street, a site later occupied by Sir James Thornhill's almshouses and where Coburg Place is now.

POWELL VILLA, Chickerell Road was the scene of an unfortunate case of accidental poisoning on 12th September 1856 when the death occurred of a son of Colonel Broughton of the Royal Engineers. 11-year old Augustus Broughton's mother had dispatched a female servant to Mr Thomas Barling's Chemist Shop at No. 67 St Thomas Street with a written order for a laxative medicine for her son – a medicine known as a 'black draught'. The servant handed the note to the two young men in the shop and returned half an hour later to collect the potion. It was duly administered to the young boy only for the family to be alarmed an hour later by the obvious distress of the lad. A doctor was summoned but Augustus died five minutes after his arrival. It was discovered that instead of dispensing a 'black draught', the chemist's apprentice had instead put 'Black Drop' in the bottle, a deadly compound of quadruple-strength opium. The evidence at the inquest was alarming to say the least – the chemist himself had not been in the shop overseeing the dispensing, there was conflicting evidence about who had actually dispensed the deadly 'Black Drop' from a clearly labelled bottle, and one of the possible dispensers was a boy not yet fourteen years old who had been employed in the shop only four months. The jury brought in a verdict of Manslaughter and two of Barling's staff – the young lad James Barrett and apprentice John Lundie who had been at Barling's for four years, were committed for trial at the next Assizes. The jury also expressed *'their disapprobation at the practice of leaving young persons, in the employ of druggists, to dispense medicines, until they are properly qualified by experience to do so'*. Appearing in court in March the following year, both of Mr Barling's assistants pleaded not guilty. It was decided not to proceed with the case and they were discharged. The house is now known as Ivy Bank.

PRAM RACE An annual Boxing Day event run over a two mile course from the Embassy Hotel to Chalbury Corner and back in Fancy Dress. Started in the 1950s. Competitors had to consume three pints of beer and biscuits and cheese en route.

PRESBYTERIAN MEETING HOUSE According to a Rental dated 1732 there was a 'New Presbyterian Meeting House' on the west side of St Thomas Street. Its location is unclear but it may have stood on the site of the present No. 69 St Thomas Street.

PRESTON The great tithes of Preston and Sutton were anciently appropriated to the prebend of Preston in the cathedral of Sarum (Salisbury), hence the place name 'Preston', or, 'Priest's Town'.

On 11th September 1925 a big auction sale took place of the Weld Estate lands in the Preston area. The Welds were selling a big slice of land owned by them since at least 1789, the money raised being required to pay death duties. Much

of Lodmoor, Southdown, Preston and Sutton Poyntz was up for sale, some 2063 acres in all, including six dairy farms, residential properties, coastguard cottages and land and ground rents. The sale also included property at Wool and East Burton, Winfrith Newburgh, Lulworth Cove and West Lulworth, which were part of the Lulworth Castle estate. Due to the high prices paid for Weymouth portion of the sale, it was actually stopped before some property was auctioned. Land at Lodmoor with a frontage onto Preston Road of over 2400 feet was bought by a Mr Ramuz of Southend. Jordan Farm bought by a Yeovil man who also bought Southdown Dairy. West Marsh and Upwey Wood went to the tenant Mr J. T. M. Guppy. Tenant Mr Hugh

Preston Road, 1900s.

St Andrew's Church, Preston, before and after (below) the addition of the lych gate.

An early view of Preston Road – note the cottage front doors well below street level.

Diment secured Sutton Farm and the freehold dairy farm of Coombe Barton and Tout. Northdown Farm was secured by the tenant Mrs Saunders. Court Farm was not sold. The six coastguard cottages were sold for good prices as was the land in front of them, despite jokes about how much further the sea would encroach. Overcombe House was also sold, plus various unnamed houses and cottages.

PRESTON. BRIDGES The small stone bridge off Bridge Inn Lane was once thought to be Roman but now seems more likely to be a mediaeval pack horse bridge.

Preston's old bridge.

PRESTON. BRIDGES, Preston Road The local press reported from Weymouth in 1824 that *'We are happy to observe that a new bridge for the better safety of travellers has been built across Preston River, situated on the high road to Wareham. The work has been well executed by Mr H. Woodward, builder of this town. Mr J. M. Fooks was the architect'.*

PRESTON. BRIDGES, Preston Road A prefabricated steel footbridge was put in position on Preston Road by the Bridge Inn on 21st August 1966. It has since been relocated to Buxton Road alongside the bridge which crosses the former railway line (now the Rodwell Trail).

PRESTON. MANOR COTTAGE Once the home of John Wesley, father of Samuel Wesley and grandfather of John Wesley, the founder of Methodism. Grandfather John Wesley was persecuted for his non-conformist views in the 1660s and was driven out of Weymouth, settling in Preston after being offered refuge there at what is now known as Manor Cottage, although forced to move from there too when the Five Mile Act of 1685 decreed that non-conformist teachers were forbidden from living within five miles of anywhere that had a minister, after which he moved from place to place. Samuel Wesley grew up in Preston, but had left it before his sons John and Charles, another prominent Methodist, were born. The old cottage was in a dilapidated state at the beginning of the 20th century, but was restored by local architect Ernest Wamsley Lewis in the 1930s.

The design of the Roman pavement at Preston.

PRESTON. ROMAN HISTORY Jordan Hill is the site of the Preston Roman Temple. Although often called Clavinio or Clavinium as in the Ravenna Cosmography, there is no evidence to support this name for the location. It became popularly used when Thomas Hardy used the name 'Clavinium' in his novels for the Jordan Hill Roman temple. Documented Roman finds in the area date back to 1812 when ploughing threw up an urn containing several hundred coins of the Roman Empire. In 1843, James Medhurst, who had previously investigated ancient sites elsewhere, saw on Jordan Hill an area where crops had failed and he unearthed the temple site with stone foundations some 35 feet square and a cemetery nearby. He displayed (and sold!) many of his finds in his 'Museum of Antiquities' on the Esplanade. In 1928 another coin hoard of some 4000 Roman coins was found. By this time The Weymouth Bay Estate Company was building houses in the area and were owners of the temple site: the company presented it to the

nation and it is now an easily accessible Ancient Monument off Bowleaze Coveway. Medhurst is an interesting character, an antiquarian and a manufacturer of Tunbridge Ware (he originally came from Tunbridge Wells). More about him can be found in *Bumper Book 1 under* MEDHURST, James and TUNBRIDGE WARE. He excavated sites at Radipole and also discovered the Roman villa site at Preston, although it was the 1850s before farmer John Scutt and the Vicar of Preston uncovered its mosaic pavement. Although a structure was built over it the pavement deteriorated, its mosaic tiles were taken as souvenirs and by the 1920s it was beyond saving and is now covered over. What had once been a substantial stone building was excavated on the cliffs at Bowleaze in 1969, but the remains were insufficient to indicate its purpose. *See also* COIN HOARD, Roman

PRESTON. SCHOOL A CofE village school and school house were built in 1850. Preston children now attend St Andrew's School, on Littlemoor Road, opened in 1992, which shares a site with Westfield Technology College.

PRESTON. (proposed) SEWAGE WORKS In 1935 proposals were put forward to erect sewage tanks in the Jordan Valley, distribute sludge over the land and carry the tank effluent out to sea. Protests ensued, the scheme was not carried through and alternatives found to take sewage to the main sewer.

PRESTON. VILLAGE HALL Dedicated to the memory of the women of the village who had played their part in WW2. It was officially opened on 30th May 1962.

PRESTON COTTAGES, (Nos. 1-4), Franklin Road, Westham were for sale by auction in July 1905.

PRESTON ROAD, No. 245 This cottage near the junction of Preston Road and Sutton Road was demolished

No 245, Preston Road is on the right. Also demolished a few years later was the adjacent thatched cottage.

in December 1960, to improve the sight line at what was a dangerous junction and accident black spot. A large barn at the Church Lane/Osmington Hill junction was also taken down, and the junction staggered.

PRETOR, Alfred, MA (1840-1908) Author of novels and short stories, *Ronald and I*; *The chapel on the hill*; *My pretty Jane*. Lived at No. 2 Camden Place, Wyke Regis. Brother of Captain S. A. Pretor (died 1907) of Belfield House.

PRIDEAUX, W. de C. A Weymouth dentist, Mr Prideaux was employed by the War Office in 1915 and was the inventor of a machine gun belt widely used by the British and Allied Air Forces during World War I.

PRIDE'S BEER HOUSE was opposite Steward's Court in the 1860s.

PRINCE FREDERICK public house was on the north side of High Street in the 17th/18th century. The pub was known successively as the Queens Head Alehouse, the Prince Frederick, the Prince's Head Alehouse, and the Ship Alehouse before becoming a private dwelling.

PRINCE GEORGE was the first steamer to be built at Weymouth. It was built by Cosens and Co. and launched in June 1898, then towed to the company's works in the Backwater for boilers and engines to be fitted.

PRINCE OF WALES PUB, St Edmund Street of the 17th century may be the present Duke of Cornwall pub. The current 'Prince of Wales' is in Park Street.

PRINCE'S HEAD ALEHOUSE was on the north side of High Street, Weymouth in the 17th/18th century. The pub was known successively as the Queens Head Alehouse, the Prince Frederick, the Prince's Head Alehouse and the Ship Alehouse before becoming a private dwelling.

PRISON The town gaol was underneath the Guildhall. In November 1626 it was stated '...*that the shop under the newe building at the Townehall shall be converted and made a prison*'. This would seem to indicate that the Townehall (Guildhall) had been recently rebuilt or extended. The present Guildhall dates from 1838.

PROSPECT public house When under construction in 1959, it was planned to call the new pub at Chapelhay the 'Hawk Inn' but the name changed to The Prospect before the pub opened on 1st May 1959. It closed in 2008 and the building or the site will probably be used for housing.

PROSPECT TERRACE is in Ilchester Road, Westham.

PUCKETT'S STORES off Commercial Road were converted to become the Queen's Cavalry Barracks in the 1790s. John Puckett was a corn merchant and at one time

one of the wealthier citizens of Weymouth. It has been suggested that he built Nos. 81 and 82 St Thomas Street (now the Barracuda Bar) and lived in one of them, but this is as yet unproved. Puckett ran into difficulties when he was building a house at the southern end of the Esplanade (*see* Bank House), failed to complete an agreed portion of the quay wall there and was eventually declared bankrupt. The Barracks, no longer required by the military by the 1820s, were sold to G. C. Welsford in 1835, then to William Wharton Burdon about 1865. *See also* BURDON, William Wharton (for a photograph of the building); KENNEDYS STORE

PUMPING STATION, Sewage Works, Westwey Road opened 17th July 1897. The long-running problems of dealing with the borough's 19th century sewage problems are under SEWERAGE in *Bumper Book I*.

PUTTON as a place name derives from 'The farm of Pudda's descendants' and in the 13th century was 'Podintone'.

PYE HILL the area around Chickerell Road nearest to the town is strangely named and it has been suggested that the 'Pye' may derive from old names for 'an insect' or 'a magpie'. It is a place name worthy of further study. There were once brickworks here, but all trace of them disappeared with the construction of the railway embankment of the Weymouth and Portland Railway in the 1860s.

Traffic lights now govern the very narrow thoroughfare under the bridge of the old Weymouth and Portland Railway at Pye Hill.

PYE HILL ESTATE The building of houses in Tennyson, Bradford, Baycliff and Emerson Roads began in 1915.

PYEHILL COTTAGE was near the Old Borough Arms, Chickerell Road.

Qinetiq

Q

QUEEN'S HEAD ALEHOUSE was on the north side of High Street, Weymouth in the 17th/18th century. The pub was known successively as the Queens Head Alehouse, the Prince Frederick, the Prince's Head Alehouse, and the Ship Alehouse before becoming a private dwelling.

QUEEN'S HOTEL (once known as the Albert Hotel), on the corner of Park Street and King Street was pulled down and completely rebuilt in 1938-39.

The first Queen's Hotel on the corner of King Street and Park Street (once known as the Albert Hotel). It was rebuilt in the 1930s.

QINETIQ (formerly DERA), Bincleaves Plans were put forward early in 2007 for the redevelopment of the site – to demolish existing buildings on the Breakwater and redevelop the area to include residential use, a hotel, car parks, business premises etc. To date (2009) no redevelopment has taken place.

QUAKERS *see* SOCIETY OF FRIENDS; FOX, George

QUAKERS GROVE Butts Grove, or Quakers Grove led to The Lookout.

QUEEN VICTORIA STATUE Renovation work on the statue was carried out in 2008 following that on the King's Statue, by the same company, Osirion Conservation.

QUEEN'S ARMS pub was on North Quay in the 19th century.

QUEENS BARRACKS *see* PUCKETT'S STOTRES

The Queen Victoria statue was unveiled in 1902. Seen here in the 1920s.

Rackmead

R

RACKMEAD, Watery Lane A neglected old house which was due to be demolished in 2008. It was not considered to be of sufficient interest for listing.

RADIPOLE BUS GARAGE Road Motors, a firm which operated in Weymouth from 1921, opened Radipole Bus Garage in 1923. It was taken over by Southern National in 1925 and the building now houses a furniture store – London Lounge.

RADIPOLE COURT is sheltered housing. Built in 1965 in the grounds of Radipole House, which was destroyed by WW2 bombs in 1941.

RADIPOLE LAKE DEVELOPMENT SCHEME The word 'Backwater' in 1933 was being ousted by the more picturesque 'Radipole Lake' for the water above Westham Bridge. Landscape experts Messrs. Deane and White had drawn up ambitious plans for the 1933 Radipole Lake Development Scheme. It was intended to carry out the work in stages over a period of 15 years until World War 2 brought everything to a halt. The 1933 plans were the extension of a scheme which had already begun with reclamation of land from the Backwater for Radipole Park Drive with its adjacent woodland gardens and the laying out of Melcombe Regis Gardens, tennis courts, bowling green and Council greenhouses on infilled ground in the late 1920s. Reclamation at the northern end of the Park Drive provided tennis courts, paddling pool and a children's playground. Much more was envisaged with the further reclamation of some 70 acres from the Lake without interfering with the course of the River Wey. Bandstands, fountains, tennis courts, children's boating pond, model yacht pond, bowling greens, cricket ground, football and hockey pitches, golf and putting courses were all in the plans. At the Radipole end of the Lake a landing stage was to be built for a possible future water bus service. A new road would run on the western side of the lake, linking to Spa Road and Radipole Park Drive and also to Westham Bridge, providing a road right around the Lake, the top end of which would form a bird sanctuary. Post-war the plans began to get under way again and in 1949 tipping began to provide new paths across the Lake, planned to be 'shore to shore' across it, much of the tipped stone being brought from the ruins of bombed Chapelhay. More tipping was carried out in 1954 to enlarge the Swannery car park. That the scheme was never totally carried through is today perhaps an advantage for no other town has a tranquil nature reserve so close to its

One of the first developments of the Radipole Lake scheme was the infill for Radipole Park Drive which was built along the shoreline shown here. The chimney of Radipole brickworks is on the right (demolished in 1933) and the original Abbots Court is in the left background.

centre. The road along the Lake's western shore (Weymouth Way) was built – but not until the 1980s, more than 50 years after it was originally envisaged.

RADIPOLE LANE was known in the 18th century as East Chickerell Road.

RADIPOLE. MANOR HOUSES The 'Old Manor' next to St Ann's Church, is thought to have been rebuilt in the 16th century by Richard Watkins and incorporates part of an earlier structure possibly once belonging to Cerne Abbey. The initials 'R. W.' are carved in stone above the entrance doorway. The house later became the farmhouse of Manor Farm. Radipole Manor, also on Radipole Lane, is of Victorian date. William Eliot, whose sons brought about the failure in 1897 of the Weymouth bank he had founded, bought the land from the Henning family and built the house sometime after 1840. It was also known as Westmead and one of his banker sons Richard ffolliot Eliot lived there. *See also* MANOR HOUSE ESTATE, Radipole.

RADIPOLE RECTORY, Radipole Lane Became a Christian Care Centre known as the 'Old Rectory' in the late 1970s after becoming redundant as a rectory on the establishment of a team ministry in Weymouth and Melcombe Regis.

RADIPOLE. SCHOOL The former village school opposite St Ann's Church was built on land given by William Eliot in 1850. It closed in 1964, once the buildings of the new Radipole Primary School in Radipole Lane began to come into use.

RADIPOLE. WOOD *see* JUBILEE WOOD, Radipole Lane.

RADLEY COURT, Preston Road was built in 2004.

RADNOR VILLAS were in Milton Road.

RAFMOOR This Air Ministry vessel was a familiar sight in Weymouth Harbour from 1952 until she headed off to the breaker's yard in 1961. She was involved in towing targets and marker buoys, maintenance work and aircraft salvaging. Originally a Red Funnel Line tug operating in Southampton waters named the *Albert Edward*, she changed her name to *Joy Belle II* as a passenger-carrying ship plying between the Channel Islands and finally became *Rafmoor* when taken over by the Air Ministry. She was succeeded at Weymouth by an ex-Admiralty minesweeper, *Airmoor 1*.

RAIL MOTORS were first used at Weymouth 1st May 1905. One class, no smoking steam rail motors on the Weymouth-Abbotsbury and Weymouth-Dorchester lines.

RAILWAY The railway to Weymouth opened on 20th January 1857, the first GWR train on the broad gauge taking the Mayor and Corporation to Yeovil and back. The London and South Western service started a few days later – the track being dual gauge until 1874. On the 100th anniversary of the opening in 1957 Mayor Charlotte Wootton in full robes and chain 'drove' the be-flagged 9.35 am *Glasfryn Hall* Western Region train to Swindon half the length of Weymouth Station platform under the watchful eye of Driver Puckett before it continued its journey. 125 years on the opening was commemorated with a plaque at Weymouth station and the 150th anniversary of the railway's arrival was celebrated on Saturday 20th January 2007 with events at Dorchester, Maiden Newton and Weymouth, where actors dressed in 19th century costume to recreate the first run.

Local railway history has been covered in depth in numerous books and publications and does not require summarising here. Weymouth railway station (replaced in

The opening of the long-awaited railway to Weymouth in 1857 was celebrated by the construction of these greenery-swagged arches at the King's Statue. A bleak scene, but it was January.

1986) has seen the occasional derailment and its locos were knocked about in WW2 air raids, but there were a couple of early incidents which caused some excitement and alarm. The first occurred on 26th August 1862 when the locomotive *Victoria* on the down train suffered brake failure and ran through the buffers and into the street, stopping perilously close to the Somerset Hotel. The second, on 2nd January 1886, could have had a similar result when a runaway train flew down the line. Early in the morning a colossal noise was heard which was assumed to be an explosion but was in fact the runaway train crashing at some 30-40 miles an hour into a line of stationary carriages at Weymouth railway station. It sent them into the fortunately stout buffers, since they too could have ended up in the street just yards away. Two men had been on a small engine engaged in bringing a large goods engine out of the engine shed, several hundred yards from the station. Before coming down the line it was necessary to change the points and both men had jumped off the small engine to do this, each oblivious of the fact that the other had got off. Hence the engine started off down the line unattended, despite valiant efforts by one of the men, a lad of 17 named Charles Cutler, to regain control of it as it passed him. His leg was crushed in the attempt and his foot later had to be amputated. He was the sole unfortunate casualty of the incident, apart from damage to the station building, the carriages and the tramway engine itself.

A few dates may be of interest: The turntable at Weymouth was constructed in 1925. Its removal has meant that the popular 'Seaside Special' steam trains which make regular visits to the town in the summer months have to steam up to Yeovil Junction to be turned around before coming back to Weymouth for the return trip. February 1952 saw diesel loco 10201 at Weymouth on an experimental run. The introduction of diesels on the Weymouth-Waterloo service began later in the 1950s and their introduction cut short the plans to build two more long platforms similar to the present one, which is 930 feet long and when completed in 1958 was intended for steam trains.

On 1st December 1952 the line to Abbotsbury closed, having opened in 1885. Upwey Station was retained for a while as a goods station (but is now a builder's yard containing the original station building) and Upwey Junction station was renamed Upwey and Broadwey. Also in 1952 the Weymouth and Portland Railway closed to passengers, its goods traffic continuing until 1965. Part of this line, from Westham to Wyke Regis, can now be walked and is known as the Rodwell Trail. In 1954 the railway bridge dating from 1900 across the A354 road at Ridgeway was replaced by the present bridge. Work took several months, the span being rolled into place on Saturday/Sunday night 4/5th December 1954. Although the new bridge gave six inches more headroom for road traffic, today it is not unusual for lorries to wedge themselves beneath it, causing long traffic tailbacks. This problem should disappear when the new Relief Road currently (2009) under construction is completed. In 1987

Not an accidental derailment – this scene at Weymouth was caused by enemy action during a WW2 air raid in 1941.

Landslips along the cliffs on the Weymouth and Portland line caused occasional problems. This slip near Sandsfoot occured in January 1909.

permission was given to demolish a thatched home in Upton Fort Road, Osmington Mills, which was a converted former LSWR dining car from the 1890s. *See also* FLYING SCOTSMAN; RAILWAY STATION; RAILWAY LINES THROUGH THE STREETS; WEYMOUTH HARBOUR TRAMWAY

RAILWAY HOTEL, No. 721 Dorchester Road, Broadwey has been converted to housing.

'RAILWAY LINES THROUGH THE STREETS' *see* WEYMOUTH HARBOUR TRAMWAY

RAILWAY STATION Work began on the construction of Weymouth's Brunel-designed Railway Station in 1855, built on land originally reclaimed from the Backwater to form a public park (*see* FOOKS, **Charles Berjew**; PARK DISTRICT). The railway opened on 20th January 1857. A walkway around the platform ends was added in 1885. The station originally had an overall timber and glass roof. The glass was taken out in 1939 as a precautionary measure ahead of WW2 bombing and work on removing the roof began in November 1951. It was decided to replace the station in the 1930s but war ended expansion plans and the original station remained in use until the 1980s. Demolition began in August 1984 and passengers used temporary facilities until the present station opened in July 1986. The sculpture on the station forecourt is by Andy Kirkby and commemorates the electrification of the Bournemouth-Weymouth line in May 1988.

RAINIER, Peter Mount Rainier, a volcanic peak in the state of Washington, was named after the then Rear Admiral Peter Rainier, RN in 1792. He was born in 1741 and entered the Navy in 1756. He was involved in a number of successful sea battles and in 1799 was promoted to Vice-Admiral. He was stationed in the East Indies 1794 until 1804 and continued to advise of matters relating to the East India station after his retirement. In 1805 he was advanced to the rank of Admiral. He was elected an MP (not local) and died in 1808. This was the year that his brother, John Rainier, paid for the cutting of the White Horse at Osmington Hill on land belonging to Robert Serrell Wood, but any local connection with the Rainiers has not yet been established.

RALEIGH, Sir Walter It is thought that he owned a Weymouth privateer and the story goes that one of his ships brought in a vessel with negroes on board, one of whom was given to Lady Raleigh as a page. Fact or fiction? 500 years on it is difficult to substantiate stories like this. He certainly had Dorset connections, living for some years at Sherborne Castle.

RAMBLER VILLAS are in Old Castle Road, Rodwell.

RANDALL, Harold D A marquetry craftsman working in the 1950s -1970s at Wyke Regis.

RANELAGH ROAD was tree lined until January 1965 when 30 trees were felled on the railway side as they had grown too big. *See also* COX'S FOUNDRY

RANELAGH TERRACE is the first terrace of houses in Ranelagh Road at the Queen Street end.

RATCLIFF HALL, Queen's Road, Radipole Mrs Ratcliff, of Alberta, Dorchester Road, Radipole gave the hall in 1901 and placed it in the hands of the Rector and trustees. It was enlarged in 1926.

RECTORY WAY is part of the 1980s development which stands of the site of Glebe House, Cross Road, a former vicarage of Holy Trinity Church.

RED CROSS CLUB *see* AMERICAN RED CROSS CLUB

RED HOUSE is Nos. 14-15 Bond Street, on the corner with New Street. It has long been known by this name, not because of red bricks, but due to its shop front having been painted red for many years.

RED INDIANS *see* AMERICAN INDIANS

RED LION INN Today's Red Lion pub is in Hope Square but in the 17th century there was a pub of this name in Maiden Street. Also one at Chickerell.

REDLANDS Close to the main road until 1947 was the 'Nottington Barrow', excavated in 1938 and found to contain cremated remains and fragments of a Bronze Age riveted dagger. It is now the site of No. 425 Dorchester Road.

REDLANDS COMMUNITY SPORTS HUB with new owner Weymouth College, was officially opened on 1st November 2008 by Peter Shilton, England's most-capped footballer. This is the former Redlands Sports Centre, which opened in September 1974, having grown out of Weymouth Sports Club, whose first Pavilion was a second-hand Nissen hut.

REEMA HOUSES The Reema Construction Company produced hollow precast concrete wall units which had no steel reinforcement. In this area the units were produced at Weston Road, Portland in the early 1950s. Reema houses and flats can be found in the Southlands area of Weymouth and Verne Common Estate, Portland. It was estimated that the number of man hours in building a Reema house was about half that required for a traditionally built house. In recent years mortgage companies have been unwilling to lend on these structures.

REES JEFFREYS ROAD FUND Many people stop their cars on the seaward side of Abbotsbury Hill to gaze back at the views of Chesil Beach and Weymouth and Portland from the lay-by at the top of the hill. The lay-by contains a metal plaque which reads *'For your enjoyment of the view. WRJ 1872-1954. THE REES JEFFREYS ROAD FUND'*. W. Rees Jeffreys was a renowned authority on Highways and Transport and the Fund he established dealt with many aspects of road use, education and related topics. It also included the provision of several dozen lay-bys at vantage points such as that on Abbotsbury Hill, which surely must be one of the best views in the county, if not the country.

REFUSE DESTRUCTOR This was an incinerator installed in 1904 in the Corporation Yard at the Westham Bridge end of Westwey Road (a site unrecognisable today as the flats of Harbour View were built here after the council depot departed to premises at Chickerell in 2003). It was worked in conjunction with the pumping station of the borough's sewerage system, the steam generated by burning rubbish being used to drive the machinery for pumping the town's sewage and thus saving on coal bills. Old photographs show two tall chimneys in this area – the smaller was that of the sewage works, the taller one was part of the electricity generating station on an adjacent site.

REGATTAS were once very popular events in Weymouth. A Charles Barclay claimed in 1908 that he was one of those who participated in Weymouth's first regatta in 1841, but this must have been a revival as they were held at least as early as the 1820s.

REGENT GARAGE On the corner of Lower Bond Street and Commercial Road the garage was built around 1929-30 and replaced a tenement block, Burdon's Buildings. In 1943 the garage played a part in the planned D-Day invasion when it temporarily became an experimental workshop for No. 1 REME in October 1943 when the testing of manufacturers' waterproofing schemes was being carried out. These were to enable army fighting and support vehicles to land from naval landing craft into the sea and onto the French beaches. Large scale exercises were mounted in Weymouth Bay. When the tests and data were complete the unit closed and moved to North Devon. The Regent Garage became Bell's Garage in 1946. For the later history of the site *see* KENNEDYS STORE. For what stood there before, *see* BURDON, **William Wharton**; PUCKETT'S STORES

RELIEF ROAD Work on the £84 million relief road finally began in late summer 2008. The civil engineering contractors Skanska set up a site compound at Littlemoor and archaeologists from Oxford Archaeology began advance investigations on the Ridgeway. As work progressed in June 2009, an ancient burial site containing over 50 skulls of beheaded males was discovered.

RELIEF ROAD (proposed, along the Weymouth & Portland Railway line) was officially deleted from Dorset County Council Structure Plan in 1983. This is now the route of a scenic walk, the Rodwell Trail.

RENDEL, James Meadows The celebrated engineer was in overall charge of the Portland Breakwaters project, his resident engineer at Portland was John Coode. The project officially began with the laying of the foundation stone on 25th July 1849, although preliminary surveys were carried out several years earlier. On Rendel's death in 1856, John Coode was appointed Engineer in Chief, a post he retained until the work was declared complete on 10th August 1872.

RENSCOMBE was an alternative name used in the mid 1950s for Stormount, the children's home on Buxton Road near Foord's Corner.

RIDGEWAY The lone house which stands on the A354 at the top of Ridgeway (currently called 'Swallows Rest') has in the past also been known as 'Edward House' and 'Harenhounds'. It was originally planned to be part of a small estate but the development was stopped after construction of the present house (for a Mr Guy, who worked for the railway) had begun. It was completed, but no further development was allowed.

RIDGEWAY DISASTER On Saturday, 5th August 1922 a coach belonging to Fancy Brothers of Portland was returning from an outing to Bridgwater late on a Saturday night. Bert Fancy, driving it, shouted as the coach came down Ridgeway *'It's all up boys, the brakes have given out'*. He managed to avoid crashing over the 30-foot drop at the side of the hairpin bend, but caught the wall, turning the vehicle over on the road. Hearing screams, rescuers rushed to the scene, including some who had just alighted from a train at Upwey Wishing Well Halte, the station then beside the bridge over the A354 road at Ridgeway. Police and ambulances arrived at the scene taking all 14 injured passengers and the driver to hospital. Sadly, one 81 year old man, on his first-ever coach trip, died a few hours later. The fact that some of the injured had to wait two hours at the accident scene before receiving medical attention led to calls for the setting-up of a St John Ambulance Brigade in the town, and this was founded later that year.

RIMBURY Rimbury was a burial ground of the later Bronze Age, after the time when people were buried in individual barrows. It lies below Chalbury Hill but still on high ground. Nearly 100 urns containing burnt bones were excavated here but nothing can now be seen. The name survives in 'Rimbury Coppice'.

The RINGS This was the name of the reclaimed ground on which the Alexandra Gardens would be laid out in the late 1860s. The name seems to originate from early in 1819 when it was agreed that the ground facing Pulteney Buildings was *'to be made into a circle'*.

RINGSTEAD The huge dish-shaped wireless aerials at Ringstead, which were communication links in the USAF Troposcatter Station, were dismantled during January-March, 1975. *See also* AMPTHILL, Lord and Lady

ROBIN HOOD (presumably a pub) was at No. 18 Little George Street.

The Ringstead aerials.

ROBINSON, Robert caused something of a furore in 1957 when he wrote an article in a Sunday newspaper criticising Weymouth. He was writing as its film critic and commenting on the location work done here for the film 'The Key'. His comments on the lines of *'The guest houses resemble Victorian orphanages...'* and quoting actor Trevor Howard's remarks that Weymouth was the worst location he ever went to did not go down at all well in the resort.

ROCK FACTORY *Correction to the main entry in Bumper Book I:*

The owner of the Rock Factory in Caroline Place was Mr Alfred Michaels.

ROCK HOTEL *Update of the main entry in Bumper Book I*

In 2008 the Function Room which had been built in 1926 on the site of the Rock Hotel's former stable block was demolished and houses of Orchard Mews are now (2009) being built on the site.

ROCK MISSION, Rock Assembly Rooms, Westham A Gospel Mission began meeting regularly at the Rock Hotel – it appears to have started in 1904. As the Westham Cottage Mission celebrated its 4th anniversary in 1908, it seems likely that these were one and the same.

ROCKS CLOSE, Westham was up for sale for development in October, 1882 – at that time it was in use as allotment gardens. The name is perpetuated in Rocks Terrace, the Rock Hotel etc. There are also Rock Cottages between Nos. 686-688, Dorchester Road.

RODWELL What was known as 'Rodwell Well' was close to Rodwell House, now the Rodwell House Hotel.

RODWELL AVENUE A small lawned area on the south side of Rodwell Avenue was presented to the town during his mayoralty by Robert Stone Comben and is known as Alderman Comben's Garden. He was mayor for three years, 1915-16, 1916-17 and 1917-18.

No. 14 Rodwell Avenue achieved brief notoriety in 1915 during the 'Brides in the Bath' trial of George Joseph Smith who murdered three of the women he married by drowning them in the bath. One of the dead women, Bessie Mundy, had wed Smith at Weymouth in 1910 (he used the name Henry Williams as he already had a wife) and they lived for a while at No. 14 Rodwell Avenue. He left her, but two years later she met up with him again and while the couple were living in Herne Bay she became the first of his three victims. Smith was hanged in August 1915.

Four bungalows for widows were officially opened on 21st November 1957 to replace four small dwellings (since demolished) on Wyke Road. They were built under the terms of the Jonathan and Rebecca Edwards Charity.

RODWELL COLLEGE This was a school established in 1861 as Weymouth Commercial School at Nos. 5 and 7 Frederick Place. The school moved to Rodwell at the end of 1910, renaming itself Rodwell College in 1911 and occupying a house known for years as 'The Blue House' on the corner of Rodwell Road and St Leonard's Road. Headmaster was Dr Percy Pankhurst. Some time later, probably around the end of WW1, Dr Pankhurst returned to the town proper and opened Weymouth Esplanade School for Commercial and Technical Instruction at No. 4 Royal Terrace, Esplanade, which seems to have lasted until the early 1930s.

Rodwell College from a 1917 guidebook advertisement.

RODWELL HOTEL, Rodwell Road was renamed The Mighty Hood on 24th April 1982, part of Maritime England Year commemorations. It is named after the famous battle cruiser which sank in May 1941 in the Denmark Straits. The pub's renaming coincided with the unveiling of memorial plaques to *HMS Hood* and *HMS Delight* at the Royal Naval Air Station, Portland and two memorial seats at the Nothe Gardens to *HMS Hood* and *HMS Barham*. More than 2000 men died in the three incidents. The Rodwell Hotel has since reverted to is original name.

RODWELL LODGE today is a modern apartment block on the east side of Rodwell Road, midway between St Leonard's Road and Rodwell Avenue. It stands on the site of a demolished mansion set in extensive grounds which was called Rodwell Lodge (and sometimes Rodwell Villa) once the home of Sir John Groves and later Alfred Owen Swaffield. It was converted to a hotel in 1973 which was later demolished to provide the site for the present flats. An early 20th century picture postcard of an impressive house called 'Rodwell Lodge' was a recent puzzle as it resembled no local building. It was discovered that it was the home in Wiltshire of the Rodwell-born wife of a Wiltshire man (married at Holy Trinity, Weymouth in 1858) who presumably carried the memory of her childhood in the area to her new home.

RODWELL VILLA *see* RODWELL LODGE

ROGERS, Agnes Ann, formerly of Weymouth In the 1850s this apparently beautiful and certainly enterprising young woman had achieved a certain notoriety in Weymouth. She was the daughter of parents described in the local press as being of 'dissipated character' and left the town to live in London after the death of her father, reinventing herself as Agnes Willoughby or Lady Agnes Willoughby. There, whilst out riding, she met William Frederick Windham, age twenty-one, who fell for her and married her in 1861. This was to the dismay of his relatives, for young William had inherited an immense fortune and vast estates in Norfolk, with a further estate which would be his on attaining the age of twenty-eight and which, under the terms of his father's will, would be lost to his relatives if he produced an heir. Attempts to prevent the marriage failed and it was then alleged that William was suffering from lunacy, the family claiming that his lifestyle was extravagant, the company he kept was unsuitable and that he indulged in boyish pranks. Although not untypical behaviour of a young man inheriting a fortune, William's upbringing, despite being the son of one of Norfolk's leading families, had been erratic, his schooling almost non-existent and his behaviour uncouth and unsuitable for polite company. On inheriting his vast wealth he embarked on a spending spree which resulted in huge debts and a diminishing estate, to the alarm of the family. Agnes had at first refused to marry him but after a financial agreement was arranged they were wed on 30th August 1861. They parted a month later, she leaving with £14,000-worth of jewellery he had given her. She returned and left at intervals until the lunacy hearing was heard in December. Various unconvincing reasons were given as to Mr Windham being of unsound mind – he had a huge appetite, snored loudly, cut down a lot of trees on his estate and had dressed up as a railway guard to drive a locomotive engine. The case became something of a real-life soap opera, with opinion divided as to whether 'Mad' Windham was really mad or his relatives were more concerned with losing what was left of his diminishing fortune. The case lasted many weeks and at the end of it William was adjudged to be of sound mind. He continued with his rackety lifestyle and Agnes flitted in and out of his life, having become the lover of an Italian opera singer. Divorce proceedings were commenced and dropped, she bore Windham a son and he was declared bankrupt. Felbrigg Hall in Norfolk was sold, Mad Windham died and

the paternity of his son was disputed (Agnes won this one, her son remained the Windham heir and inherited another of the family's estates). Agnes Windham, the golden-haired girl who grew up in Weymouth, settled down in Norfolk and became 'respectable'. She and her son both died in 1896.

ROLLER SKATING Popular in Weymouth since the 1870s, roller skating has now been superseded by skateboarding with facilities at **The Front** skatepark at

FOR THE

RITTER ROAD SKATES.

————————

SKATES ON HIRE. SKATING TAUGHT.

————————

FRANKLIN & WATHEN,

ALEXANDRA CYCLE DEPOT,

WEYMOUTH.

...they would have been rather hampered by Victorian skaters' boots.

Young Weymouth roller skaters entertaining at the Pier Bandstand in the 1950s...

...were known as the 'Roller Revellers'.

Lodmoor. Roller skating was a popular attraction at the Pier Bandstand in the 1950s when local teenagers put on shows.

ROPERS BUILDINGS are between Nos 694-696 Dorchester Road, Upwey.

ROSE COTTAGES A place name choice which vies with 'Myrtle' for popularity. There were Rose Cottages in Walpole Street; Upwey (part of Prospect Place); Littlemoor (between Nos. 504 and 508 Littlemoor Road); Westham (probably Nos. 103-107 Abbotsbury Road) and Wyke Regis. Rose Terrace became Nos. 2-36 Granville Road, Rose Hill Cottage was in St Leonard's Road. No doubt there are more!

ROSEBERY, Lord was on his yacht at Weymouth in 29th June 1902 for a concert at the Alexandra Gardens given by the band of the Italian battleship *Carlo Alberto,* also attended by **Marconi.**

ROSEMARY LANE An ancient street name in the town, location unknown.

ROSSI'S ICE CREAM PARLOUR, The Esplanade Begun in 1937 by the Figliolinis and owned by 3 generations of the family.

ROUND HOUSE There was an earlier Round House than the present ones associated with the name – No. 1 The Esplanade and the houses at the King's Statue. In 1662 a house in Melcombe was called the Round House, and a deed of 1731 mentions a property *'once part of a house called the Round House'.*

ROUNDHAMS was the name of a large field off Chickerell Road.

ROWE, John G. worked in the drapery trade before opening his own store in St Mary Street, extending it as adjacent properties became available until by the 1890s he occupied Nos 13, 14, 15 and 16. He demolished a little terrace of houses behind No. 14, known as 'Snug Corner'.

The northernmost part of his shop eventually became the site of Woolworths building; the adjacent part slightly set back in the street still has its original façade above street level. Woolworths left the town in 1985 (returning in 2000 to New Bond Street before finally closing in 2009) and the St Mary Street building was much remodelled and now houses individual shops.

...and Woolworths which replaced it. The shop opened here in 1923 and the large store shown above dates from 1938.

ROWLAND COURT, Greenhill Flats built in 1965 were demolished in February 2008. New apartments currently (2009) under construction are to be called Hutton Apartments.

ROYAL BRITISH LEGION *see* BRITISH LEGION

Rowe's Victorian drapery department store...

The famous John Nixon cartoon of King George III's first bathe at Weymouth in 1789 - 'Royal Dipping'.

ROYAL CANTEEN pub was in Barrack Lane, adjacent to the Burial Ground at the Nothe. Existed in the 1850s, 1860s.

ROYAL CRESCENT SURGERY, Crescent Street was built in 1986. The site was once occupied by an old house known as Belvidere Cottage.

'ROYAL DIPPING' is a cartoon by John Nixon of King George III's first sea bathe at Weymouth, in July 1789. In most details it does correspond Fanny Burney's description of the occasion in her diary of the 1789 visit.

ROYAL HOTEL *see* SPROULE, Andrew

ROYAL OAK PUBLIC HOUSE, Upwey. The pub closed in 1965 but was not demolished until April 1968. There are two Royal Oak pubs in Weymouth at the present

The 'Royal Oak' at the bottom of Ridgeway, closed in 1965 and was demolished in 1968.

time – on Custom House Quay and on Dorchester Road, Lodmoor Hill.

ROYAL OBSERVER CORPS Underground and above ground posts for the ROC Weymouth crew were constructed near the Riviera Hotel in 1961.

ROYAL SOCIETY FOR THE PROTECTION OF BIRDS information centre at Radipole Lake was built in 1982.

ROYAL STANDARD pub, Upwey dates to the mid-19th century.

ROYAL VISITORS There is a long list of dates of Royal Visits to Weymouth in *Bumper Book I*, and it includes all King George III's holidays in Weymouth 1789-1805. The list below is a supplement.

June 1852 Queen Victoria on the royal yacht *Victoria and Albert* entered Portland Roads. Prince Albert and the children were taken by royal barge to visit the Breakwater works. Meanwhile a diver descended into the sea at the stern of the boat and selected some pebbles and shells to present to Her Majesty. She did not land.

September 1860 The Duke of Cambridge was in Weymouth, arriving by train en route to Portland to meet the Lords of the Admiralty.

April 1870 The Duke of Cambridge arrived by train to view the Nothe and Breakwater works. He was Commander in Chief of HM Forces.

June 1882 Rear Admiral the Duke of Edinburgh arrived by train to take command of the Fleet.

May 1887 The Duke of Cambridge arrived to review the Queen's Own Dorset Yeomanry Cavalry.

June 1897 His Imperial Highness the Grand Duke Cyril of Russia, cousin of the Czar, arrived in the war ship *Russia,* on which he was a lieutenant. He left by train for London for the Queen's Diamond Jubilee celebrations.

July 1898 The Duke of York (later King George V), commander of *HMS Crescent,* arrived in Portland Harbour and visited the Royal Dorset Yacht Club in Weymouth. The Duchess arrived by train on Sunday afternoon. Mr Montague Guest had placed Devonshire House, Devonshire Buildings at the royal visitors disposal. During the visit the Duchess bathed from one of the machines on the Sands, apparently unrecognised.

August 1902 King Edward VII and Queen Alexandra were in the new Royal Yacht in Weymouth Bay on 21st and 22nd August 1902. It was a private visit and they did not land. The town was illuminated, bands played, and crowds turned out but the only ones to glimpse the King were on Cosens steamers, the Company running trips out to view the new vessel.

May 1903 Princess Victoria daughter of Edward VII, was on board the Royal Yacht on 4th, 5th and 6th May 1903 in Portland Harbour. She left the yacht and cycled, apparently incognito, from Portland through Wyke and into Weymouth. She also went for a cycle ride in the country on the Tuesday and was cheered on her return to the quayside at Weymouth in the evening. The yacht left on Wednesday.

December 1904 Prince of Wales visited Abbotsbury with Lord Ilchester's shooting party.

April 1904 Princess Victoria on the royal yacht *Osborne* was in Portland Harbour briefly in April 1904 but doesn't appear to have landed.

March & May 1905 Queen Alexandra was on board the royal yacht *Victoria and Albert* when it put into Portland Harbour. She did not land. She was on a prolonged sea trip and returned in May, again without coming ashore before leaving for Portsmouth.

May 1906 The Prince and Princess of Wales were on board *HMS Renown* and returning from an Indian tour when fog in the Channel brought them into Portland Harbour. They did not land.

July 1906 Princess Henry of Battenberg visited Weymouth.

August 1911 The battleship *HMS Hindustan,* arrived at Portland with the Prince of Wales (later King Edward VIII) on board. He had just started his naval career as a midshipman. He came ashore and strolled on the Esplanade but was not in uniform and apparently not recognised.

May 1912 This visit by King George V to review the Fleet is listed in *Bumper Book I* but it was a great occasion in the town, being the first official visit by a reigning monarch since the visits of King George III ended in 1805 and the crowds turned out in force despite rather miserable weather. The Admiralty yacht *Enchantress* arrived with First Lord of the Admiralty Winston Churchill on board

accompanied by ex-Prime Minister Arthur Balfour, Prince Louis of Battenberg and Lord Morley of Blackburn. Prime Minister H. H. Asquith joined them later, arriving by train. The King, accompanied by Prince Albert (later King George VI) steamed down the lines in the royal yacht. Highlight of this Review was the aerial display. Naval air ace Charles R. Samson's plane suffered a mishap and fell into the water – he and the hydroplane were speedily pulled out and he was soon in the air again. His flight, circling the Royal Yacht and skimming the waters around it, was the highlight of the aerial show. Then civilian aviators Claude Graham-White and Benny Hucks arrived from London with a Nieuport monoplane and a Bleriot monoplane and provided more displays. Churchill and Balfour went for an underwater trip on a D-type submarine in Portland Harbour, the D3 and D4 submarines then being the largest afloat. The King went for his first underwater trip in submarine D4. The sub, of 800 tons displacement and carrying a 12-inch gun dived, travelled a couple of miles underwater and then surfaced to bring the King back to the royal yacht. Later in the week the King and Prince Albert joined *HMS Neptune* and steamed out to sea with other important guests for firing exercises, curtailed due to the heavy mist. The weather continued to be a problem and a mock battle between ships in the Bay had to be cancelled due to the all-enveloping fog, but the King was later able to proceed out to sea where the postponed battle practice was held. Mayor Bartle Pye was informed that the King accompanied by Prince Albert would land at Weymouth on Saturday morning, May 11th and motor through the town before proceeding by royal train to London.

King George V steps ashore at Weymouth in May 1912.

October 1913 Prince Albert, midshipman on *HMS Collingwood,* arrived at Portland on 12th October. Played rugby at Portland the next day.

July 1922 King George V was in the royal yacht off Portland prior to sailing to Torbay with the fleet. Whilst here, he boarded *HMS Queen Elizabeth* to watch exercises in the Channel including the destruction of the ex-German cruiser *Nurnberg* by gun fire and bomb. These operations were secret and no details of them appeared in the press.

July 1930 After opening Weymouth Town Bridge, the Duke of York (later King George VI) toured Whiteheads Torpedo Works at Wyke Regis.

June 1938 The entry for July 1938 in *Bumper Book I* should be June 1938.

May 1944 King George VI and high-ranking British and American naval officers inspected the assembled invasion fleet in Portland Harbour on 25th May.

June 1978 The Duke of Edinburgh visited Portland.

July 1981 Princess Anne visited Portland Naval Base.

February 1985 Prince Michael of Kent was here for a day, Arrived by helicopter and was winched down and back up again after seeing ships of the Task Force exercising.

August 1985 The Queen, Prince Philip, the Prince and Princess of Wales and their children, Princess Anne and her children and Prince Edward were all on the royal yacht *Britannia* in Portland Harbour, where Prince Andrew was joining them. Prince Philip reviewed the Sea Cadet Corps fleet as their Admiral.

October 1988 Princess Anne arrived at Portland to watch speed sailing championships.

July 1999 The Duke of Edinburgh commemorated the laying of the first stone of Portland Breakwater in 1849.

April 2007 Duke of Gloucester opened Nothe Fort improvements.

September 2008 Duke of Gloucester opened Holy Trinity Primary School's new environmental garden and toured the school. The same day he unveiled the plaque commemorating the restoration work on King's Statue (his great-great-great-great grandfather).

June 2009 The Queen and the Duke of Edinburgh visited Weymouth and Portland National Sailing Academy and Weymouth.

RUSSIAN FISH FACTORY SHIPS were in the Weymouth Bay in the winter months of the 1990s. Known locally as Klondykers, they left in 1997.

RUSSIAN GUN The gun and carriage presented to the town in 1857 after the Crimean War ended was moved around on the seafront and eventually ended up on the pier. It was still there in 1940 when the Council decided to hand it over for use in war munitions. *See also Bumper Book I*

The Russian Gun, a Crimean War relic, on the pier in 1887.

RUTLAND, Squadron Commander Frederick J, DSC, RN (1886-1949). As a Flight Lieutenant he became known as 'Rutland of Jutland' following the daring rescue of an injured man almost certain to be crushed between two naval vessels during the Battle of Jutland in May 1916. The previous day he had carried out a reconnaissance trip in a Short seaplane from the deck of *HMS Engadine* and accurately reported the enemy's position and course by wireless (the first time this had been achieved between an aircraft and ships engaged in a fleet action) despite coming under fire from the guns of four light cruisers. For this action he was awarded the Distinguished Service Cross. For his single-handed rescue of the dying man (in defiance of orders) Rutland received the Albert Medal, First Class. He was born in Park View (now part of Queen Street) in Weymouth's Park District on Trafalgar Day, 21st October 1886, joining the Royal Navy as a boy entrant in 1901 at the age of 15. On gaining his pilot's certificate in the eventful pioneering days of flying, he joined *HMS Engadine*, which had been converted to a seaplane carrier. After a service career which included much experimental work on improving the take-off and landing of planes on ships' decks, he left the Navy in 1923. His career then took him to Japan where he worked on organising the Japanese Naval Air Service, a task begun two years earlier when he was seconded to that country, then an ally of Britain, with the full approval of his service bosses. It was the link with Japan which would implicate him in later years when he was accused of spying.

Was he a spy in the World War II years? It seems that none of those who knew him well believed him to be anything but a British patriot, despite some mystery about his prosperous lifestyle. Following the Japanese attack on Pearl Harbor on 7th December 1941 and the sinking by Japanese torpedo-bombers of three British battleships three days later, Rutland, who had earlier returned to Britain from the United States, with, he claimed, information to impart on the possible Japanese involvement, was arrested and interned in Brixton Prison. No charge was ever brought against him despite the intervention of senior naval men who simply did not believe the gallant officer capable of betraying his country. Rutland, transferring between Brixton and a prison on the Isle of Man, was released towards the end of 1943 and went to live in Wales, making no real effort to clear his name. On 28th January 1949 he was found dead in a gas-filled London hotel room, the coroner's verdict being that 'Deceased did kill himself while the balance of his mind was disturbed'. MI5 files released in 2000 reveal that he had been paid by the Japanese to set up a spy base in Hawaii.

Further reading: *Rutland of Jutland*, by Desmond Young. (Cassell, 1963.)

RYAN'S ACRE is a housing development on the south side of Littlemoor Road, the first house being completed in August 1984, built by Ryan of Wimborne.

RYDAL SCHOOL, Rydal Lodge, No. 27 Spa Road was a private school founded by Mrs Charlotte Wootton in the 1930s (she was Mayor of Weymouth 1956-57). It closed in the late 1960s, the head then being Miss M. McFarlane Watt.

RYLANDS LANE RAILWAY BRIDGE was removed and replaced by a new bridge in April 1957.

SDT

S

SDT *see* SOUTH DORSET TRADES MINERAL WATER COMPANY LTD

SAILORS HOME originally run by Miss East *see* EAST, Frances E.

SAILORS RACE was held in June 1903. It was a run from Weymouth to Dorchester by sailors from HM ships in Portland Harbour.

SAILORS REST, St Thomas Street was run by the British Women's Temperance Association. It began around 1899 but closed in 1906, possibly because the new purpose-built Sailors' Home in St Nicholas Street was due to open early in 1907.

SAILORS RETURN INN in Chapelhay Street may be the same as the Sailors Home Inn as both appear to be in the same street. The present Sailors Return pub is at No. 1 St Nicholas Street.

ST ALBANS, Duke of He had a property on the Esplanade, but accounts of where it stood differ. In 1790 he was *'permitted to erect a seat on the Esplanade, opposite his house, and also to make steps to the sands there'*. Historians Arthur Gill and Bryan Little suggest his house was built in 1782 (following the building of the Duke of Gloucester's house in 1780) and was in Charlotte Row, the building with colonnaded front which was to become Harvey's Library and Card Assembly in King George III's time, and the Royal Dorset Yacht Club in more recent years (it is currently a pub). William Bowes Barrett suggests the corner house of Clarence Buildings and St Alban Street where a Mr Warne, surgeon, later pulled down and rebuilt Nos. 11 and 12 (now the Clarence Hotel).

ST ANDREW'S CHURCH, Preston *see* PRESTON

ST ANDREW'S CofE VA School, Littlemoor Road opened September 1992.

ST AUBYN'S SCHOOL, No. 5, Carlton Road North A boarding and day school for girls founded 1919/1920, which moved in the 1940s to No. 63

Dorchester Road and closed around 1950. A house at No. 10 Abbotsbury Road was also known as St Aubyn's.

ST CHARLES RC CHURCH, Sunnyside Road, Wyke Regis The final Mass at the church was held on 18th June 2004 and the building was demolished in 2008. Houses are currently being built on the site. The church had opened on 10th May 1956.

ST JOHN'S COURT on the corner of Dorchester Road and William Street, stands on the site of St John's Schools, demolished in 1974. St John's Church of England VA Primary School relocated to Coombe Avenue in 1974.

ST JOHN'S GARDENS A shelter in the gardens was erected from money left by Dorothy Gray of Weymouth Bay Avenue *'as a thanksgiving for 40 years of residence in the beautiful surroundings of the borough'*. It was constructed in 1964. The gardens, on land given by Sir Frederic Johnstone, opened on 20th July 1904.

ST JOHN'S MISSION HOUSE, Chelmsford Street opened December 1892. In the latter part of the 20th century it became Park Church Centre and services are held there in conjunction with St John's Church.

ST MARY STREET, No. 18 The building on the corner of St Mary Street/Upper Bond Street was demolished in 1923 and replaced by the current HSBC bank (then the Midland Bank). The older building had housed draper and outfitter T. H. Williams and Sons.

ST MARY STREET, No. 45 This historic building was demolished in April 1883. It stood on the south side of Church Passage at its junction with St Mary Street. Dating from the 16th century, just a few architectural details were preserved and incorporated in the present building on the site.

ST NICHOLAS SCHOOL, Broadwey The school building stands almost opposite the Church on Dorchester

The old village school, Dorchester Road, Broadwey, now converted to housing.

Road. It was built in 1839 with additions in the late 19th and early 20th centuries. The school closed in 1972 and moved to new buildings on the same site as Wey Valley School, changing its name to St Nicholas and St Laurence School 'in 1976 when it accommodated pupils from the old village school of St Laurence at Upwey which closed that year.

SALADIN was a War Office balloon which flew over the Bridport cliffs in December 1881 and disappeared. On board was MP Walter Powell, whose body was never found.

SALT HOUSE *'once stood on the Coneygar'*, according to 18th century deeds. This was the land north of the town's main streets, later to be developed as the Esplanade.

SALT PANS John Benjamin Kerridge, writing in the 1850s observed *'The ravages made by the sea on the shore at Smallmouth have lately brought to light what is evidently one of the salt pans or salinae in use by ancients for the manufacture of salt. It is a circular trough 6 or 7 feet in diameter formed of well puddled clay it has two openings lined with slabs of Kimmeridge shale to a thickness of almost 2 inches, one of these channels being covered by a slab of similar material. The outer edge of the bourn sloped for about 2 feet until it reached the level of the ground. About 50 yards distant was uncovered some masonry, apparently of Saxon construction but unfortunately it was destroyed almost as soon as discovered and the stones carried away...'.* A later writer notes of the Smallmouth area *'in the winter of 1868-69 there was exposed an ancient salt pan...'*

SANDESFORT HOUSE was demolished in 2003. It was built as a private house and later became Thornlow Senior School, which closed in 1998. The school had added buildings, including a swimming pool, but the whole site was cleared and Sandsford Place and Thornlow Close flats and houses now fill it.

SANDFORT COTTAGES are listed in an 1891 Rate Book and are in the Park District.

SANDPIPER, HMS In September 1983 Weymouth 'adopted' the Navy ship *HMS Sandpiper*.

SANDSFOOT CASTLE'S 'BLACK CAT' The graffiti-ed 'Black Cat' or 'Old Nick the Devil' which can still just be seen high up on an inner wall of Sandsfoot Castle is believed to have been painted in the early 1920s by a local lad for a dare.

Further reading: *By-the-Wey, The Quarterly Newsletter of 'Friends of Weymouth Museum'*, May 2008, page 4.

SANDSFOOT CASTLE *Additions to the main entry in Bumper Book I*

The bridge between the gardens and the castle earthworks was replaced in the autumn of 2007 – *see* SANDS-

Sandesfort House stood at the junction of Buxton Road and Rylands Lane.

Sandsfoot Castle ruins have always been a popular subject with artists…

…and provide a good spot for an outing or picnic.

FOOT GARDENS. In December 2008 it was reported that the Castle was urgently in need of restoration work.

The stonework shown here near the cliff edge has long since tumbled into the sea.

SANDSFOOT COVE 'WRECK' Some boat-shaped timbers lying half buried at the base of the steps leading down to Sandsfoot Cove were often referred to as the 'wreck'. They were the remains of one of the old torpedo targets in Portland Harbour which came ashore in a gale many years ago.

SANDSFOOT GARDENS The Tudor-style ornamental gardens were laid out in front of the Castle in 1931 and a shelter was added in 1964, funded by his wife in memory of John C. Talbot, who enjoyed the gardens. Weymouth-born, he was the auctioneer and estate agent who once occupied offices at Statue House. The shelter has since been replaced by a café. A new oak timber footbridge spans the lower level footpath at the Gardens, a previous softwood footbridge having rotted away. It links the Castle with the gardens and opened on 15th November 2007.

SAPSWORTHS OF WEYMOUTH The firm started with a shop in Westham Road in 1939, moving to Great George Street in 1947. In May 1948 the food factory was established at Camp Road, Wyke Regis and at the same time the firm amalgamated with local butcher Lawson Jones. Fresh meat and manufactured meat products were distributed over a wide area. The factory was in 'Bridge Close' now at the end of Mandeville Road. Currently (2009) Value House store.

SCOOTERS May Day Holiday weekend scooter rallies at Weymouth were organised by the National Scooter Rallies Association in the early 1980s.

SCOURCE, Alfred Weymouth scrap merchant who died in 1961 following a fall from his horse while hunting. Born at Wyke Regis, he spent his early years farming at Park Mead Farm. In 1923 he opened a scrap car business in Putton Lane and in 1938 opened a garage in Benville Road, Lanehouse, later known as Fiveways Garage.

SCOUTS The new HQ of the 9th Weymouth (Holy Trinity) Scout Group opened in February 1955 in the grounds of the Sidney Hall. The hut is long gone, the Sidney Hall and buildings around it being demolished in 1987 to make way for the supermarket at the foot of Boot Hill. The Scout Hut in Radipole Lane opened 26th September 1959, HQ of the 1st Radipole Scouts.

SCUTT MEMORIAL HALL at Preston opened in December 1909 in memory of the late Mr Charles Scutt, JP of Wyke Oliver Farm who drowned on Lodmoor the previous year.

SEA FESTIVAL *see* WEYMOUTH SEA FESTIVAL

SEALS Seals still exist which were used by the boroughs of Weymouth and Melcombe Regis dating back to mediaeval times.

One of the borough seals – this one belonged to Melcombe, long before the union of the two towns.

SELWAY TERRACE (Nos. 1-6) was owned by Henry J. Selway and was in Prince of Wales Road.

SEWARD, Edwin, FRIBA The architect of numerous important public buildings in South Wales where he lived in Cardiff from 1869-1915. Not Weymouth-born, but he retired here in 1915 and died at No. 12 Victoria Terrace on 21st June 1924. No family link has as yet been traced to Weymouth photographer Edwin Seward (1877-1954).

SEYMER STREET seems to be an alternative name for Seymour Street. Seymers were in business in the town in the 18th century.

SHAMBLES Mentions of the Shambles go back to the 16th and 17th centuries. On the Weymouth side of the

The Shambles in Melcombe would have been outside the Guildhall – this is the predecessor of the current building on the same site in St Edmund Street.

harbour the Shambles adjoined the Town Hall and in Melcombe, the Guildhall. The name 'shambles' originally defined a market area where fish and meat were sold.

SHARRAW BUILDINGS are Nos. 66-77 Dorchester Road.

SHEARS ROAD runs from No. 43 Beaumont Avenue to No. 66 Weymouth Bay Avenue.

SHELTON, Anne appeared at the Alexandra Gardens Theatre, summer 1960.

SHEMARA The 1000-ton luxury yacht of Sir Bernard and Lady Docker was in Weymouth in May 1956.

SHEPHARD, Brigadier General Gordon Strachy, DSO, MC (died 1918) Of the Royal Flying Corps. A distinguished flying ace in the early days of aviation. The Shephard family once owned Shortlake House at Osmington. In its grounds stands a memorial cross to Shephard, who died on 19th January 1918 when attempting to land his plane in France, where he is buried. The cross is in the form of an aircraft propeller. The house at Osmington is now a children's holiday activity centre. The wording of the cross spells the surname incorrectly as Sheppard, so perhaps it was repainted at some time in almost 100 years since his death.

SHEPPARD, Brigadier General Gordon Strachy, DSO, MC (the spelling is incorrect) *see* SHEPHARD

SHEPSTONE'S GARAGE on Dorchester Road at Upwey is now Wey Valley Mazda, the Shepstone family having retired in 1970, when the business was acquired by Win Percy, international motor racing enthusiast and British saloon car champion in 1981.

SHERBORNE TERRACE is now Nos. 23-28, Chapelhay Street.

SHERRICK'S STEPS are difficult to locate. They appear to have led from High West Street down to North Quay.

SHIELDHALL Steamship which is a regular visitor to Weymouth owned and operated entirely by volunteers and often open to the public. Built in 1955 by Lobnitz and Co. of Renfrew for Glasgow Corporation to carry effluent out to sea for dumping. Sold in 1977 to Southern Water based in Southampton. Sold in 1988 to The Solent Steam Packet Ltd, a group of preservationists. Length 268', breadth 44'.7", draught 13' 4".

SHIP INNS and SHIP ALEHOUSES not surprisingly abound in Weymouth. Today's town pub of the name is on the corner of Maiden Street and Custom House Quay. In the 17th century there was a Ship Inn in St Mary Street. A Ship Alehouse on the north side of High Street, on the Weymouth side of the harbour was known successively as the Queens Head Alehouse, the Prince Frederick, the Prince's Head Alehouse, and the Ship Alehouse before becoming a private dwelling. There was Ship Inn at the west end of Radipole village and the Ship Inn at Upwey is now known as the Old Ship. Preston's Ship Inn is now the Spice Ship. Most unfortunate of all was the Ship Inn at Shrubbery Lane, Wyke Regis where bombs fell on 28th June 1942 demolishing the pub and killing five people, including the landlord's wife.

The present 'Spice Ship' pub at Preston under its former name.

SHORT, John Joseph Rolls Found guilty in December 1902 in a lengthy commercial fraud case which involved the collapse of five well-known City firms with liabilities of £300,000 and assets of £15,000. Of 8 defendants, 6 were acquitted but Short and another man were found guilty on two counts, one on the general conspiracy charge, the other of obtaining an advance on false pretences. Sentenced to 9 months imprisonment. Short had been a bank manager in Weymouth and a stone quarry agent at Portland.

SHOWNIGHT *see* VICTORIAN SHOWTIME

SIDDONS, Sarah Great tragic actress of the Georgian era. She came to Weymouth to liven up the performances at the Theatre Royal on Weymouth Esplanade where the entertainment at the time *'was quite in the barn style; a mere medley – songs, dances, imitations – and all very bad'*. Unfortunately, the great tragedienne turned her hand to comedy at Weymouth without much success. Said Fanny Burney in her diary of the Royal visit to Weymouth in 1789 *'She looked too large for that shepherd's dress'.*

SIGRIST, Frederick Millionaire who made his fortune in the Hawker-Siddeley aircraft industry. He lived in Weymouth as a child and was educated at Henry Roger's **Weymouth Commercial School** in Frederick Place in the 1890s. His father was an insurance company's superintendent, and the family lived in East Street. Frederick's daughter 'Bobo' Sigrist made headlines when she eloped to marry Gregg Juarez in January 1957.

SILLY HOW FARM was in the Fleet area. 'How' being the name for a piece of plough land and 'Silly' a surname in the parish registers for the district.

SILVER STREET on North Quay, Weymouth was demolished in the 1930s. There is also a Silver Street in Sutton Poyntz.

SKATE US Atomic submarine. Arrived at Portland 5th March 1958 having made the fastest ever crossing from the USA to Europe. Also here in 1960.

SLAPTON SANDS *see* EXERCISE TIGER

SMITH, Frederick Sefton (1857-1924) Proprietor of the Burdon Hotel (now the Prince Regent Hotel) for more than 30 years. Mayor in 1908-09.

SMITH, William Johnson, MD (died 12/4/1885) Founder member of the British Gynaecological Society. Nephew of **Sir Edward Johnson**. Graduated at Edinburgh in 1842. In Weymouth he appealed for funds to set up a hospital for women, despite his uncle's opinion that he would be would make himself unpopular with all the medical men in the town and wouldn't manage to raise a penny towards the hospital – he proved Sir Edward wrong and his uncle subsequently donated to the fund. Smith opened the Weymouth Sanatorium in Clarence Buildings in 1848, moving to larger premises there in 1863. The Sanatorium closed in 1902 when a new hospital was built in Melcombe Avenue.

SMITH'S COURT (Nos 1-3) was between Nos. 21 and 22 New Street.

SMUGGLERS INN at Osmington was formerly the Picnic Inn. It was known in earlier times as the Crown Inn.

SNUG CORNER *see* ROWE, John G.

SOCIETY OF FRIENDS A rental of 1732 suggests that a house in Maiden Street was 'late the Quakers meeting house'

An early picture of the Smugglers Inn at Osmington Mills, then known as the Picnic Inn and much extended since.

SOCKETTY HOCK was a farm name in the Fleet area. Believed to derive from sock, an Anglo-Saxon word for plough.

SOMERSET HOUSE, No. 8 Greenhill is now the Greenhill Hotel. Nos. 8-16 were formerly known as Somerset Place.

SOUSA'S BAND played at the Jubilee Hall in the early 1900s.

SOUTH BELFIELD, No. 60 Buxton Road is the former stable and coach house of Belfield House.

SOUTH DORSET TRADES MINERAL WATER COMPANY LTD. Founded in 1903 by a group of local licensees to produce mineral waters and soft drinks. Known as SDT. First premises were in Edward Street, now the site of the Bus Garage. Moved the factory to Nos. 31-33 Holly Road in 1923.

SOUTH PARADE COURT Nos. 1-7, Elma Cottage, Flora Cottage in South Parade Court and other unoccupied houses in the Court were closed as unfit for habitation in February 1912 until made fit for the purpose.

SOUTH VIEW, All Saints Road, Wyke Regis A popular house name, also used at No. 44 Abbotsbury Road and No. 91 Newstead Road.

SOUTHAMPTON was a Royal Navy frigate on duty at Weymouth for royal pleasure and protection when King George III holidayed here 1789-1805.

SOUTHBROOK, No. 26 Church Street, Upwey Dates from c.1820, possibly a rebuild of an earlier farmhouse. One of an impressive group of four properties built around the junction of Stottingway and Church Street — **Eastbrook, Westbrook,** Southbrook and **Upwey Manor.**

SOUTHERN NATIONAL GARAGE, Chickerell Road, Charlestown Formerly the Greyhound bus company's garage, it was used by Southern National following an air raid of 21st October 1940 on the Edward Street bus garage. It was sold in 1959 to Universal Engineering but when the company relocated to the Granby Industrial Estate its premises were demolished and now the houses of Lloyd Terrace fill the site.

SOUTHFIELD VILLAS are in Alexandra Road.

SOUTHILL Radipole and Southill Community Association's Hall was opened early in 1958. It was replaced in 1974.

SOUTHILL PRIMARY SCHOOL, Sycamore Road opened in 1973.

SOUTHLANDS ESTATE Dates from the 1930s. The builder was K. Openshaw.

SOWERBY, James (1757-1822) A botanical artist of the 18th century who is thought to have painted at least one view of Weymouth.

SPA CRESCENT was at the end of King's Road Radipole, west side, and has since been renumbered as King's Road.

SPA HOTEL, Dorchester Road, Radipole was built in the 1890s and in recent years has been renamed The Old Spa.

SPA HOUSE, on the corner of Spa Road and Dorchester Road, Radipole These were tea rooms and a shop in the former Pig and Whistle public house, which was renamed the Bridge Inn before its conversion to a café in around 1912. Now a takeaway.

SPA TERRACE is in Spa Road.

SPEAR HEDGE An old Radipole place name: *'a part of Radipole parish, contained within a line drawn from the Old Sluice to the Spear Hedge and along the Spear Hedge to the Backwater has also been considered within the borough...'* Vagrants were once ordered to be flogged out of town *'...as far as a gate which is situated at Radipole, at the Spear Hedge...'*

SPIES Henry Christian William Schutte had lived in Weymouth for a number of years and worked at Weymouth cargo stage. He was arrested in August 1914 and charged with conveying information to an enemy which might be of use to that enemy. See *also* RUTLAND, Frederick J.

SPIRIT a local pilot cutter which sank on 15th January 1910 after being hit by Danish steamer *St Ian.* James Zelley, serving as an extra hand, was drowned.

SPIRIT OF THE SEA A nine-day festival first held in Weymouth and Portland, 5th-12th July 2008.

SPRAGUE BROTHERS of Upwey Sons of Edward Sprague, an Upwey miller. Of his six children, three sailed for America in 1628 or 1629 – Ralph, Richard and William. Ralph was accompanied by his wife Joanna and two small sons. They settled in Massachusetts in the what later came to be known as Charlestown.

SPRING BOTTOM INN was at Sutton Poyntz.

SPRING COTTAGES are in Church Street, Upwey.

SPRING PLACE was the first terrace of houses to be built in Rodwell Avenue, at the Hope Square end. Now Nos. 2-14 Rodwell Avenue.

SPRINGFIELD NURSERIES were in Holly Road, Westham in the early 1900s.

Mr Charles Robert Clay, first landlord of the Springhead Hotel, Sutton Poyntz, surrounded by his family.

SPRINGFIELD TERRACE (Nos. 1-14) is now Nos. 58-88 Chickerell Road. In the 1901 Census the enumerator's sequence is: Prince of Wales Road, Ilton Terrace, Selway Terrace, North View, Melrose Terrace, Chickerell Road, Lilac Cottage on the Marsh, Coburg Terrace, Fermain Terrace, Lulworth Terrace, Springfield Terrace and 16 houses at the back of Lulworth Terrace, Arch Terrace and cottages, south side of Town Lane.

SPRINGHEAD HOTEL, Sutton Poyntz The first landlord was Charles Robert Clay (1851-1902), who was the licensee from 1898-1902. He died there 22nd May 1902. After Army service, Charles Clay went into farming and then the pub trade when agriculture declined. His death certificate records him as being Licensee and Veterinary Surgeon and he died from heart trouble shortly after being called out to treat a sick animal.

SPROULE, Andrew Already well established as a builder in Bath, Sproule clearly saw development possibilities in Weymouth once the town began to establish itself as a health and pleasure resort. Fashionable visitors looking for places to stay wanted somewhere which was a cut above the inns and lodging houses of a coastal port. In 1770 he applied to lease a piece of land on what was *'formerly called the Coneygar and afterwards Townsend, Townsend's Field or Townsend's Ground'*. This land would have extended northwards from where the Masonic Hall stands in St Thomas Street today and was where the future Esplanade terraces

would be built. Sproule planned to build his hotel on this empty land facing the Bay: he realised that visitors would prefer to overlook the sea rather than the streets of the town, and also that they would require convenient Assembly Rooms in which to socialise within the building. He tried to acquire quite a large area of land but was allowed to build on less than half of the ground he originally requested.

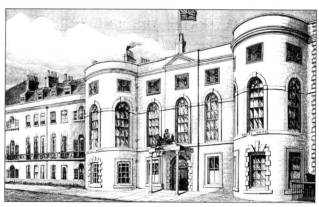

The first 'Royal Hotel' built by Andrew Sproule of Bath.

Perhaps the Corporation was also realising that the town's future expansion might be along the seafront, although no-one at this stage, in the days before the Duke of Gloucester built his residence and King George III made Weymouth famous, could have realised just how important 'The Esplanade' would become. Sproule built his hotel, which opened in 1773. It was known initially as Stacie's Hotel after its first manager, but became the 'Royal Hotel' when the Duke of Gloucester's house was built close by. It was an elegant building, bow fronted, with a ballroom where *'a hundred couples could dance with ease'*. Sadly, the hotel, which became the centre of the town's social life in the Georgian period, was allowed to become run down in the late 19th century and was demolished in 1891. An untidy seafront site remained empty for six years as plans for a new hotel came and went, and it was 1897 before the foundation stone of the present Royal Hotel was laid.

SQUASH CENTRE Newstead Road was officially opened on 11th September 1981.

SQUIRE'S KNAP is the area of Preston Road just beyond Overcombe Corner.

STAGG, James One of Westham's earliest residents, Mr Stagg lived in a house on wheels in what became Abbotsbury Road. It must have been quite a substantial property as he put it up for sale in October, 1895, when it was described as *'Hampden Place. Mr James Stagg's garden, portable dwelling house, vinery or tomato house heated with hot water and outbuildings on a quarter of an acre, walled on all sides… Bounded on the west by the new church in course of erection {St Paul's Church} 63½ foot frontage to the road and a prime building site'*.

STANDARD COTTAGES were in Laurel Lane, Broadwey.

STAR COFFEE HOUSE was in King Street in the 1860s.

STAR INN Today's Star Inn stands on the corner of Gloucester Street and Park Street but a 17th century Star Inn was on the other side of the harbour, probably in the High Street/North Quay area.

STATUE HOUSE. *Correction to the entry in Bumper Book I:*
   Statue House at the end of Johnstone Row and its companion at the start of Coburg Place were transposed in *Bumper Book I.* The entry should read: Statue House and its companion at the entrance to the town's main streets were built to plans Sir William Pulteney had put forward in 1802. His death in 1805 probably delayed the project and Johnstone Row was not built until 1812, finished with Statue House, the 'round house', which has been little altered. This was once known as 'Croydens Corner', as Victorian shop proprietor and auctioneer R. H. Croyden's name was emblazoned in large letters high up on the building. More recently, Statue House will be remembered as a model railway emporium but since 1982 it has been a café. Its companion building at the end of Coburg Place dates from a little later and in 1815 paupers living in almshouses on the site (built, but not endowed by Sir James Thornhill) were evicted so the area could be re-developed. This action was questioned by some who wanted to know how Pulteney and subsequently the Johnstone Estate, had acquired the property. Nevertheless

Coburg Place was built as was the 'round house' to match Statue House, although this building has been much altered at street level with plate glass shop windows. It is perhaps interesting to note that Statue House was up for sale in 1965 and there were proposals to put a preservation order on it but these were rejected, councillors describing the building as *'Hideous, an eyesore and a broken down relic of a bygone age'.* Fortunately opinions change and this fine building is now Grade II* listed.

Statue House in its 'Model Railway' days.

STEPHEN STREET is mentioned in 17th century town records, but not located.

STEPHENSON, Humphrey Meigh MRCS, LRCP, MC, BA. Born in Weymouth 1882. Author of *Death in the Deep, Three Missing Partners'* and other works of fiction.

STEPHENSON, Major General Theodore Edward was given a civic reception on his return from the fighting in South Africa, 28th March 1903 and also granted the Freedom of the Borough. He was Weymouth-born, the son of the Reverend Canon Stephenson of St John's Church.

STEWARD FAMILY Influential in local politics in the 18th century, at a time when only freeholders were able to vote and ownership of property was a deciding and corrupting factor in election results. Gabriel Steward (1731-1792) was an East India Company captain who settled in Weymouth. He came into property by his marriage to the

Nottington House, the Steward family home. Built in 1817, now demolished.

The former entrance to the house in Nottington Lane. Nottington Court flats have since been built here.

niece of local man John Tucker. Tucker had been left property in Weymouth by George Bubb Dodington and had added to it, but he died without heirs and his property went to his brother, whose daughter inherited it and thus it passed to her husband Gabriel Steward. Steward also purchased a large amount of local property from William Chafin Grove. In 1790, two years before his death, Steward sold all his local property to Sir William Pulteney and he, too, added to it and was able to control the affairs of the borough to a large extent. This became known as the Johnstone Estate (*see* JOHNSTONE, Sir Frederic). Gabriel Steward and his sons Gabriel Tucker Steward and Richard Tucker Steward all represented the town in Parliament and were Mayors at various times. Richard Tucker Steward built Nottington House in 1817. The Stewards are also known to have owned a house in St Thomas Street where they entertained the Prince of Wales (later King George IV) when he visited Weymouth, possibly preferring it to Gloucester Lodge, the residence of his strait-laced and disapproving father King George III. This house is described as a '*Mansion house, outhouses, stables and garden in St Thomas Street, west side...*', but its location has not been established. Late 19th-century historian William Bowles Barrett suggested two possible sites – the present No. 67 St Thomas Street, where the Post Office is today, or a larger site, the present Nos. 73-76, now premises adjacent to and including the present Natwest Bank, also all of much later date.

A glimpse on the far left hand side of the photograph of one of the buildings suggested as the Stewards house in Weymouth – demolished in 1920 when the Post Office was extended.

STEWART-SMITH, Lionel was the architect of the Riviera Hotel and had a practice at No. 9 Royal Terrace, Esplanade in the 1930s.

STOCKS The use of stocks as a punishment died out in mid-nineteenth century. This uncomfortable and humiliating form of punishment was meted out in earlier centuries for a variety of minor crimes. In 1616 a local man, J. Luke, was condemned to sit in the stocks for six hours for stealing three quarts of train oil [whale oil]. Two years later three of the town's watchmen who were found sleeping on their watch had to sit in the stocks for *'one hour and upwards'*. In January 1704 J. Parker *'swore four oaths'* and was *'sate in the stocks'* as a punishment.

STONE PIER *Addition to main entry in Bumper Book I:*

Probably lost to view when later work was carried out on the Stone Pier, a commemorative stone was laid in 1877 when extensions to the pier were completed. On the upper surface of the stone was the following inscription:

Weymouth Breakwater Extension. This Stone, in commemoration of the valuable assistance rendered by H. Edwards, Esq., M. P., was laid by John Lundie, Esq., Mayor, December 5 1877. J. Jackson, Contractor. W. B. Morgan, Engineer. R. Greenwood, Weymouth.

The *Southern Times* added a historical note *'The extension of the Breakwater for the protection of the harbour during easterly gales is erected on the rubble ground first deposited in 1827, under the direction of the late Sir J. Cubitt...'* More extension work was carried out the following year.

Work in progress – extending the Stone Pier, 1877.

STOPES, Marie (1880-1958) The birth control pioneer was a regular visitor to this area from the 1920s to the 1950s having bought Portland Higher Lighthouse as a holiday home. She sold it early in 1958.

STREET NAMES The Weymouth Telegram reported in June 1861 *'Weymouth is following the example of all other towns in having the names of the streets written up at the corners. Our wonder is that so necessary and important a work has not been done years ago.'*

SUBMARINE INCIDENTS AND LOSSES In the days when Portland was a submarine base there were occasional collisions and several losses. Among them on 10th January 1924 submarine *L.24* was lost with all hands after colliding with *HMS Resolution*. The same day two submarines *K2* and *K12* collided and suffered damage, but there was no loss of life. On the morning of 5th November that year *K22,* formerly *K13,* struck rocks near the Breakwater and was not refloated until the evening. No lives were lost, but as *K13* she had previously sunk in the Clyde and on that occasion not all her crew were saved. In January 1932 *M2*, a seaplane-carrying submarine, dived off Portland and never resurfaced, being lost with all hands. Her sister ship *M1*, equipped with a huge gun, had been lost off Start Point in 1925 after a blow from a merchant ship. A catastrophic explosion on board the *Sidon*, moored alongside the depot ship *Maidstone* in Portland Harbour in 1955, led to the loss of thirteen lives. In 1956 submarine *Scorcher* collided with a merchant ship but made it home, although damaged. The *Thule* was damaged in naval exercise in November 1960, *Odin* hit the seabed and returned with a damaged rudder in 1962, and *Tiptoe* was in a collision in 1965. A Dutch submarine, the *Tijgerhaai*, went aground on sand about a mile and a quarter off shore in Weymouth Bay in a gale on 19th October 1955. She refloated on the flood tide.

There were also incidents of a less serious nature. In 1932 during Weymouth Hospitals Carnival, submarine *H33* was moored in Weymouth Harbour and could be visited but she got stuck fast when the tide went out and had to be towed off by tugs from Portland. The paddle steamer *Premier* had a brush with a submarine that year when she was rammed by *HMS Rainbow,* fortunately without injury to her passengers and crew. The next year saw a dummy submarine being towed around Weymouth waters by the *Premier* during the making of the film *Jack Ahoy.* A replica submarine of a more serious nature was made at **Tod's** in 1940. Built in wood

Submarine M2 *lost in 1932.*

and a perfect copy above the waterline, it was moored in Portland Harbour and was realistic enough to be attacked by Luftwaffe planes. *See also* U-BOATS

SUBWAYS The old subway under the Weymouth and Portland Railway at Littlefield Crossing, Abbotsbury Road, opened 16th September 1922 and closed in 1985. The current Westham subways date from 1985 during the construction of Weymouth Way and the Swannery Bridge in the 1980s. Steven Jurado painted the murals on the subways at the Swannery, Esplanade and Manor Round-about. He was presented with an award by Weymouth Civic Society, offered to young people for original public art, in 2008.

SUEZ CRISIS 1956 saw army vehicles on Chesil Beach car park prior to being loading into a tank landing craft at Castletown bound for the Mediterranean area.

SUMMERCLOSE GARDENS and **SUMMERCLOSE PLACE** became part of Dorchester Road, Broadwey.

SUN FISH A specimen was found off Portland Cove in June 1846. 6 feet 6 inches long, it was displayed at Portland and Weymouth.

SUN INN The Sun Inn today stands at the junction of King Street and Crescent Street but earlier Sun Inns existed on the Quay in Melcombe in the 17th century and in High Street, Weymouth in the 1700s.

SUNNYBANK HOUSE AND STABLES John B. Cole was a local jeweller and builder of houses in Stavordale Road where he lived in a house and grounds known as Sunnybank, which he sold to the Council in October 1901 as a site for the town's electricity generating station. It appears that the council already had an interest in Sunnybank as they had set up stables there in order that the town could carry out its own street watering, haulage and scavenging. More permanent stable blocks followed in 1903. These were the beginnings of many years of use as the Corporation Yard off Westwey Road (since relocated to Crook Hill, Chickerell). The last of the horses employed there left in 1949, two men of the same family having worked with them since 1903, Jack Davis succeeding his father.

SUNNYSIDE COTTAGES are in Sutton Road, Sutton Poyntz. Also in Hope Street, Weymouth.

SUPERMARKET Weymouth's first supermarket, Maypole, Ltd. opened 28th May 1963 at Nos. 72/73, St Mary Street. In the same street three years later smaller grocers Pearks and Liptons closed, transferring business to the Maypole store, all three being owned by the same company.

SUTTON POYNTZ. CHURCH At Sutton Poyntz there was once a chapel of ease to Preston, but only traces remain – a few bits of architecture incorporated into the old school building of 1867.

Sutton Poyntz – a view from the 1920s.

SUTTON POYNTZ. COURT HOUSE Long after it ceased to have any judicial role, in later years when the villages of Preston and Sutton Poyntz became the property of the Weld estate, this was the estate office. The Welds held a big auction sale of their holdings in Preston and Sutton Poyntz in 1925 to pay substantial death duties (*see* PRESTON). The building was severely damaged in the Sutton Poyntz fire of 18th April 1908.

SUTTON POYNTZ. FIRE The fire broke out on 18th April 1908 and gutted a number of buildings – almost a quarter of a mile of them on one side of the street – before it was brought under control.

SUTTON POYNTZ. POND It is hard to believe today but the cottages beside the mill pond were dilapidated and unsightly in the 1960s and the pond itself was weed choked, smelly and mosquito ridden.

SUTTON POYNTZ. WATERWORKS Here was installed part of the funnel of Brunel's *Great Eastern* steamship after a tremendous explosion blew it out of the ship when she was on her acceptance trials in the Channel in 1859. It served as a filter until 2005 when it was no longer required. It has since been taken to the *Great Britain* site at Bristol.

SUTTON ROAD EVANGELICAL FELLOWSHIP Originally met in the 1930s in a room in a house in Seven Acres Road, known as the Gospel Room, and then moved to the Preston Gospel Hall in Sutton Road which was renamed the Sutton Road Evangelical Fellowship.

SUTTON'S Grocers A long-established grocery and bakery business which was founded in 1878 in Governor's Lane. By the 1890s the grocery business had moved to No. 22 St Alban Street and in 1916 moved again to No. 6 St Alban Street. Now run as a coffee shop, Suttons still has its distinctive shop fascia.

'SWALLOWS REST' *see* RIDGEWAY

SWAN INN, No 567, Dorchester Road, Broadwey Now closed, the pub is a late 18th century rebuild of an earlier structure. There was also a Swan Inn in Chamberlaine Road, Wyke Regis. Today's town centre Swan Inn at the lower end of St Thomas Street takes its name from an earlier pub on the site.

SWEETE LANE was another name for Buxton's Lane, and may indicate all or part of the present day Cross Road and Buxton Road between Cross Road and Foord's Corner.

SYMES LANE was an alternative name for Boot Hill.

Weymouth Fire Engine at the Sutton Poyntz fire, 18th April 1908.

Tamarisk Court

T

TAMARISK COURT Stavordale Road takes its name from the Tamarisk Hotel formerly on the site.

TAR BOAT A regular visitor to Weymouth's gasworks on Westwey Road was the *LIDO*, which moored in the Inner Harbour and collected tar via a pipe under Westwey Road. The tar, some 150,000 gallons a year, was a by-product of the gasworks and was sold for road dressings.

TELEPHONE EXCHANGE The National Telephone Company's Exchange opened in Weymouth in 1887 with its office at No. 55 St Thomas Street. The first automatic exchange was opened on 15th December 1966 and it was replaced by the present electronic exchange in June 1984, officially opened on 5th July 1984.

TELERECTION Elliott's factory buildings, Lynch Lane were taken over by television aerial manufacturers Telerection Ltd., of Cheltenham in 1959.

TEMPERANCE HALL, Broadwey was built in 1878. Now No. 619, Dorchester Road.

TEMPERANCE HALL, Park Street The Temperance Society took over the Park Street premises in April 1861.

TEMPLEMAN'S MILL *see* HELEN LANE in this volume and TEMPLEMAN, Thomas John (1848-1919) in *Bumper Book I*

TERRITORIALS An advert in the local press in April 1887 appealed for recruits for a new battery of the 2nd Volunteer (Dorset) Brigade, Southern Division, Royal Artillery. The battery formed was a unit of the Hants and Dorset Volunteer Artillery. From this originated the local TA unit known in recent years as R Battery of the 250 (Queen's Own Dorset and West Somerset Yeomanry) Medium Regiment, Royal Artillery, but the unit underwent many name changes before that, although the local HQ was always in Weymouth, at the Drill Hall in Lower St Alban Street, built in 1891. The 'citizen army' came into its own in the Transvaal War with Volunteers being asked to go out on active service and a number of these men were granted the Freedom of the Borough in recognition of their time in South Africa. On the election of a new government in 1906 the Volunteer Force became known as the Territorial Army. In World War I the local units landed in France in 1915 and were engaged in heavy action, a significant number of men being decorated. More volunteers were called for in the late 1930s and as the international situation worsened the Dorset Heavy Brigade RA (TA) was called out for service. Volunteers formed Nos. 1 and 3 Super Heavy Batterys, RA. Both went out to France in 1940 and distinguished themselves before being evacuated from Dunkirk. In 1947 there was another reorganisation and the Dorset force became 421 (Dorset) Coast Regiment, RA (TA) amalgamating with the West Somerset Yeomanry in 1957 as 255 (West Somerset and Dorset Garrison, Medium Rgt RA (T). (R Battery, Weymouth). As R Battery of the 250 (Queen's Own Dorset and West Somerset Yeomanry) Medium Regiment, Royal Artillery the regiment was granted the Freedom of the Borough in 1966. A year later the Territorial Army became the Territorial and Army Volunteer Reserve. The Drill Hall site is now filled with the flats of Beaufort Garden Mews and Martello Mews, as the TA is no longer Weymouth-based.

THOMAS, Leslie His novel *Bare Nell*, published by Eyre Methuen in 1977 has scenes set in Weymouth.

THOMAS, Rowland, JP (1815-1903) A Bridport man who took on a bakery and confectionery business formerly owned by Peter Green at premises in Bond Street which later became the London Hotel (currently a pub called the Twenty Twelve Bar), subsequently transferring to the premises known as the **Red House** in Bond Street. Mr Thomas was one of those who took action when the gasworks run by Burdon were providing inadequate supplies of gas for lighting the town and he was a prime mover in setting up a Limited Liability Company to purchase the Gas Works from Burdon. He became the first chairman of the Weymouth Gas Consumers Company in 1867. On the Council for many years, he was Mayor in 1884 (and for a short time in 1894 when Sir Richard Nicholas Howard became Town Clerk and stepped down from mayoralty).

THOMSON LOCAL DIRECTORIES for the West Dorset area commenced publication in 1982.

THORNHILL in Broadwey was originally a small farm.

THREE MARINERS pub was at Chickerell.

THRESHER FAMILY *see* CORFE HILL HOUSE

THRESHER'S COURT appears to have been in New Street or East Street in the 19th century.

THUNDERCAT RACING The Weymouth Thundercat event, high speed powerboat racing, began in October, 2006.

THURMAN, Michael Jerrard (1822 -1906) Ran an ironmongery business at No. 68 St Thomas Street. On his death in 1906 the premises were sold but the business continued under the Thurman name until 1967 when the whole building was demolished and rebuilt, with the condition that above street level the façade had to exactly match the original, using the dismantled stonework. At ground level plate glass took over. Currently (2009) Iceland store.

The long-established ironmonger in St Thomas Street – street level windows have now been replaced with plate glass.

TILLEYS Having taken over the business of W. Cogle at **Alexandra House** on the Esplanade in 1901, Tilleys built up a large cycle business and were to stay in these premises as a garage until 1943 when they transferred to Frederick Place. In 1907 the firm opened a large new purpose-built garage 'Tilleys County Garage' in Victoria Street, designed by local architect Alfred J. Bennett. The garage was requisitioned for war work in the early 1940s by Westland Aircraft. Wadham Stringer later took over the garage but it closed in 1982 and was demolished. Flats went up on the site in 1984. In the 1950s the firm also had a car showroom at No. 60 St Thomas Street.

TIMOTHY WHITES AND TAYLORS LTD was a hardware store chain once to be found in High Streets throughout the country. In Weymouth the shop originally occupied Nos. 81 and 82 St Mary Street and No. 24 St Thomas Street, now Boots walk-through shop, the two having swapped premised in 1980. Relocated at Nos. 69 and 70 St Mary Street, it was announced that Timothy Whites would close in March 1984.

TITANIC The best-known Weymouth survivor of the *Titanic* disaster on 14th/15th April 1912 was crew member George T. M. Symons, whose parents lived in Franchise Street. He was the lookout in the crows nest at the time the iceberg was sighted. His evidence regarding the actions of those in the lifeboat he manned following the sinking was controversial at the time and is still discussed today. His fellow crewman in the lookout was Frederick Fleet, not a local man, but well-known in Weymouth. He, too, was saved. Men with local connections who drowned were steward Percy Deslandes, whose parents lived in Victoria Street; R. G. Smith and P. P. Ward, also stewards. Richard Otter, son of the late Mr W. H. Otter of Avalanche Road, Portland, was a second class passenger travelling back to America after visiting friends on Portland: he drowned.

TIZARD, Captain Thomas Henry, CB, FRS, RN (1839-1924) Hydrographer and oceanographer. Born in Weymouth. Navigating officer on *HMS Challenger* during her epoch-making round the world expedition in 1872-76. Assistant Hydrographer to the Navy 1891 until his 1907 retirement, after which he continued to do work for the Admiralty, producing tide tables for the English coast. Son of Joseph Tizard of Weymouth, well known coal merchant.

TOBACCO HOUSE A house on the north side of Petticoat Lane was known as the Tobacco House in 1759.

TOD, W & J, Boatbuilders, Ferrybridge, Wyke Regis The firm was founded in the 1930s. During WW2 Tod's switched from pleasure craft to producing numerous small motor vessels, survey and harbour launches, motor cutters and assault landing craft for the Admiralty and Air Ministry. One job in 1940 was a dummy submarine of the 'S' class, built in wood and a perfect replica from the water-line up. In Portland Harbour it looked like the real thing and was attacked by Luftwaffe planes as such. Assault craft built at Tod's were among the first to be used by British naval forces in Norway, Sicily and the famous Lofoten Islands raid and were used in every theatre of operations from Europe to the Pacific. In the 1950s the firm were very successful in producing glass fibre craft and the P&O Liner *Oronsay* came into Weymouth Bay in 1957 to pick up a prototype glass fibre lifeboat for trials- so successful that 20 were ordered for the liner *Oriana* launched in 1959. The Wyke yard closed in 2002, by then having moved on to other fibreglass products and the houses known as 'Tod's Yard' now fill the site, built 2008-2009.

TORPEDOES occasionally went astray during local trials. In 1933 a 30-feet long Admiralty torpedo leapt through the sea and ended up on Greenhill Beach with its propellers still running, from whence it was speedily collected by Admiralty tugs, fortunately without damaging anyone. Quite a few local people remember similar incidents when torpedoes went off course during test runs.

TOWN BRIDGE A pictorial survey

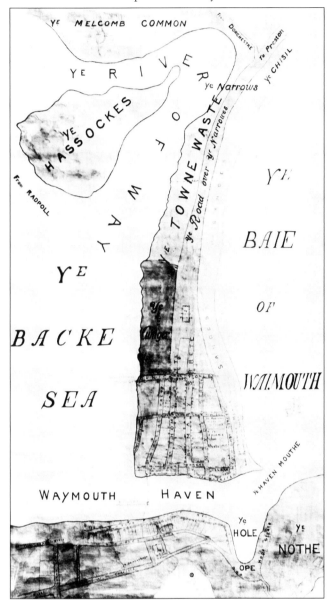

In 1770 a new Town Bridge was built, again in timber, but on a site west of the traditional one at the end of St Thomas Street. This one crossed the harbour at the end of St Nicholas Street, a move which slightly enlarged the Outer Harbour but was not popular with the townspeople.

Weymouth in Tudor times, when only a ferry boat crossed the harbour between Weymouth and Melcombe Regis.

1824 brought the opening of the first stone Town Bridge, reverting to the St Thomas Street site.

The first Town Bridge of 1597, a conjectural reconstruction from contemporary descriptions by Eric Ricketts. Constructed of timber and with a central draw-bridge, it must have been in need of frequent repairs (there were charges for iron-wheeled carts passing over it) but there are no mentions of another bridge until 1713 when the borough's four MPs funded a new one. This may have been replaced in 1741 but there is little documentation regarding either of these bridges and no illustrations exist.

The 1824 bridge has to be paid for and tolls were in force for many years. By the 1880s it was proving inadequate in handling increasing road traffic: the approaches were steep and the roadway too narrow for two vehicles to pass. Improvement work began and a new flat swing section, reducing the rise in the bridge by 5 feet 6 inches, was installed. The picture below shows a temporary bridge being put in place for pedestrians to cross the harbour while work was in progress. The improved bridge re-opened on 14th May 1881. Tolls were introduced once more to meet the bill and remained until 1889.

Opposite and overleaf, the bridge improvements of 1881 – which lasted until 1928.

1928 brought the decision to completely replace the Town Bridge and on 4th July 1930 the present bridge was officially opened by the Duke of York (later King George VI). Once more a temporary timber footbridge had been provided for foot passengers to cross the harbour. In 1938 a second arch was added under the bridge and the line of the Weymouth Harbour Tramway was re-routed under it.

Today the raising of the Town Bridge every two hours in summer to allow boats up and down the harbour is something of a tourist attraction. Formerly this service was a charge on boat owners but a public inquiry in 1983 ruled that all charges were to be abolished.

TOWN CLERKS from the 19th century to date:
Charles Bowles appointed 1787
Henry Hayes Tizard appointed 1824
Henry Hayes Tizard (the younger) appointed 1836
Frederick Charles Steggall appointed 1842
Pelly Hooper appointed 1879
Sir Richard Nicholas Howard appointed 1894
H. A. Huxtable appointed 1905, died suddenly 10th April 1915, Walter R. Wallis was a Committee Clerk who took over as Town Clerk temporarily until July 1915. Then he retired.
Frederick Fernihough appointed 1915
F.T.V. Isherwood appointed 1923
Percy Smallman appointed 1926
Edwin J. Jones appointed 1956 and stayed in post until 1974, when the borough amalgamated with Portland and the post was re-named 'Chief Executive'

TOWN FIRE The 17th century Town Fire which destroyed much of Melcombe Regis occurred in July 1665, not 1666 as in *Bumper Book I.*

TOWN LANE This name for Chickerell Road was still being used in the 1890s.

TOWNLEY TERRACE (Nos. 1-8) was in Horsford Street.

'TRIP' is the term used to describe the exodus of workers in July from the GWR's Swindon works when it closed for

Tumbledown farmhouse can be seen in the background of this photograph of the 1955 floods. It was demolished in the early 1960s.

An early picture of Tumbledown Farm.

the annual holiday. The railway workers were given a free travel pass to any GWR destination and Weymouth was the favourite of many – some 6000 workers and their families arriving in special trains throughout the morning on 'Trip Day' which some of the visitors extended into a week oreven a fortnight's stay. 'Trip' lasted from around the 1880s until WW2 and recommenced in the post-war years but numbers arriving by train steadily declined as coach and car travel and foreign holiday destinations took over.

TROWS are flat-bottomed craft used for crossing or working in The Fleet and transporting fish catches from Chesil to the mainland. (or, in days past, smuggled goods and the looted cargoes of wrecked ships). Trows are around 15 feet long, with a beam of some 5 feet. They have no mast and are towed, rowed or punted.

TUMBLEDOWN FARM stood almost opposite the junction of Radipole Lane and Causeway.

TURK'S HEAD INN, Chickerell was bought by Devenish brewers in 1834, the deeds dating back to 1777, although there was an even earlier brew house on the site. New tenants when the pub was renovated in 1963 were Eric and Joan Sealy Poole – his grandfather, the Reverend Sealy Poole was Rector of Chickerell for 42 years until his death in 1935.

TURTON VILLA, Turton Street This unusual stone-built house bears a date plaque of 1771 but is thought to be of later date. It does not appear on the 1864 Ordnance Survey maps of the town.

TWELVE APOSTLES *see* NEWBERRY CLOSE

TYPHOON The Portland based ocean-going tug served in the Falklands War with a crew from Weymouth and Portland in the South Atlantic Task Force. In South Georgia ferried supplies between ship and shore and while in the Falklands towed the ill-fated *Sir Galahad* out to sea to be sunk as a war grave. *RMAS Typhoon's* crew arrived home in July 1982.

U-Boats

U-BOATS A captured German U-boat was taken around the coast after WWI and this area also saw U-249, the first U-boat to surrender at the end of WW2, brought in escorted by *HMS Amethyst* and *HMS Magpie*.

UNION ARMS public house was on the south side of S Leonard's Road in the late 19th century. The terrace in which it stood was destroyed in WW2 bombing. Another Union Arms Inn stood on Dorchester Road until 1855 (when it was up for sale) and was demolished and replaced by Lodmoor House (later **Lodmoor High School**).

UNION YARD was at the rear of No. 117 Dorchester Road, Lodmoor Hill.

UNITED STATES NAVY BASE The de-commissioning of the American World War 2 Weymouth and Portland Naval Base was announced in the *Echo* on 21st May 1945.

UPPERTON HOUSE No. 37, Rodwell Road is on the corner of Rodwell Road and Rodwell Street, opposite the Rodwell Hotel. It was part of the considerable property in that area owned by Sir John Groves (died 1905) of the brewery and was sold in 1906 after his death.

UPTON FORT is on the coast between Osmington Mills and Ringstead. It was the last of the Victorian forts built to protect Portland Harbour and Weymouth Roads, part of the Nothe Fort/Verne Citadel/Breakwaters defences, although it was not actually completed and ready for action until 1902. It was armed during the Great War and brought into use again in WW2, notably on 21st March 1944 firing on German F-boats on the edge of Weymouth Bay. It was decommissioned in 1956 and is now a private residence.

UPWEY (Below) *The church of St Laurence.* (Overleaf) *Contrasting views of Church Street, not far apart in years.*

Summertime at the tearooms around 1950 and summertime in the disastrous floods of July 1955. (Above) The village more than a century earlier.

UPWEY CHARITIES Payne's Charity for the Poor dates from 1779 when a Mrs Payne left a sum of money, the interest to be paid to the poor of the parish. The Kitchen Plot and Poor's Plot were areas where the poor were allowed to cut furze for fuel. Daniel's Charity was money invested with the dividends to be spent on beef and flour for the poor of Upwey – Mrs Daniel, owner of Westbrook House, bequeathed the money. Miss Jackson left £500 to be invested for Upwey School.

UPWEY HOUSE The original Elizabethan Manor House at Upwey was demolished in the 19th century and the Gould family built the present Upwey House to the west of the original site.

UPWEY MANOR was originally built in 1639 and has been extended since. It is one of an impressive group of four properties built around the junction of Stottingway and Church Street – **Eastbrook, Westbrook, Southbrook** and Upwey Manor. Once owned by **Warren Lisle.**

UPWEY READING ROOM Was the gift of Canon Gildea. Opened 1st November 1906.

UPWEY SCHOOL The village school of c.1840 closed in 1976. It stands beside the Wishing Well and has been converted to a Village Centre. Children of the village now attend St Nicholas and St Laurence School on Dorchester Road at Broadwey.

UPWEY in Victoria, Australia. A village 25 miles from Melbourne. At first named Glenlissa but renamed Upwey, after a family named Tulledge who came from Upwey in Dorset.

The first Upwey House, demolished in the 19th century. Seen here in the 1790s.

VALUE HOUSE STORE, Mandeville Road, Wyke Regis For the site's previous history *see* SAPSWORTHS

VAN COURTLANDS, Bryants Lane, Wyke Regis This unusually-named house took the Van Courtland surname of a 19th century owner.

VANDELEUR FAMILY Several members of this family were known to live in Weymouth in the 19th century. Alice Vandeleur married Augustus Burdon, the heir to **William Burdon.**

VAUDEVILLE THEATRE on the Sands It appears that Vaudeville Theatre, the concert platform on the Sands, first appeared there in 1923 as the local newspaper that year noted '*The concert platform which has been erected on Weymouth sands is the best that has ever been there… substantial structure… The Vaudesques is the party in residence this season…*' Val Vaux and his Vaudesques were a popular attraction between the wars. Prior to WW1 there was a Sea View Concert Platform on the beach. *See also* BROWN, Ballard

VAUGHAN, Frankie The singer was at a Pavilion Ballroom Dance to raise funds for Weymouth Boys Club on 29th October 1961.

VE DAY STREET PARTY – WORLD'S LARGEST The party, held on 7th May 1995, to commemorate the 50th anniversary of VE Day, was held on Weymouth seafront between the King's Statue and the Alexandra Gardens.

VERNE VILLAS (Nos. 4-1) appear to be in the Chickerell Road area in the 1890s.

VESPA A team of four girls riding Douglas Vespa motor scooters were on a countrywide tour in July 1953 and visited Tilleys in St Thomas Street, the machine's sole distributor in the district.

VICTORIA ARMS, Ferrybridge is now the Ferrybridge Inn. It has been known as the Victoria Inn, the Royal Victoria Hotel and the Ferry House Inn.

VICTORIA COTTAGES or VICTORIA BUILDINGS were in West Parade (Park Street). Cottages of the same name were in the Newstead Road/Abbotsbury Road area.

VICTORIA INN, Knights in the Bottom, Chickerell Various theories have been put forward regarding the naming of this location, the most likely one seeming to be that a family called Knight lived there at some time.

VICTORIA VILLA, No. 47 Lennox Street is now known as Lennox House.

VICTORIA VILLAS are in Roman Road.

VICTORIAN SHOWTIME A modern version of the 19th and early 20th century Shownight, this is a Christmas event re-started in the 1980s as a late-night shopping evening. The name was changed in 2008 to Victorian Showtime as it became a daytime event held from noon to 6pm. Organised by Weymouth Community Academy.

VIGONIA HOUSE was in Lennox Street.

VINE, Edward Artist. Born in New Street, Weymouth, 1943. Paints many Dorset scenes and has held exhibitions in the county.
Further reading: *Edward Vine's Dorset.* (Halsgrove in association with the Peter Hedley Gallery, Wareham, 2002.)

VINE COTTAGES in William Street may take their name from W. Vine, a builder who lived there.

VINES PLACE *see* LANEHOUSE ROCKS FARM

VINING Robert This Rodwell-based Weymouth builder/architect worked with the better-known James Hamilton and because of this association, tends to be over-looked. He was working at the end of the 18th/early 19th century and a complete listing of buildings he designed would be interesting – so far discovered are the Clavell Tower, Nottington Spa House and the Rectory at Langton Herring, all dating from around 1830. He also rebuilt the Esplanade (he'd worked on its construction with James Hamilton in 1800), following the severe damage caused by the Great Gale of 1824. He owned Middlehill Brickyard (Sudan Road, Rodwell) and lived nearby, at Elwell Manor.

VIXEN FORGE was in Ranelagh Road. Flats of Heron Court have been built on the site. Another Vixen Forge was in Mill Street, Broadwey.

Waby House

W

WABY HOUSE the name is derived from Waia Bayeux, the French cathedral town and the family de Baieux, once lords of the manor of Upwey.

WADSWORTH'S FARM Wadsworth was one-time tenant of Radipole Farm, also known as Nangle's Farm, from another occupant. *See also* RADIPOLE FARM in *Bumper Book I*

WALL CLOSE, Westham was up for sale for development in October, 1882 – at that time in use as allotment gardens.

WALL COTTAGE appears to be in the Chickerell Road area in the 1860s.

WALL MEAD is the site of the 1856 Melcombe Regis cemetery. Additional land was purchased for the extension of the cemetery later in the 19th century.

WALLIS, John (1861-1935) Ferryman and boat proprietor of Weymouth. Retired in 1929 and his business was taken over by his son Edgar Wallis, later to become the proprietor of the Mon Ami Hotel and the Grand Hotel and Mayor in 1960-61.

WAR MEMORIAL, Melcombe Regis Cemetery The Portland Stone Imperial Cross stands close to Newstead Road and is a replica of many in the Flanders cemeteries. It appears to have been completed early in 1925.

WAR MEMORIAL, Weymouth Cemetery. This cross is the same design as that in Melcombe Regis Cemetery. It commemorates the sailors, soldiers and a nurse who died in the Great War. It was dedicated on 20th January 1926. The nurse was Nurse F. L. M. Hook.

WAR MEMORIAL, Wyke Regis Unveiled on 30th November 1919 in the new burial ground at the cross roads opposite Wyke Regis Church, it is an obelisk of Portland Stone with tablets on which are inscribed the names of 52 Wyke Regis men. The memorial was restored in March 2009. *See also* HAIGH, Captain Francis Evans Percy, RN (its designer)

WARD, Albany (1879-1966) Later famous for his cinema chain the 'Albany Ward Circuit', he established his first permanent cinema in Weymouth – the Palladium on the Town Bridge, in 1909 (in the building currently (2009) the Rendezvous pub). He had property in Weymouth – a house in Holland Road – and in the 1920s he also owned Burdon's Buildings at the time when it was closed due to overcrowding (*see also* BURDON, **William Wharton**; KENNEDYS; PUCKETT'S STORES). He was an enthusiastic fund raiser for the local lifeboat.

WARD, Charlotte Alice Deputy Medical Officer of Health, Weymouth Borough. Daughter of Robert Conway, Head of Weymouth College where she was taught by the masters and, unusually at that time, gained enough knowledge of science to be accepted by The London School of Medicine for Women. After travelling abroad with her husband she returned to Weymouth in 1939, as deputy to Dr Gordon Wallace and as Medical Officer of Health while he was serving in the Army during WW2. Ran first aid, birth control and baby clinics and was registrar at Weymouth and District Hospital. Retired in 1964.

WARD'S COURT in New Street may have be named after the disgraced MP for Weymouth, John Ward of Hackney, who was expelled from the House of Commons in 1726 for forgery. He owned property here.

WAREHOUSES Most of the old harbourside warehouses have now been successfully converted to other uses and a few have been lost. Kingfisher Marine in Commercial Road currently (2009) occupy the last one in industrial use but it appears that when the firm relocates to premises nearby, the warehouse will be demolished.

WARREN, Henry This artist produced a view of Weymouth Harbour in the 1830s. It has been something of a puzzle ever since, as his picture shows Holy Trinity Church – but on the wrong side of the water! It may be that he painted the original early in the 1830s, but by the time it was produced in print form the church had been built. Not being a local man, Warren may have assumed that it

Henry Warren's mystery view of Weymouth Harbour. The white building rising above the rest on the left hand side wrongly represents Holy Trinity Church.

was sited on the north side of the harbour and thus added it incorrectly to the left hand side of his original view.

WARRY'S GROVE COTTAGE, TEA AND FRUIT GARDENS were on the Nothe in the 1830s.

WATER LILY FARM *see* BENNETTS WATER GARDENS

WATER MUSEUM The Museum of Water Supply at Sutton Poyntz opened in September 1989.

WATERLOO COTTAGES follow No. 2 William Street on the 1891 Census.

WATERLOO public house is at No. 1 Grange Road.

WATTS, Richard Caines (born 1859) married a daughter of Sir John Groves and was a director of John Groves and Sons. Mayor in 1910-11. Built Nettlecombe, his house on Wyke Road which is now the Convent of Mercy.

WAVEPIERCER In the late 1980s hydrofoils replaced the traditional ships which took passengers and cars to the Channel Islands and France. In 1991 the world's largest passenger-only Wavepiercer was introduced on the route and now even larger Wavepiercer craft also transport cars.

WAVERLEY ARMS pub was renamed the Waverley Hotel in 1937 after a total rebuild.

WAVERLEY ROAD was originally known as Reliable Drive. It changed its name in the early 1930s.

WAVERLEY TERRACE, Abbotsbury Road appears to be the houses adjacent to the Waverley Arms pub. Some houses may have been demolished when the pub was rebuilt and extended in 1937.

WAYBAIOUSE or WEYBAYOUSE and other spelling variations. This is an alternative name, no longer used, for Upwey, the family of Baieux or Bayouse once dwelling here. John Bayouse founded a chantry at Upwey in 1243.

WEATHER Weymouth has the distinction of being the first seaside resort in the country to set up a weather station. It was established by local chemist **T. B. Groves** in 1880 at Nothe House. Sunshine records were fiercely contested in the days before holidaymakers flew off to warmer climes for their summer breaks and newspapers published 'league tables' showing which resorts had the best weather. Rainfall figures can be found in the annual *Proceedings of the Dorset Natural History and Archaeological Society* where they have been published since 1888.

WEBB, MAJOR & COMPANY The early history of the company dates back to 1890 when it was established as Bagg and Frampton, Mr Webb joining the firm as manager in 1891. The Bagg/Frampton partnership was dissolved towards the end of 1891 and the company was then styled Bagg and Sons, later Bagg and Sons Ltd. A recession in the building trade coupled with John Bagg, the original founder, living way beyond his means led to his bankruptcy, the end of his connection to the company and the formation of the new company of Webb, Major & Co. Ltd. in 1910. The firm had a large store in St Thomas Street and was well known for its huge timber sheds in Commercial Road (see **BETTS, George William** for the previous history and current history of this site). In 1965 Webb, Major & Co., Ltd. was taken over by the Devon Trading Company Ltd.

WEIGHBRIDGE The public weighbridge was once in the roadway outside the Esplanade Tea Cabin and the lessee of the café had to operate the weighbridge. His duties came to an end shortly before WW2 when the mechanism failed. The weighbridge then transferred to the former Corporation Yard on Westwey Road and is now relocated to Weymouth and Portland Borough Council's depot at Crookhill, Chickerell.

WELBOURNE'S LANE seems to have been an early name for Boot Hill.

WELCOME INN in St Nicholas Street was also known as the Welcome Home Inn and the Welcome House.

WELCOME TO WEYMOUTH signs with a Georgian theme were erected on Preston Hill and Ridgeway in September 1957. They were the work of F. G. Biles, sign-writer of Bridport. They were replaced when Portland came into the Borough in 1974 by 'Welcome to Weymouth and Portland' signs but the Ridgeway welcome is now a 'pineapple gateway' – two Portland stone pillars topped with pineapples either side of the A354, erected by Weymouth Rotary Club in October 2005. These will be relocated when the Relief Road is completed.

WELDON LODGE, Rodwell Road This is the 1948 conversion of Holy Trinity Vicarage's stables and coach house as a residence for the curate. Named after Canon Weldon, one time vicar of Holy Trinity.

WELLINGTON, Duke of A portrait of the Duke of Wellington was presented to Weymouth Corporation on 4th June 1858 by Sir John Lethbridge. It is stored in Weymouth Museum but is not currently on display.

WELLINGTON ARMS, St Alban Street Near here in 1836 was found a funeral urn containing ashes and burnt bones, buried in shingle, six feet below the surface. Another 'Wellington Arms' pub was at Charlestown, now converted to a shop and post office on Chickerell Road.

WELLINGTON PLACE *see* NEWBERRY CLOSE

WELSFORD FAMILY Long established local family, all

active in local politics, all with the forename George. George (Culverwell) Welsford was an Alderman in 1839 and died 12th January 1854. His son George Culverwell Welsford, who died 22nd October 1865 was Mayor in 1849 and 1856 and had married a Miss Boulter in 1830. He was a timber merchant and ship owner. Their son was George Boulter Welsford (1833-1913) solicitor, Mayor in 1874 and 1875, who died unmarried at Greenhill in 1913.

WEMBLEY EXHIBITION 1924 A non-stop excursion train ran to Paddington for the Wembley Exhibition on 18th June 1924. It had almost 800 passengers on board and many shops and businesses closed for the day to allow employees to make the trip.

WESSAGUSSET was the original name of Weymouth in Massachusetts. Founded in 1622 and renamed Weymouth in 1635, the year 100 settlers arrived from Weymouth, Dorset. Part of the Massachusetts Bay Colony, it was originally a fishing and farming community. In 1837 the Weymouth Iron Works was founded and when that closed a shoe industry was started. That also ceased and the town now relies on smaller business and industrial operations.

WEST CHICKERELL is today's Chickerell. East Chickerell became Charlestown in the 19th century. *See also* EAST CHICKERELL

WEST QUAY in Weymouth was once the name of North Quay. West Quay in Melcombe was the part of today's Custom House Quay west of the Town Bridge, which extended round Ferry's Corner into what is now the southern end of Commercial Road.

WEST STREET There were once West Streets on either side of the harbour. In Weymouth, West Street was renamed High West Street. In Melcombe, West Street still exists but much altered. Derelict properties were demolished in 1982, and the whole area was redeveloped in 2003.

WEST VILLA appears to be another name for Westville, on Chickerell Road.

WESTBROOK HOUSE, Church Street, Upwey One of an impressive group of four properties built around the junction of Stottingway and Church Street – **Eastbrook**, Westbrook, **Southbrook** and **Upwey Manor**. Westbrook was originally built c.1620 by Sir Thomas Freke, partly demolished c.1730 by William Freke and largely rebuilt c.1740-50 by William Floyer. It retains many early features despite further alterations in the early 19th century. By 1867 it was owned by Henry Charles Goodden of the Upwey Gould family. It has a beautiful setting with fine entrance gates and a bridge over the river.

WESTDOWNE HOUSE, Chickerell Road The early 19th century house lost some of its grounds to new houses in 1997. Also known as Westdowne Lodge, it was probably built in the late 1830s by Eliza Orton, one of the major landowners of Wyke Regis, although not as her residence.

WESTFIELD TECHNOLOGY COLLEGE opened in 1976 as Westfield School. It has been known by its present name since September 1999.

WESTHAM Westham grew rapidly, perhaps too rapidly, for in its early days there was little but housing, the main aim of its developers being to cram in as many houses as possible. This new development of hundreds of houses close

St Paul's Church, Westham.

to the town also added to Weymouth's outdated and already overloaded sewerage system. Having failed to persuade the Rural District Council (within whose boundaries Westham lay) to do anything about the drainage question, the solution was to bring Westham within the borough boundary (it was previously part of Wyke Regis) on 9th November 1895 and, at long last, to overhaul Weymouth's sewage disposal methods. *See also* SEWERAGE in *Bumper Book I*. A new parish was formed in 1901 and St Paul's Church, building of which had commenced in 1894, was finally completed in 1913.

Further reading: *Westham over the bridge of time: a short history of Westham, Weymouth* by Debby Rose (2008).

WESTHAM CAMP Some 10,000 Australian troops were in the Weymouth and Portland area between 1915 and 1919. They were first based at Montevideo House, Chickerell before camps opened at Westham, Littlemoor, and at the Verne Citadel, Portland. Many of the men had been wounded, some very seriously, during the unsuccessful Gallipoli campaign and, later, on the Western front. Those who were fit enough returned to the front line, others were repatriated. At the end of 1918 the Weymouth camps were used as holding areas for the Australians as not enough ships were available to transport them all home – some waited until 1919. Westham camp's buildings, equipment, horses etc. were being sold off in 1919 and 1920 and in the autumn of 1919 plans were already underway to fill the site with local authority housing.

WESTHAM CINEMA A Cinema was established at Westham prior to World War I by local entertainments promoter and garage owner Thomas Moore. When the Australian Imperial Forces set up their convalescent camps in the vicinity he let the building to the AIF Entertainments Board. Post-WWI the building had a variety of occupants including use as a dance hall, church, a clothing sale venue and as a garage for Jeanes' motorbuses and furniture vans. In early 1950s the site was converted to retail units, now Nos. 155-159 Abbotsbury Road. Mr Moore, who died in July, 1929, later owned garages in Dorchester Road and Greenhill and was a councillor from 1924 until his death at the age of 53.

WESTHAM COTTAGE MISSION *see* ROCK MISSION

WESTHAM CRICKET CLUB was the new name in 1902 for Goldcroft Cricket Club.

WESTHAM LIBERAL CLUB closed down in June 1914.

WESTHAM SUBWAYS *see* SUBWAYS

WESTHAM WORKING MEN'S CLUB opened in October 1904 at No. 1 Cromwell Road. It appears to be a replacement for the **Arch Liberal Club**, closed by magistrates in November 1903 for six months due to drunken and rowdy behaviour.

WESTHAVEN BUNGALOWS for the elderly The first one opened in March, 1950.

WESTHAVEN HOSPITAL The old buildings of 1902, originally a 2 ward, 40 bed iron building with a separate isolation hospital nearby (never used for this purpose) were added to over the years and became totally inadequate. The foundation stone of the redevelopment of the hospital was laid in May 2007. It provides health care services for older people, with purpose-built accommodation for therapy services, a community rehabilitation team, and a 36 bed inpatient unit which is to replace inpatient beds at John Talbot Ward at Weymouth Community Hospital.

WESTHAVEN SCHOOL *see* CONIFERS PRIMARY SCHOOL

WESTMEAD was an alternative name for Radipole Manor, the Victorian house with two lodges off Radipole Lane. *See also* RADIPOLE. MANOR HOUSES

WEY VALLEY SCHOOL AND SPORTS COLLEGE, Dorchester Road The first phase of the school opened on 2nd May 1949 as Broadwey Secondary Modern School. It changed its name on the introduction of comprehensive education in 1985.

WEYMOUTH, Lord Weymouth gave title to Thomas Thynne of Longleat in Wiltshire, son of Sir Frederick Thynne. He was created Baron of Warminster and Viscount Weymouth on 11th December 1682.

WEYMOUTH, Nova Scotia Village on the River Sissiboo. First settled by Loyalists under a Mr Stickland from Weymouth, Massachusetts during the American War of Independence. Timber from surrounding woodlands enabled them to build boats and it became a thriving little port. Gradually larger ports took over the shipping trade and it is now land of vacationists, anglers and sportsmen. A tourist resort, like Weymouth, England.

WEYMOUTH. ROYAL NAVY SHIPS' NAMES
Weymouth. 14-gun Royalist ship *Cavendish* captured 1645 by Parliament. Sold 1662.
Weymouth. 4th rate 48. Built 1693, rebuilt 1718. Broken up 1732.
Weymouth. 4th rate 60. Built 1736. Wrecked 1745 (Antigua).
Weymouth. 4th rate 60. Built 1752. Broken up 1772.
Weymouth. (ex-East Indiaman *Earl Mansfield*, purchased on stocks). 4th rate 56. Storeship 26 guns 1798. Wrecked 1800 (Lisbon Bar).
Weymouth (ex-Indiaman *Wellesley*) 5th rate 36. Purchased 1894. Storeship 26 guns 1811, convict ship 1828. Sold 1865.
Weymouth. Wooden screw corvette. Laid down 1860, cancelled 1861.
Weymouth. 2nd class cruiser. Built 1910. Sold 1928.

Presented with a set of ornate silver by the town which was later presented to Weymouth and Portland Borough Council. When the ship was broken up in 1929 the Hughes Ship Breaking Company of Blyth presented the town with a bronze crest mounted on teak.

Weymouth. Frigate. Built 1961. Renamed *Leander.* Expended as target 1989.

Weymouth. Trawler. Requisitioned 1915-1919.

Further reading : *Ships of the Royal Navy : the complete record of fighting ships of the Royal Navy from the 15th century to the present day,* by J. J. Colledge and Ben Warlow. (Chatham Publishing. Rev. ed. 2006.)

WEYMOUTH AND MELCOMBE REGIS PROVIDENT INSTITUTION FOR THE INDUSTRIOUS POOR was founded in January 1832.

WEYMOUTH AND PORTLAND NATIONAL SAILING ACADEMY The Academy was opened in June 2005 by Princess Anne. Its completion as an Olympic venue for the 2012 Games was celebrated in November 2008 with an official unveiling by two Olympic gold medallists – triple jumper Jonathan Edwards and Laser sailor Paul Goodison, of Wyke Regis.

WEYMOUTH AND SOUTH DORSET ARTS CENTRE The building in Commercial Road closed in April 2004 for refurbishment with intended future use by Surestart on the ground floor and the Arts Centre on the first floor. Despite re-opening in 2006, in 2007 it became obvious that the Arts Centre (the charity having by now set up a limited company known as Weymouth Arts Centre Ltd) would not be able to take up the lease of the building with Weymouth and Portland Borough Council due to the high annual running costs. The limited company existed until September 2007 and the charity closed in 2008, its assets being distributed among various local charitable causes and its records being deposited at the Dorset History Centre in Dorchester. Weymouth College took over the first floor of the building, re-opening it on 7th June 2008 as The Mulberry Centre.

WEYMOUTH AS A WATERING PLACE with a description of the Town and Neighbourhood, The Breakwater and its Construction, The Portland Quarries, The Chesil Beach etc., etc., for the use of intending and actual Visitors. Printed by D. Archer. 1857.

WEYMOUTH ASSOCIATION FOR PREVENTIVE AND RESCUE WORK This may have been the original name of St Gabriel's Mission, later St Gabriel's Home as both began in the 1880s in Great George Street. St Gabriel's was a home for unmarried mothers. It closed in 1973, having been at No. 18 Dorchester Road since 1952.

WEYMOUTH BAY ESTATE this was a newer development off Preston Road just beyond Overcombe Corner,

Overcombe Corner in the early 1920s, before any of the Weymouth Bay Estate developments had begun.

The garage at Overcombe, the site redeveloped as housing in the latter years of the 20th century.

built in the early 1960s, which continued the name of the original 1920s and 1930s estate at Overcombe (when Bowleaze Coveway and houses along Preston Road were built). The new roads led off Melstock Avenue. *See also* WEYMOUTH BAY ESTATE in *Bumper Book I*

WEYMOUTH BAY METHODIST CHURCH The Church stands on the site of the demolished **Christian Science Church**. It was built to replace the fire-gutted Maiden Street Methodist Church, which was too costly to restore. The new church is a multi-purpose building and as well as serving as a church it will be available as a performance and exhibition space and a meeting place for local groups. It seats up to 240 people. It held an open weekend 4th and 5th April 2009. Current plans are to turn Maiden Street Church into a restaurant and flats when the current economic climate improves.

WEYMOUTH BELLE The first *Weymouth Belle* was a motor boat built for pleasure trips round the Bay in 1923.

WEYMOUTH BELLE Built in 1943 by Bolsons of Poole, was named *Bournemouth Belle* and did trips round Poole and Bournemouth. Bought by R H Wills and Son and arrived in Weymouth in May 1967 and was renamed *Weymouth Belle*. Sold in 1975 and renamed *Souters Lass* and ran a ferry service in the Orkneys transporting oil rig workers. Sold in 1976 and still in service giving cruises on the loch at Fort William.

Members of the Bicycle Club gather at the King's Statue.

WEYMOUTH BICYCLE CLUB was founded in 1874.

WEYMOUTH BOXING CLUB was founded in the late 1940s and purchased a building in Hardwick Street as HQ in 1951.

WEYMOUTH BOYS CLUB building on Chickerell Road dates from 1963, although the club is much older, having started in the early 1940s. Post-war it was based in the bomb-damaged Holy Trinity School at Chapelhay. Extensions to the Chickerell Road premises were opened on 23rd October 1982 by astronomer Patrick Moore. Further refurbishment was completed in the early 1990s.

WEYMOUTH COLLEGE achieved public school status in the 1880s during the Reverend Dr John Miller's time as headmaster (1885-1901). *See also Bumper Book I*

WEYMOUTH COMMERCIAL SCHOOL, No. 7 Frederick Place was established in 1861. Its headmaster from the 1880s was H. J. Rogers, the school having originally been in Turton Street. The school moved to Rodwell at the end of 1910, renaming itself **Rodwell College** in 1911 and occupying a house known for years as 'The Blue House' on the corner of Rodwell Road and St Leonard's Road. Headmaster was Dr Percy Pankhurst.

Weymouth College left the town in the early months of World War 2. After further use by other educational establishments, the buildings were converted to housing.

WEYMOUTH CRICKET CLUB Weymouth in 1905 had two town cricket clubs – St John's and Lansdowne. They amalgamated that year, Weymouth Cricket Club being the name chosen for the united clubs. A previous Weymouth Cricket Club had gone out of existence some time before.

WEYMOUTH FOOTBALL CLUB The club fell on hard times early in 2009, losing £9000 a week and owing £300,000. Its new Chairman is Ian Ridley, a former chairman, who is leading a new consortium of local businessmen in their efforts to save the club.

WEYMOUTH GRAMMAR SCHOOL, Alma Road
The 'New Wing' opened in 1935, linked to the older building by a covered way. A pair of very imposing and decorative iron gates were presented to the Grammar School in 1936 by Weymouth Corporation to stand at the end of Holland Road, the entrance to the New Wing. The gates were formerly at the Jubilee Hall and were probably removed during its 1926 transformation into the Regent Theatre and Dance Hall. All the Grammar School buildings were demolished in 2002: since the school's removal to Charlestown in the 1960s they had been used by Weymouth College (formerly South Dorset Technical College) but were redundant following the College's move to Cranford Avenue. Houses of College Heights now fill the site, but the gates remain in Holland Road.

WEYMOUTH HARBOUR TRAMWAY every so often a subject for discussion is Weymouth's railway lines which used to take trains through the streets from the railway station to the quay- should they stay or should they go? *See also Bumper Book 1*

A cyclist decides the best way to avoid the railway lines is to ride on the wrong side of the road.

The fine gates, ex-Jubilee Hall, and Weymouth Grammar School's 'New Wing'.

WEYMOUTH INDEPENDENT EVANGELICAL CHURCH services are held at the W. I. Hall, Gallwey Road, Wyke Regis. The church was founded in 1997, although it members had met as a Christian fellowship for several years before. (Prior to W. I. ownership the building was the chapel of the Primitive Methodists.)

WEYMOUTH MOTOR COMPANY was a bus company formed in May 1919 by four local garage proprietors – E. W. Tilley of Crescent Street, Percy a'Court of Gloucester Mews, George Bugler of Rodwell Garage, Boot Hill and Henry Bell of Franchise Street. Bugler resigned soon afterwards and was replaced by Arthur Hodder of Royal Crescent Garage. The company stayed in business until 1924 when it sold out to the National Omnibus and Transport Company, which rebuilt the Edward Street premises of the Motor Company in 1929 (the garage had to be rebuilt again following its demolition in a 1940 air raid), now the First National HQ in the town.

WEYMOUTH PINE *Amendment to the entry in Bumper Book I:*

Lord Weymouth planted large numbers of *Pinus Strobus*, the Weymouth Pine, on his estate at Longleat early in the 18th century and has long been associated with the naming of the tree, but the variety was already well known in the

United States having been discovered in Maine the previous century by a merchant called George Weymouth. J. B. Kerridge, writing in about 1860 noted that at Radipole around the church '...*here that graceful tree known as the Weymouth Pine flourishes and in the immediate vicinity may be seen some magnificent specimens...*'

WEYMOUTH POTTERY was run by Leonard Stockley. Started in 1961 in a tiny building in Augusta Place, Esplanade.

WEYMOUTH ROWING CLUB Local rowers founded the club in 1855 and by summer 1856 had 4 four-oared galleys and 2 skiffs. Initially successful, the club collapsed in 1867 and the boats were sold. Revived in 1871 and in 1874 they built their first boathouse but membership was dropping in the late 1870s and funds non-existent. There was another revival in 1883 but in 1885 there were mounting debts and the club closed in 1886. It reopened again in the summer of 1887 and appears to have existed in some form until 1923 when enthusiasm was at an all-time low and the club may have closed again that year.

WEYMOUTH SEA FESTIVAL The event, which has combined Weymouth's Waterfest and Trawler Race over the late-May Bank Holiday since 2006, was cancelled due to

Edwardian rowers line up outside their clubhouse for a group photograph.

The White Hart Inn, in Lower Bond Street, renamed New Bond Street in 2000.

lack of sponsorship in 2009. For 2009 it was replaced with a Trawler Race Music Festival of local bands.

WEYMOUTH TOWN BAND Originally the Weymouth Military Band of 1922, it reformed after WW2 and changed its name to Wyke Regis Military Band and was renamed Weymouth Town Band in 1953. It no longer exists.

WEYMOUTH TOWN SOCIETY Dr Christopher Childs put forward proposals for setting up a local society for the study of Art, Literature and Science at a public meeting in Weymouth in 1883. It would provide lectures, debates concerts and exhibitions with the ultimate aim of establishing a museum and a library, and was aimed at all classes of society. Speakers were engaged and exhibitions laid on and the society met with mixed success. By 1889 its originator Dr Childs felt that the Society wasn't maintaining its standards and was becoming just a source of entertainment – although his proposal to disband the society was rejected and it continued for a few more years. Funding was always a problem and the Weymouth Town Society seems to have faded away by 1892.

WHITE HART INN of today stands in Lower Bond Street (now known as New Bond Street). There may have been earlier inns of the same name as there is more than one early reference to a White Hart in St Mary Street. There was also a White Hart Inn on the Weymouth side of the harbour, demolished when Holy Trinity Church was built in the 1830s. Wyke Regis had a 17th century White Hart Inn, thought to have been on the site of the Social Club in Chamberlaine Road. *See also Bumper Book I*

WHITE HORSE, Osmington '*...about 2 miles from the town of Weymouth on the road to Wareham is a village called Preston, above which is a large hill on the side of which is an image cut out, representing King George III on horseback. It takes up an acre of ground. The image was cut out in the year 1808, a great many men were employed and were from the beginning of May in that year till the beginning of August completing it*' An entry from the diary of Thomas Oldfield Bartlett of Wareham, now in Dorset History Centre.

A correction to the details in *Bumper Book I* regarding the Osmington site Mr John Wood, bookseller of Weymouth, was active in getting the project off the ground but it was cut on land belonging to Robert Serrell Wood of

King George III has been riding his hillside White Horse for more than 200 years.

Osmington. A probable family relationship between the two Woods has not yet been established.

The White Horse is the only hill figure to carry a rider.

WHITELEE COURT, No. 207 Preston Road was built in 1985 on the site of Whitelee Garage.

WHITEWAY, William One of the leading 17th century Burgesses of Dorchester with an estate at Martinstown. His diary, covering the period from November 1618 to March 1634, is in the British Museum. Although mostly about Dorchester, and especially interesting regarding an outbreak of plague there, it also contains some references to the Weymouth area including:

On 2nd October 1621 he reported *'This same day came down certain commissioners with the broad seal of England to dig in a hill at Upway near Dorchester for some treasure that lies hidden underground, but having spent three days about it, they went away having found there nothing but a few bones, saying they meant to dig at Bincombe and under that pretence went away'*

More Weymouth news comes in August 1623 *'The twenty-fifth of this month the King's ships arrived in Portland in their voyage for Spain to bring home the Prince and his lady, they reported that the Prince was married the 24th ditto and was to come from Madrid four days after, and at the end of 20 days to be at the sea side to take shipping. The Earl of Rutland is Admiral of the Fleet. With him are divers Lords. They departed from Weymouth the next day about midnight. The Prince Royal bearing the Admiral is a vessel of wonderful bigness strength and beauty'.* [This refers to the proposed marriage between Charles, son of King James I and Isabella, daughter of King Phillip III of Spain and known as the 'Spanish Match', which never took place].

On October 2nd 1624 he reports storm and shipwreck *'This night there was an extraordinary storm of rain and wind which blew down many houses and threw many great trees and cast away many ships in all parts. Amongst them were four at Melcombe two of these were Frenchmen; there were eleven Frenchmen drowned in the same'* And again on 24th January 1631 *'This day there was a mighty tempest at Weymouth with thunder and lightening. Eight men were dangerously hurt with it in the Pilgrim, and two slain.'*

On 17th April 1634 comes reference to emigrants to the New World *'Mr Newburgh of Marshwood Vale, and many others set sail from Weymouth towards New England; and the 29th of the same Mr John Humphreys, with his wife the Lady Susan, set sail likewise foe the same place. This summer there went over to that plantation at the least 20 sail of ships and in them 2,000 planters.'*

Further reading:Annotated extracts from William Whiteways Diary by the Rev. W. Miles Barnes can be found in the *Proceedings of the Dorset Natural History and Archaeological Society, Vol. XIII.*

WILLIAM HENRY pub, No. 1 Frederick Place The pub opened in 2008 in the premises previously occupied by the Hogshead pub and before that for many years by Forte's Ice Cream Parlor. It takes its name from William Henry, Duke of Gloucester and younger brother of King George III, who built Gloucester Lodge on the Esplanade. The Lodge originally had a long garden stretching down as far as today's School Street and **Frederick Place** and Royal Terrace were later built on it.

WILLIS, Browne *Notitia Parliamentaria, or, an History of the Counties, Cities and Boroughs in England, Wales...1716.* A short description and history of Weymouth and Melcombe Regis is contained in it.

WINDHAM, William Frederick *see* ROGERS, Agnes Ann.

WISDOM, Norman Appeared at The Alexandra Gardens Theatre in a 1955 fund-raising concert for the families of those lost in the Sidon disaster (*see* SUBMARINE INCIDENTS AND LOSSES) and also filmed scenes for *The Bulldog Breed* in Weymouth.

WITCHES Occasional references to women being accused as witches occur in the town records. In 1647 Edith Bull deposed that she heard Damaris Harvey say Avice Miles was a witch '*... and that Amy Cotton, Aunt to the said Avice, never prospered after she was cursed by the said Avice Miles*', and in 1716 '*John Jerard deposed that Richard Webb of this town, Blacksmith, called Jerard's wife an old witch and said she bewitched his child to death, and that he would murder her.*'

WITHAM was the harbour dredger in the early 1900s.

WOMBWELL'S MENAGERIE OF WILD BEASTS was a Weymouth attraction in 1823 and returned to the town in the 1840s.

WOODFORDE, Parson The Diary of Parson Woodford is well known. Written by the Reverend James Woodford, it described his travels during the period 1758-1802. He was in Weymouth in July 1779 and '*supped and slept at the King's Head*' [the inn formerly on the site of Maiden Street Methodist Church] which he found to '*be a very good Inn and very civill people*'. Weymouth he found '*was quiet with little company in it.*'

WOOLLAND FURLONG is on the 1797 Inclosure map and gave its name to Wooland Gardens built in 1994 on the site of the demolished Wyke House Hotel.

WOOLWORTH, F. W. The announcement that all Woolworths stores would cease trading came towards the end of 2008. The firm had first opened a shop in St Mary Street in 1923, building a new store there in 1938. This closed in 1985, the building then being greatly altered to provide four individual shop premises. Woolworths returned to a new store in the New Bond Street redevelopment in 2000, which closed for good on Tuesday 6th January 2009. *See also* ROWE, John G.

WORLD HERITAGE SITE status was awarded by UNESCO to the East Devon and Dorset Jurassic Coast in December 2001.

WRIGHT'S ENGLISH NAPLES STORES, No. 50, St Mary Street was a large grocery business at the lower end of St Mary Street, founded in the late 19th century by R. J. Wright and later taken over by his son. It moved to No 54 St Thomas Street, becoming Northovers in the late 1930s.

WYKE CASTLE *see* FENHOULET, Andrew Chadwick

WYKE LODGE *see* BOULTON VILLA

WYKE REGIS. BOUNDARIES *see* BOUNDARIES

WYKE REGIS. BREWERY In 1863 Alfred Gray removed his brewery from High Street, Weymouth to '*roomy and eligible premises at Wyke Regis*'. Orders were to be addressed to Alfred Gray, Brewery, Wyke Regis.

WYKE REGIS. CHARITIES In his will proved in 1647 Bernard Mitchell left various sums to aid the poor in a number of Dorset parishes as well as ten bushels of sea coals to the poor of Weymouth and Wyke Regis annually and six bushels to six poor widows of Melcombe annually. The Wyke coal later became a sum of 10 shillings distributed by the rector of Wyke to the ten poorest families at Wyke at Christmas. Martha Beach's will of 1823 left a sum, the dividend to be divided between 6 poor women over the age of 60 in Wyke Regis parish, also distributed at Christmas.

WYKE REGIS. FAIR The last one before more recent such events was held in 1875. It stretched all along Portland Road to Kaye's Lane from the Church and along Chamberlaine Road to Wyke Square. Fairs and markets were granted or confirmed at Wyke in 1221, 1248, 1250.

WYKE REGIS. GARDENS on Portland Road. The gardens opened at Whitsun, 5th June, 1938, built on Home Close and sometimes known as Home Close Gardens.

WYKE REGIS. JUNIOR SCHOOL The CofE Junior School, High Street, Wyke Regis opened in the late 1980s. It replaced the school buildings of 1897 on the same site, which had a main entrance in Victoria Road.

WYKE REGIS. LIBERAL CLUB was in Victoria Road, currently the site of Wyke Regis Working Men's Club.

WYKE REGIS. MANOR FARM *see* MANOR FARM, Wyke Regis

WYKE REGIS MEMORIAL HALL *see* WYKE REGIS. PARISH ROOM

The Parish Room on the right of the photograph was replaced by the present red-brick Memorial Hall more than a century ago.

WYKE REGIS. MILLENNIUM 988 – 1988 Wyke Millennium Celebration Week was held from 2nd to 9th July 1988, commemorating Wyke's 1000 years of history since King Ethelred II granted to his minister Atsere a certain part of land in the place called by the inhabitants 'Wyck'. This charter still exists and it describes the boundaries of Wyke. *See* BOUNDARIES

WYKE REGIS. NICKNAMES A 19th century resident recalled Wyke residents being known as 'Cutbirds'. The more usual term is 'Wykeite'.

WYKE REGIS. PARISH ROOM In November 1906, work had commenced on pulling down the old parish room and the adjoining Chamberlaine Room and intervening cottages. Architects of the new parish hall (Wyke Regis Memorial Hall) were Crickmays, the builder F. Selby.

WYKE REGIS. POORHOUSE was in High Street.

WYKE REGIS. RECTORY The early 19th century rectory of All Saints Church went on the market in August 1954 when a new Rectory was built opposite the church in Portland Road.

WYKE REGIS. REGATTA Held at the end of July in Portland Harbour, Wyke Regis Regatta seems to have been a very jolly affair in 1901: sailing, pulling and swimming contests; aquatic sports, field sports, fireworks; and dancing in Mr Groves' field near Ferrybridge.

The former rectory still stands, converted to private housing.

WYKE REGIS SOCIAL CLUB, No. 5 Chamberlaine Road Believed to be on the site of the 17th century White Hart Inn, the premises became a private residence in the 18th century when owned by John Orton Swaffield. In the 19th century this was bought by Devenish and became the New Inn, and for a short time a coffee tavern in the days when the temperance movement was strong. Eventually sometime before WW1 it became Whitehead's Social Institute and finally Wyke Regis Social Club.

WYKE REGIS TRAINING AREA is part of the Defence Training Estate South West and is located on 3 sites: Two of these are on the northern side of The Fleet. – the Bridging Camp, established by the Royal Engineers in 1928 for training in bridge and ferry building and other military exercises, and Chickerell Camp and rifle range, used for field training and marksmanship.) The third site is at the Verne Yeates, Portland and is used for bridging and signals training.

WYKE REGISTER is an informative monthly magazine delivered free in the Wyke area. Publication began in May 1991.

WYKE SQUARE won Weymouth's Civic Society's plaque in 1995 for sympathetic enlargement and remodelling of the square.

WYVERN SCHOOL is on the same site as Wey Valley School and Sports College and St Nicholas and St Laurence Primary School in Dorchester Road. Officially opened 18th May 2007, the children having transferred from Cacique on Chickerell Road.

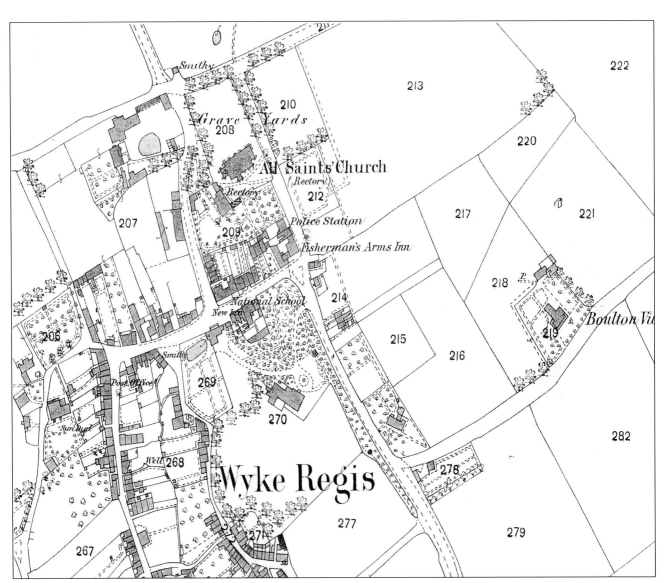

Wyke Regis in the 1860s. A section of the 25"=1 mile Ordnance Survey Map.

Y.M.C.A.

Y.M.C.A. The Weymouth branch of the Young Men's Christian Association seems to have found premises in Weymouth early in 1905 when they set up at No. 8 Frederick Place, but they struggled financially. They organised one or two 'athletics' events locally which they called 'Dromemas', apparently a Greek word for racecourse. The light-hearted races were of a novelty nature (Cycle potato planting race, Thread the needle race, Feather race etc.) and these were held courtesy of the local gentry in the grounds of houses such as Belfield and Radipole Manor in 1905 and for a few years after. Attendances were a little disappointing.

A gathering at Radipole Manor for one of the YMCA-organised 'Dromemas'

YACHT CLUB HOTEL, Melcombe Regis is listed in Kelly's 1855 directory.

YANKEE The America's Cup winning American yacht here was racing in Weymouth in August 1935 and was beaten by Tommy Sopwith's yacht *Endeavour.*

YARLANDS or YEARLANDS farm was up for sale in February 1859. It was around 50 acres of land including Farmhouse, Barn, Stables etc. at Putton in the parish of West Chickerell with *'many eligible plots for building'*. Also in the sale were lands called Lake Close, Calves Close, Rowlands Close, and a piece of land commonly called Crook.

YORK VILLA, Alexandra Road Formerly part of the Georgian Radipole Cavalry Barracks, off Dorchester Road. Now converted to two semi-detached bungalows, Nos. 24 and 26 Alexandra Road. Built for officers, possibly for the barrack master. *See also* RADIPOLE BARRACKS in *Bumper Book I*

YOUTH ACTIVITIES CENTRE on the Marsh opened in August 1964. It was a dual purpose building also housing the Youth Employment Centre.

YXPILA one of the graceful timber ships which were a familiar sight in Weymouth Harbour in the first half of the twentieth century. One of her crew regularly performed the daring feat of diving off her topsail into the harbour.

The Yxpila *in Weymouth Harbour.*

The tradition of sending a postcard from the seaside has long been popular. These comic cards date from the early 1900s.